MW00778372

LIFE UNDERGROUND

LIFE UNDERGROUND

ENCOUNTERS WITH PEOPLE BELOW THE STREETS OF NEW YORK

TERRY WILLIAMS

Columbia University Press   *New York*

Columbia University Press
Publishers Since 1893
New York   Chichester, West Sussex
cup.columbia.edu

Copyright © 2024 Columbia University Press
All rights reserved

Library of Congress Cataloging-in-Publication Data

Names: Williams, Terry M. (Terry Moses), 1948– author.
Title: Life underground : encounters with people below the streets of
New York / Terry Williams.
Description: New York : Columbia University Press, [2024] |
Includes bibliographical references and index.
Identifiers: LCCN 2023032859 (print) | LCCN 2023032860 (ebook) |
ISBN 9780231177924 (hardback) | ISBN 9780231177931 (trade paperback) |
ISBN 9780231556941 (ebook)
Subjects: LCSH: Underground homeless persons—New York (State)—
New York—Social conditions. | Underground homeless persons—
New York (State)—New York—Economic conditions. |
Upper West Side (New York, N.Y.)
Classification: LCC HV4506.N6 W55 2024 (print) | LCC HV4506.N6 (ebook) |
DDC 305.5/692097471—dc23/eng/20230831
LC record available at https://lccn.loc.gov/2023032859
LC ebook record available at https://lccn.loc.gov/2023032860

Printed in the United States of America

Cover design: Julia Kushnirsky
Cover image: Jocelyn Chuang

Dedicated to Bernard Monte Isaac, a.k.a the Lord of the Tunnel

CONTENTS

PROLOGUE

*While I thought I'd interviewed the last person living under-
ground after the aught years rolled around, I ran into a man
named Jean Pierre near the tracks who told me the underground
was his and that nobody else lived there. He said, "I own the
underground now." Apparently this may not be true. I'll have
to go there to find out for myself.*

        —Terry Williams, field note (2009)

*Well, people are still in the underground. Junior lives in one
of those bunker type alcoves you know up in those levels above
the tracks. Well, he's still there and Katy the cat lady is still
there too. That underground will always have people in it, I
don't care who says different. Also, Chris Pape [Freedom] lives
not too far from 96th street and he's around. I'll try to find
him for you.*

        —Bernard, personal correspondence (2012)

*Homeless people feel most at home when they are living in spaces
that are hidden from public view. The underground provides
a form of release from harassment and staring eyes, from police*

taunts, social workers who want to place them in shelters, from
teenagers who want to torch them while they sleep.

—Terry Williams, field note (2015)

Though this book charts a dispossessed space of New York City, one of many underground locations—tunnels, hidden passageways, abandoned railroads, shelters, and dungeons—inhabited by a group of people considered disposable.

Although the underground I recall here is not the engineering wonder of the Canal du Midi, nor does it have the history of two centuries behind it, it does give the strong sense of a haunted past.[1] Many of its inhabitants mention the Devil when they speak of it. There is mystery as you move down its walled-in spaces and traverse its graffiti-sprayed corridors. The people who live in these spaces are often invisible to other New Yorkers. As I explored these spaces, I couldn't help but see in the underground a metaphor for or symbolic representation of the unconscious: we lock the doors of our minds—and of our society—to the unfamiliar or unpleasant, like the vagabond, the poor, the homeless tramp, the mentally ill, the stranger, relegating them to forgotten, unknown spaces. The underground reminds me of the pioneering American psychiatrist Harry Stack Sullivan's concept of the "not me."[2] "As long as it is *not me*, or my family, or my part of town, I will pay it no mind" is a common refrain. But there is a Latin phrase, "*de te fabula narratur*," which translates roughly to mean "at the outset what I am about to say seems of little concern to you, but do not fall asleep, for *this story is about you*." For Sullivan, the "not me" is no less a part of the person than the "good me."

The work that follows is based on hundreds of visits underground I conducted between 1991 and 1996 and then sporadic visits during the years 2000 through 2020. Some contact was made during the four gap years, and I also conducted interviews from 1996 to 2000. The resulting narrative looks at the underground from different perspectives, including anecdotal material, world literature, field observations and notes, autobiographical writing, biographical displays, photographs, drawings, transcribed conversations with residents, and excerpts from personal journals. I intend this book to be an ethnographic collage, a rendering of lives pieced together from impressions, encounters, scraps. I specifically engage these vistas through an ecological approach; these locations are treated as part of a natural, organic arena.[3] The ethnographic material compiled here is more than a collection of accounts of individual suffering or personal musings; together it emphasizes neglect as a constant fact of life for poor people and, at the same time, shows how people without shelter actively strive to make a place for themselves through a kind of oppositional culture and personal resistance to capitalism, challenging the values of a democratic society as they struggle for dignity amid despair.

What follows presents the day-to-day activities of a small group of people discovered living literally under the streets of one of the richest, most populated spaces on Earth: an area between West Seventy-Second and West Ninety-Sixth Streets in Manhattan. But merely providing a description of the lives of people underground does not adequately tell the whole story or illustrate the transformations that members of this community have undergone during these years.

This story is not only about the specific people living in this underground but about those living a shelterless life in this city.

The classic stereotype of the unhoused as vagabond is just that, a stereotype. In fact, the people we will encounter in this book live in a wide and surprising range of ways. I think the key here for readers is to understand that being underground does not mean one must eschew all relations with folks in the world above. Every underground person is linked within a web of overlapping social worlds. By delineating these social networks—in essence, learning about who knows whom and interacts with whom—we can gain a greater sense of the social organization of the folks living underground. In this respect, *Life Underground* hopes to provide a sharper view of how underground residents interact and intersect and to give readers a better understanding of what life under such conditions entails. The *micro* approach (geography), the *meso* perspective (cultural), and the *macro* approach (economic, social, and psychological) each play their role. I realize at the same time the complexity of these common areas of interest, how they cannot be generalized, and how they raise significant sociological questions in turn.

The underground is a relatively calm environment, overlaid with a general mood of depression, though occasional confrontations and altercations do occur, usually because of a need to quench a drug-related thirst but also over food, water, possessions, or territory. For the underground folk, the important thing is to try to establish a sense of place, and their actions and responses have much to say to us about how we all understand, interpret, remember, and, most importantly, *long* for a place, any place to call our own. We form an almost spiritual bond to a place, and many residents have established such a bond to the underground.

In conducting this retrospective ethnography—what some might call a hybrid memoir/ethnobiography, rather than auto-ethnography, since the research centers on my own experiences and reflection—I attempt to explore the underground space as a sociologist might do for the first time.[4] I might add that this idea of ethnography involves a wide range of research and analytic methods but is grounded in the participant-observation approach, which uses one's self to organize a personal, reflective, subjective narrative.

A section of this area under study has been mined by a number of journalists, filmmakers, photographers, and writers; it is popularly referred to by graffiti artists, millennials, hip-hop lyricists, and virtual reality aficionados as the "Freedom Tunnel." It was so named after Chris Pape, also known as Freedom, an early graffiti artist who used the abandoned Amtrak tunnel as his gallery.

Although some individuals' stories have already been told by others, that does not mean that they cannot be further elucidated. These are complex people, and no one has a monopoly on their lives, save them; it is they who determine who can and cannot report on their adventures and daily habits. I do not believe any one chronicler is able to capture all the complexities that make up a human collective. This poses a challenge to the effort to tell these lives and stresses that any one account is insufficient to, of, and for the multitude of identities inhabited, expressed, and embodied by any individual over time.

Take, for instance, the idea of inventing a new self—in Sullivan's language, the turning of a "not me" or "bad me" into a "good me." People try to find ways to make up an identity that is respectable to those they meet from "topside" (above ground), who are sometimes considered their betters. I allude to several members of the residency who constantly reinvent themselves; this idea of the reinvented self is cause to rethink who the person really is. It raises a host of questions: Are they all the same person the journalist met, or the filmmaker inspected, or the anthropologist interviewed? If you happen to catch a person at the moment of reinventing themself, are they the same person who told an entirely different life story two months earlier? Were they lying then, or now? The question expands to classic, existential proportions: Who are we at any given point in time in our lives?

In my reading of both Jennifer Toth's and Teun Voeten's books about this same tunnel space, my viewing of the film *Dark Days*, and my perusal of the coffee-table book by the photographer Margaret Morton, I remain firmly unconvinced that everything about the people here depicted have been adequately described, analyzed, and explained, totally and completely for all time.

ACKNOWLEDGMENTS

I t is with pleasure that I acknowledge my obligations to several friends and colleagues. The book would not be possible without the continued support and excellent assistance of my wife, Natalia Williams, who acted as supportive friend, ardent critic, and one-woman think tank. The work related to this book has taken many engaging and exciting features over the years and benefited from the assistance of many friends, mentors, and others. The original research was made possible by a number of fortuitous events, meeting people underground, and the connections to media folks and people I met in North Carolina.

Some people shared their field notes, tapes, video recordings, unique ideas, and happenings with me. The assistance they offered provided an important contribution to the making of this book in more ways than they know. A few of my co-thinkers: Ana Cardenas Tomazic, Hakim Hasan, and the anthropologist/photographer Teun Voeten continue to assist me with photographic knowledge and wisdom and were central to making the visual images provided superbly important in the making of the book. The brilliant photographer Jocelyn Chuang worked closely with me on several projects, including the photographic images provided here.

The cartographer Rick Bunch, at UNC Greensboro, did a magnificent job constructing maps for the text, along with the drawing by Michele Albee. Tom Gerry, Jana Leo, Dara Levendosky, Errol James, Ye Lui, Jackie Oberlander, Philip Oberlander, Dave Ray, Donald Smith, Sergeant Floyd Smith, and Markus Schulz were especially helpful in providing valuable assistance. In addition, a special thanks to Chairman of the Board William Kornblum, Grand Central Neighborhood Social Services Corporation, and all other board members, especially Edith Goldenhar. And, of course, all the staff at GCNSSC who allowed me to conduct interviews and provided important voices in the making of the text. Director Brady Crain and his able staff, including Tamara Hopkins, were extremely helpful. I am grateful to my former students who provided ideas and insights, especially Dr. Scott Beck, whose assistance was absolutely invaluable; Dr. Cristina Dragomir, Dr. Rezvaneh Ganji, and Dr. Ariana Ali; Dr. Laurie Gunst and Sammye Chitsom. The New School scholars William Milberg, Kirti Varma, Monica Gomez, Siri Manasa Poluru, and Charles Whitcroft all played key roles in making the book possible

My current students in my Global Cities as a Social Construct class, Synne Jensen, Tyler St. Amant, Ida Ward York, Zoe Wolfsen, Jackson Shulman, Merve Yardim, Ella Grace Dunn, Oliver Rosenthal, Francisco de la Garza, Sequoia Valverde, Lucia Corral Saborido, and Lock Reddy, were gracious in helping me do the research. Dissertation proseminar participants who were very kind in listening to the last draft: Aura Cardenas, Malkhaz Toria, Wilhemina Agbemakplido, Maya Herman, Brian Bartholomew, Robert Proverb, Reynaldo Ortiz-Manaya. Special thanks to Kahlil Zulu Williams and Neruda Williams for ideas offered. I especially thank all the various people underground and the many I did not have the privilege of naming in the text.

Eric Schwartz and Lowell Frye, under whose guidance the work was originally pursued, have from the start provided an encouraging guiding light for all the books in this series. I warmly thank all anonymous reviewers for taking the time to read the manuscript during these pandemic times. Although all of the aforementioned assisted in some way in the completion of this book, I take complete responsibility for any of its shortcomings.

LIFE UNDERGROUND

INTRODUCTION

What we need in America is a new class of individuals, who at any physical cost to themselves and others agree to quit work-ing, to loaf, to refuse to be hurried or try to get on in the world.
—Sherwood Anderson, *Winesburg, Ohio* (1915)

Before the arrival of the railroad in the mid-1800s, the Hudson River's shores along the northwestern edge of the island of Manhattan contained a community of squatters. By the 1930s, when Parks Commissioner Robert Moses covered the New York Central railroad tracks, creating a two-and-a-half-mile-long tunnel under the promenades of Riverside Park, it had evolved into a shantytown. Eventually, certain sec-tions of the tunnel stopped being used for rail traffic. Many homeless people who currently reside here began moving into the space as early as 1974. By the early 1990s, approximately 113 tunnel residents were found by Amtrak work crews, who were renewing track in the abandoned space along and under River-side Park for passenger train service between Pennsylvania Sta-tion and Washington, DC. Sensationally depicted by the media as "mole people," those who were interviewed resented that characterization; others altogether refused interviews with the press and media representatives from what they refer to as "topside" society. When I asked Bernard, one of my main contacts, how he felt about the term, he told me he resented the implications made in the media that they were violent, unclean, and cannibalistic. All these myths made him angry. "When Jennifer [Toth] came out with her book by that name [*The Mole People*] I was disappointed. You see, I felt and hoped when you did your book, you would have a 'mole people revisited' in order to set the record straight."[1]

This book, *Life Underground*, takes its name from the original title of Maxim Gorky's play *The Lower Depths*, first produced for the Moscow Art Theater in 1902. It is a play known for characters who form a "motley, shiftless and often criminal fringe" of the populace.[2] My lifelong fascination with the alienated and others I've met in my life—the outsider, the risk taker, the beaten down, the dissenter, the upper-class beatnik, the lost and forgotten, wherever they may be—probably started when I was a kid in Mississippi. One fall day, while playing outside, I saw two strange-looking white men with dirty faces and torn trousers walking in our backyard. We watched silently as our mother handed the men a paper bag and some apples; the men then withdrew into the woods. I asked her who they were, and she said "hobos," a term I'd never heard before. I did see other hobos on occasion over the years, and I knew they were men (I never saw any women hobos) who had no jobs but rode around on freight trains looking for work. My father said a hobo was an indigent person, a tramp. Yet the self-imposed isolation and voluntary (or, more likely, involuntary) poverty of the hobo, hermit, vagabond, or shelterless person living underground, the ascetic lives of these people, often are considered (by those *not* living thus) opportunities for spiritual richness. I am reminded of John Dos Passos's U.S.A. trilogy, where in his epilogue "Vag" he captured the American vagrant as a symbol of the failed promise of the American dream: "I feel the gravel underfoot, the starlit night about me. The nose smells, the ear hears, the eyes see. 'Willfully living?' 'Why not?' Having survived up to now at least the death dealing hail of cosmic particles, the interpreting mind says 'I am here.'"[3]

Among several unidentified others, the underground residents in this book include:

Bernard, thirty-two, a Black man from Florida;

Kal, forty-four, a man of Polish descent who ran away from home at sixteen and became a drifter, part-time short-order cook, and full-time drug misuser;

Bobo, fifty, a Vietnam veteran who has lived on barges, under Grand Central Terminal, and in other underground spaces;

Beatrice, thirty-one, taken underground by her lover after her mother died and who now lives with him and twenty cats;

Kovacs, fifty, an avowed racist who has the distinction of being the oldest underground resident;

Jason, twenty-nine, a man of Puerto Rican/African descent who many say was into Santeria in the underground before the community was razed;

Tin Can Tina, aka Mary Mangoni or MM, age unknown, a white woman who drank heavily and lived with a mentally challenged group for a time at the mouth of the underground;

Jean Pierre, thirty, a Haitian man and the last person I met underground at the Seventy-Second Street location before the community was razed.

The people living underground in my narrative decided to name their own spokesperson to deal with the media: Bernard, referred to as the "Lord of the Tunnel." The individuals interviewed here lived primarily in one stretch of underground running roughly parallel to the Hudson River between West Seventy-Second and West Ninety-Sixth Streets, an area known above ground as the Upper West Side. But in the next chapter we will begin our story farther south, under Grand Central Terminal in midtown Manhattan.

To discourage living underground, officials regularly padlock entrances or weld them shut, but residents always manage to regain access. The light of the daytime world enters the underground through grates and holes, through artificial light, or, most commonly, from lamps set up for railway workers. The result is a murky atmosphere, yet the setting can be visually

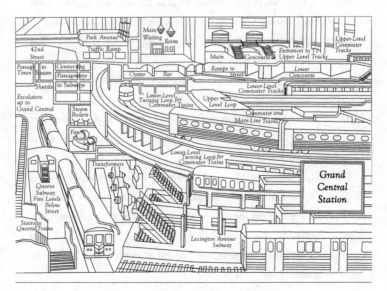

FIGURE 0.1. Grand Central Station.

powerful when rays of light stream through topside grates to illuminate the living spaces below. In many ways, underground residents are pioneers in an urban frontier, settling in places where humans have not previously lived.

The growing literature on homelessness includes little on these inhabitants; indeed, many underground residents do not consider themselves homeless—"just temporarily without proper shelter," as one woman put it—and think it inappropriate to apply the term to their situation. They consider the subterranean chambers of the underground a safer housing alternative than city shelters. It is important to stress that people have *chosen* to live here: despite its inherent difficulties and dangers, many see the underground as much safer than what is available "topside."

This book is an attempt at classic "imaginative ethnography," which is not a new idea or concept. As a matter of fact, the approach has been around for quite some time, in part because much of the discipline, since its inception, has used an imaginative approach to tell powerful stories. But the way the story is told and what the very story is are precisely what this narrative is itself about. The chapters are organized using the field note as the overarching structure, since field notes are the soul, tissue, and foundation of every ethnographic study. In pursuing this frame, this book uses a *collage ethnographic* approach, including anecdotal material, field observations, photographs, cartography, transcribed conversations with residents, and excerpts from personal journals.

Most ethnographic accounts make use of fieldwork that is both spatially and temporally bound, even when the ethnographer has remained in the field. In contrast, I deliberately construct a "collage ethnography" because of the ways my text is structured—interviews, reconstructions of events from interviews, drawings, photos, standard narrative, lyrics, poems, autobiographical prose, and biographical observations of the cityscape all intertwined. The stories in the text unfold in pieces, so the reader is spectator to the events as they happen. Rather than aspiring to objectivity, collage ethnography admits observers and participants as characters in a developing vignette, or "storiette." A source of inspiration for my approach and method has been William Kornblum's "Discovering Ink: A Mentor for a Historical Ethnography," published in the *Annals of the American Academy of Political and Social Science* in 2004. Kornblum's article and later his book serve as central landmarks for imaginative ethnography in the postmodern era. In both, he sets up a sociological time-travel treatise "in an effort to fill in a gap or two and possibly to extend our knowledge of Chicago in the early 1920s." He later states, "Using what I have learned about the fieldwork process, I am attempting to project myself, or someone rather like me, back to a time when sociology was a much newer field even than it is now."[4]

Similarly, in *Life Underground*, I want to recreate as accurately as possible an experience of Chicago fieldwork conducted in the heady days of early empirical urban sociology—like Kornblum, to project myself back to a formative period of sociological study where method was far from a settled affair, where fieldworkers put to use everything at hand to pursue their research. "Historical ethnography" is the term contemporary anthropologists often use to describe this eclectic set of methods, but it is not yet a common method in sociology. Ann Sutherland describes the central substantive focus of the method this way: Historical ethnography still takes seriously the traditional anthropological method of intensive, personal fieldwork to learn about how people think and see what they do—and learn what both what they think and what they do means to them. But today, ethnographers no longer take for granted that culture (or identity) is a given. Instead, they are problematized; that is, culture and identity are also things that have to be explained. If culture persists, or if identities of ethnicity and nation are key features of culture, then we must try to understand how they are constructed and reconstructed over time. This point is not too far from the perspective Michael Burawoy brings to the argument, that it is not possible to understand current social conditions or cultures using ethnographic methods without developing a historical understanding of the phenomenon under study as well. Ruth Behar similarly suggests that in addition to bringing in the living influences of the past, many contemporary sociologists and anthropologists recommend that "fieldworkers lend their own experience to the process of enriching and dynamizing the fieldwork material itself."[5]

These arguments fall somewhat short of making it clear what historical ethnographies and, more specifically, imaginative ethnographies are or how they differ, if at all, from some of the classics of urban ethnography, like those composed by, for example, Eli Anderson or Mitch Duneier. At stake in the distinction are questions about the state of sociology as a discipline distinct from anthropology and of sociological inquiry as a mode of historical representation. What forms of imaginative ethnographic study belong to the sociologist? Carol Ellis and Arthur Bochner began a series of creative ethnographic works in the mid-1990s to compensate for the complicated situation and what has been termed the "crisis of representation" occurring in the discipline.[6] Ellis and Bochner capture the approach as a genre of writing that displays multiple layers of consciousness connecting the personal to the cultural. Denzin, in his book *Interpretive Autoethnography*, provides perhaps the best analysis thus far on the significance of imaginative ethnographies: *this way of doing fieldwork makes the researcher's own experience the subject of investigation.* Following this line of influence, I do not shy away from reflective consideration of my place and presence in the midst of the social conditions, cultures, and lives under study.[7]

Several additional sources are important to consider as background for this work. For one, there is an exhaustive list of material on poor people without shelter; I will mention in this volume those I consider to be particularly significant. Second, I envision my hybrid approach as also taking part in the tradition of retrospective ethnography, much like Charles Tilly envisioned it as based on a concept or a belief that "individual behavior and collective dispositions make up the fundamental causes of social behavior," whereby historical occurrences are explained by "reconstructing . . . participant's motives, emotions, and states of consciousness." Seen in this way, a retrospective ethnography is formed by the "effort to reconstitute a round of life from the best historical equivalents of the ethnographers' observations, then to use the reconstituted round of life as context for the explanation of collective action." Tilly made it clear in a talk he gave in 1995 at the New School that anthropology—and sociology, for that matter—should insist on a more crucial role by encouraging the researcher to excavate feelings, influences, perceptions, and meanings in order to extend a more thorough understanding of what the field had to offer at any one point in time.[8]

PLACE AND PLACELESSNESS

The underground is a strange place or space, in a technical sense. It is not like any other place because it is not really a place to be lived in. It is not an apartment or a house, though we know there are a few people who reside down there, like Bernard, the "Lord

FIGURE 0.2. The underground, looking north, seventy-five feet below the street.

Source: Photo by Jocelyn Chuang.

of the Tunnel," and Kal, who sleep in two bunkers side by side, and that it contains spaces like the "Cubano Arms," a lean-to at the northern mouth to the underground, where the new arrivals, who happened to be mostly Cubans at the time, made a home for themselves.

I should note that these places, though makeshift *homes*, are not really *theirs*, because these are not public places. Rather, they are owned by the Amtrak Corporation, which has the power to remove/evict people who trespass at any time. And in spite of the rhetoric some of the underground residents use, such as "I am not really homeless but just temporally without shelter," which I have heard more than one inhabitant say, they are really *home-less*, because this place is not really a home. A few structures are built environments, especially the Cubano Arms, a

Frank Gehry–type construction, basically a *casita* made of found materials including cardboard, tin, wood, and tarpaulin. I peeked in one day when its inhabitants weren't around: I saw an old mattress, newspapers, and what looked like pictures of flowers on the walls. I didn't linger and quickly made my way further along the passage, hoping to see other people along the way.

This fact, that these homeless people's homes are not actually *theirs*, raises the issue of full citizenship rights for people who are propertyless and whose labor is no longer needed. James Duncan makes the important point that, despite possessing rights, lacking a home poses the homeless individual as a challenge to the maintenance of property relations and thus as a challenge to society as a whole:

> In a society such as ours, whose organization is based on individual property rights, a poor person will be viewed as a problem for the group controlling the area in which he lives. He possesses little property and hence has little stake in the existing order which functions primarily to protect property and ensure that orderly market relations take place. The "tramp" possesses all of the same problems for the controlling group that the poor local person does, but these problems are magnified as he, being an itinerant, has even less stake in the area. Not only does he lack property, but he rarely has ties with local residents. Thus the tramp feels no obligation to maintain the moral order and furthermore his mobility makes it difficult to force him to comply with it. The locals view the "tramp" as a threat and do their best to drive him away.[9]

As an unhoused individual, you simply do not have the same rights as a real homeowner. These rights are unrelated to paying rent. You are essentially a vagabond, or what was once called a "bum," a "vagrant," or a "tramp." The men living in the Cubano Arms are certainly not real homeowners: the Amtrak Corporation can remove them at any time. And they did exactly that in the 1990s.

Given these circumstances, the underground residents are considered by sociologists, among many others, as a "hard-to-reach group." When I speak of "hard-to-reach" or "hidden populations," I also have Jean Schensul and colleagues in mind, who state:

> In an epidemic, what have come to be called "hidden populations," groups that reside outside of institutional and clinical settings and whose activities are clandestine and therefore concealed from the view of mainstream society and agencies of social control . . . as well as from local community-based organizations, may be a special risk for infection and for transmitting infection to other populations.[10]

This is not to say that the residents, the squatters underground, are actually pestilential, but they certainly are viewed as if they are by the larger society; they are essentially a pariah group.

COMPARATIVE URBAN ETHNOGRAPHY

After working with Edward Preble, the dean of street ethnographers, I wanted to approach the field in a way that incorporated all of the techniques I'd learned from him, along with a few of my own. I used an "emic" (insider) approach, a kind of passive participant observation. I began using a method I refer to as "night-time behavior mapping," where I would conduct fieldwork between the hours of midnight and 6 AM. "The darkness," one longtime resident told me, "consecrates a world to many people down here. It confirms our existence. You mustn't forget we are people of the dark, forgotten and foreboding."

A central feature of ethnography is that it takes time to build and maintain meaningful relationships with people. The payoff for the time invested can be great: ethnography can provide clear descriptions of processes, everyday rituals, and lifestyles, and it can help clarify vague concepts and assist in formulating hypotheses. These strengths, combined with the techniques of using key contacts, snowball sampling, and networking, make ethnography a valuable method of inquiry. A major emphasis of this technique is a heavy reliance upon building close relationships with folk and obtaining information as complete as possible from them about the phenomena under investigation.

My interest at this time, around the mid-1990s, was on crime, drugs, teenage life, and labor market forces. Especially when asking about such matters, it is very difficult to disentangle the impact of crime or unemployment—that is, the effect of "society-level" experiences—on an individual's traits, or personality, or subjectivity, whatever language you prefer, from the effect of that individual's own life experiences. This is probably the single most difficult task facing anyone doing research in this area, and it is the subject that practically everyone who has written about these matters struggles to handle adequately. Perhaps the two levels, that of social experience and that of personal experience, can never be entirely disentangled. But nevertheless, I felt it important to ask what individual characteristics (one's temperament, intelligence, family background, age, quality of parenting) may have influenced the decision to move in one direction or another when confronted with the conditions of street life.

The life stories I capture in my writing of the men, women, and children in this city are more than accounts of individuals attempting survival and self-empowerment. These life histories and case studies are not just personal musings; they are testament to a history of exclusion and inclusion, struggle and hope, resistance and resilience. I understand addiction to be rife in America, propelled by deep currents in our culture and exacerbated by the social contrasts that exist here. Dependence on substances and compulsive behaviors are widely encouraged in our society; compulsive spending, sex addiction, gambling, workaholism, and eating disorders are all promoted through the subtexts of popular culture. In our televised universe of perpetual gratification—the denial of pain and promise of instant relief and easy answers—we are immersed in a climate that nurtures our desire for ecstasy, escape, and anesthesia. Add to the mix social and economic injustice, and you have a society in which culture, social structure, and the economic system all conspire to foster addiction at all levels. This perspective has led me to view the construction of identity, empowerment, and cultural citizenship in terms of social relations and claims for rights and equity.

In order to carry out this research, it was important for me to incorporate the voices, views, values, and writings of those I wrote about so as to render human their concerns. It was also important to me to use a language they could understand. Of course, this raises another issue: because I use so much of the language of the people I research in what I present here—their speech and even their writings—the question of who was the ethnographer became blurred. Is the whole enterprise irrevocably politically "tarnished" because I have the power to write about those who don't write about themselves? Can I protect my ethnographic work here from the more general political epistemological debates about writing and the representation of otherness? Ethnography is a sensitive method. It tells the

practitioner to experience bodily as well as intellectually. Direct
involvement became the way to continue the work—and possibly
to protect it from such critiques.

METHODS AND STRATEGIES

The group in this study consists of eight shelterless people—
Bernard, Jason, Kal, Jean-Pierre, Bobo, Beatrice, Tin Can
Tina, and Kovacs—whom I followed over several years and who
saw their limited life histories recorded. All were asked to sign
consent forms and were paid cash for formal interviews. Of the
120 people approached over the years of the study, only the eight
in the present volume remained relatively consistent, reliable
contacts. Most of the individuals in this cohort were nomadic,
staying underground for short stays before moving on to aboveground locales. Most of the interviews were conducted in the
underground but not exclusively in this setting; many were followed out as they worked, begged, ate at soup kitchens, bought
drugs, and lectured above ground.

Casual interviews with sixty-one others between the ages of
eighteen to fifty, male and female, were conducted during the
years in the underground from June 1989 to 1995. Scattered
follow-ups occurred with those who left after the destruction of
the bunkers, lean-tos, and other forms of makeshift housing took
place in 1996, when the tunnel under Riverside Park was cleared
out by the city and Amtrak.

In this study, ethnographic mapping is central in understanding the ecology of underground life and culture. I started
watching the movements of homeless people in the city as part
of a graduate-level course I taught entitled "Seminars of Engagement." The practical component of this class often required

all-night, on-site vigils, and once, at around three in the morning, while sitting on the floor of Grand Central Terminal, I noticed people leaving the floor area, out of sight, down a number of ramps. The obvious question—"where are these people going?"—was an initial catalyst of this research project.

An open-ended interview guide was developed and memorized by the researcher as an initial tool for gathering data, although a variety of data-gathering strategies were employed to obtain information. The guide was used to provide structure to the interviews and to ensure that the same "areas of interest" were covered in all interviews. But after a very short time, this strategy was abandoned for a more systematic accounting, since some residents were uncooperative, others often drunk or high. Many were simply unintelligible. Tape-recorded interviews were attempted with some success, but the most common approach was simply to listen to their stories and write them down from memory after each visit.

Selected underground residents who had proved to be reliable were given tape recorders or journals to write or tape their own stories, which were collected at a later time. Residents were asked to describe the circumstances of their current and as much of their early lives as they saw fit. Probe questions were used to add detail to their narratives. Once people left the underground, they were interviewed in a follow-up session about their lives above ground and about their future life plans. Interviews, journal entries, and tape recordings were transcribed using *hypertext*, a software program that organizes textual data. Residents who chose to write in journals were given a dollar per manuscript page. Journals were collected whenever I went back into the underground, and new journals were provided.

VISUAL WORK

The historical tradition of photographic documentation of the homeless dates back to the 1880s, with the work of Jacob Riis. Riis, initially writing about the destitution of the Lower East Side, turned to photography to reinforce his concerns about the poor and the destitute. Known as the "Emancipator of the Slums," Riis demonstrated the power of the camera as a weapon for social reform. The use of photography by field workers began in the late 1800s; around 1896, at least thirty articles in the *American Journal of Sociology* used photographs as illustrative data and evidence of their discussions. In *Balinese Character: A Photographic Analysis* (1942), Gregory Bateson first "saturated" photographic research in another culture. His book included over seven hundred photographs. Later, in 1951, Margaret Mead, the anthropologist, used photography for her child-development studies.

In one of my visual ethnography studies, I chose a location where I am a board member of a local organization, the Grand Central Neighborhood Social Services Corporation, which provides basic necessities and a range of social services to New York City's indigent population. The study outline involved five homeless individuals recruited from St. Agnes Church and part of the Grand Central Neighborhood program.

These five individuals, all of whom had at one time lived in various homeless locations, underground, in Grand Central Terminal, on the street, in subways, and in shelters, were then trained in the use of simple 35mm SLR photographic cameras. Domains pertinent to their lives were identified (financial, emotional, social support, substance misuse), and for a period of three months subjects recorded those life domains using black-and-white film. I bought the exposed film, had it developed, and asked people (subjects) to describe the photographic material (via monthly free listings) and open-ended interviewing. The description of the material, as well as the photographic material itself, was coded and analyzed via cluster analysis.

The more than four thousand images thus produced helped me gain an in-depth understanding of some of the subjects' sociocultural patterns. These images provided a comprehensive description of the subjects' self-understanding and their socio-cultural milieu. These photographic patterns inventoried some of the shelterless persons' human functions, quality of life, nature of their social relationships, and level of psychological well-being. Research findings, as well as professional prints of some selected pictures, were used, in the form of an art exhibit and local press coverage, to call public attention to some of the issues homeless individuals face in their daily lives.

The uniqueness of that research resides in the fact that, to my knowledge, no previous ethnographic research had fully explored the possibilities of recording visual data via the active participation of actual milieu-competent individuals. Recent developments in ethnographic theory seem to reflect a concern in the field regarding the scientist's authority to represent an "alien" human group's identity.[11] Concerns regarding the possible epistemological biases attached to the role of the ethnographer as an agent of representation have also been debated.

The representational scientific mechanism of ethnography seems to be an actual object of debate. From a historical perspective, it may be argued that Western presentational processes have a sort of "built-in" epistemological bias, that of the mediatization of ethnographic realities. This process of mediatization imposes the observer's historically determined intellectual milieu over the experiential or phenomenological.

The notion of anthropological colonialism, for example, as a mode of representation and description of an ethnographical reality, speaks bluntly of mediatization as a complex and evident methodological problem that was invisible just a few decades ago. This study attempted to suggest new modes of portraying ethnographic entities, particularly of those groups considered difficult to reach. By letting the participants generate and systematize their own ethnographic gaze, I hope to analyze the methodological implications that the expansion of ethnographic authority to indigenous communities may have.

JOURNALS AS CULTURAL ARTIFACTS

Collecting journals from underground residents, with the sole intention of giving people the chance to express themselves, makes the residents less "subjects" and more part of the process of defining who they are, using their own words, actions, dreams, and past experiences.

The journal could be seen as a "meta" field note, where the ethnographer writes about field notes in the journal, making it a field note, too. I have different kinds of Rhodia journals, either yellow or black. Yellow is for personal items, and black is for the field notes, yet both are used as data-gathering tools. The yellow, personal reflections, whether about myself or my feelings about the world, and the black for the larger environment that is the field, are both umbilically part of my field note storehouse.

In her illuminating chapter "I Am a Field Note" in Sanjek's 1990 *Field Notes: The Making of Anthropology*, Jean Jackson writes that no clear standard exists for what defines field notes. I have always used the notes as personal reflections, the building blocks or scaffolding of larger ethnographies, and a way to discipline my ventures out into the field. The notes are arrived at by various means. Some notes are handwritten on the spot; others are "head notes," as Jackson calls mental notations while conducting research; others were tape recorded; still other notes derived from the contacts themselves, asking them to record in journals key situations or events relevant to their lives.

In doing the fieldwork in the tunnel, my reconstructing the interviews after the fact, in my journal, was difficult; it often took several trips and interview sessions to get "complete" stories. On subsequent visits, I would show my notes to residents and ask if they would read them over and comment. It often took several tries to get the language, the inflections, the slang, and the repetitiousness of what was said down correctly. In addition, the situation demanded arriving at the right time: place and mood had to align to pull it off. But overall, I have my own standards, as most ethnographers do, as our notes represent only one moment in time, like a snapshot of where we were at this moment or that, an instamatic of what we were thinking, a flash reminder of our research goals, a photocopy of our feelings about whether or not our hunches were right.

1

DESCENT

People tend to think or believe that there are some vast underground chambers and that people are lost down there. Every nook and cranny has been searched by us. We know every place a person can hide. We've heard the Beauty and the Beast stories, the alligator in the sewer stories, but this place is more labyrinthine in myth than reality.

—Metro North employee, interview

Each venture underground stirs the same feelings: as soon as I hit the stairs and start down into the darkness, I feel I am entering something dangerous. I suppress this anxiety, fear, and hesitation, partly because I'm getting to know the people there and partly because I know that I want to write this book. But even after the tunnel residents become my friends, the fear is still present every time I go down. I realize now that the fear is not of the underground per se but of something inside me. Entering the underground evokes a primal state in my being. My antennae are suddenly alive. I am acutely aware of all that is around me: the rats scuttling about, the rocks falling, the strangers who might jump out of the darkness at any time.

FIGURE 1.1. Underneath the half-light of the grate, seventy-five feet below the surface.

Source: Photo by Teun Voeten.

There are points of sheer darkness where I can't see my hands in front of me—a momentary derangement of the senses so far removed from what I felt five minutes ago as I walked through sunny Riverside Park. The underground evokes unusual mental images and visual associations with a primal past: Namibian underwater lakes hidden for thousands of years or French caves, dark, cold places with humid air and prehistoric, mysterious drawings. In walking in parts that are entirely dark, I fear becoming entrapped. This place, like other manmade structures, recalls catacombs, tombs, vaults, dungeons, places of confinement and enslavement. In my mind the underground also recalls death and rebirth; Tolstoy noted such structures as places where the dead return to life on earth. These experiences led to my idea that the underground is the unconscious of the city.

GOING DOWN UNDER

The environments in which I first hoped to conduct research included underground spaces where the homeless sleep, eat, and stake out a claim. I initially intended to investigate three research sites: the 168th Street subway tunnel, the space under Grand Central Terminal, and the Amtrak tunnel below Riverside Park. I intended to map out the territory and the behavior of its inhabitants, to interview underground residents, and to photograph their dwellings—cardboard homes, rafter homes accessible only by ladder, and the burrows under train platforms.

Over the course of four months, I established ties with seven underground residents, one church, two police precincts, and several social welfare agencies serving the tunnel areas of West Seventy-Second Street and Grand Central Terminal. There are tried-and-true survival strategies that have developed in these spaces, and most residents make conscious, informed choices about where and how they set up living structures. Bernard, Green Tent, and the men in Cubano Arms all live in underground spaces in order to lower the risk of confrontations and hassles above ground of one kind or another. They chose locations that would help them evade interactions with police, the public, and sometimes one another; they strategically select spaces and locations underground (alcoves, nests) in order to avoid trouble with other people underground. The descent began for those in this narrative with personal tragedy, with sorrow, despair, and desperation, a spiral downward from the subway stairs to the tracks, from the park bench to the hundred steps below, from the Hudson River basin to the steel grate, from the rotting banister to the rat-infested underground lean-to.

FIELD NOTE: FIRST DESCENT
(APRIL 1991)

I began around noon, making my way down into the many levels at Grand Central Terminal. I put on an orange train reflector vest that the engineers and workers wear, given to me by Sergeant Henry, and started walking toward the tracks. It is clear why you need to wear these vests: there are many trains moving in every direction. I crossed twenty-one third rail electrified tracks during the two-hour tour and many times felt totally bewildered by the sheer complexity of the maze-like structure.

I encountered the loop of circular tracks where trains can turn without having to back up. I move down from the second level; about twenty-five feet above the tracks, there was an extended bridge-like structure, a grate of some sort just hanging there with newspapers, magazines, and cardboard covering it. The sergeant called it a "nest." The "nests" can be dated by looking at the newspapers and magazines that line them. Most are only several days old. Some are built in "colonies," where clusters of people live together in groups of twenty to fifty men and women, but no children. Plastic-filled garbage bags act as pillows.

One nest I see, spread out under one of the steel pillars that supports the Waldorf-Astoria, is made up with almost military precision. The ends are tucked in, and the blankets are smooth. At the head of the bed is a small metal chest that holds toiletries. Ten feet away from the spot is a private elevator made by the United States Secret Service for Franklin D. Roosevelt. Apparently, he was brought from Hyde Park in a private train car, then wheeled into the elevator and up to the elegant hotel.[1]

By the time I find the next underground location, I am thirty blocks up the West Side of Manhattan, in the area below

Riverside Park. Though there are several gates along the way, all were closed. Jumping over a four-foot brick wall, I walk down a sloping dirt-covered incline with evergreen shrubbery on both sides, next to a winding *S*-curve in the West Side Highway. I squeeze through a short fence before passing through a hole in an oval, latticed iron gate in Riverside Park and, from there, into an almost infinite black expanse. This gate is nearly invisible until you reach the bottom of the hill, but there a platform structure extends to a stairway with a pipe-fitted banister. Only the first few rickety steps are visible; beyond that is darkness.

The stairway into the underground shows the footprints of only a few others. With the rusting rails and broken glass, most of which look undisturbed, I could not tell there had been many feet crossing this path before. To the right of the stairs as I move further south toward the entrance, there is a group of recently deinstitutionalized men and women who would scream and holler if anyone approached. I had been told by an official at ADAPT, a grassroots group that provides outreach and psychiatric help for the homeless, that this was one such group. They are like sentinels guarding the entranceway.

Immediately at the ground-floor level, I can see dirt, cans, boxes, and assorted debris: the rubbish accumulated by the few visitors who braved the underground to live or left by the adventurous loner who came out of curiosity. Some rubbish made its way down through the grates above the park, as kids could be seen squeezing paper cups and cans through the ironwork just for fun, to see it flutter or clatter down onto the tracks.

I enter the underground of smells, odors, and scents from human bodies, garbage, burning wood, crack cocaine, tobacco fumes, food cooking, dust, dirt, mildew, rotting debris. Odors emanating from human feces can be scented along the edge of walls away from the camps or housing. Some people initially act crazy to avoid talking with me or anyone above ground, only to later act sane when they learned through the underground grapevine that I was OK to talk to and not somebody "crazy from topside." In many instances, they apologize.

FIELD NOTE: BERNARD AND THE STORY OF THE UNDERGROUND (2016)

The prose of this section comes from a field note I wrote in 2016. The story of the underground could not have been recorded without my first meeting Bernard Monte Isaac, who hollered out from the Ninety-Fifth Street grate, what he called his "intercom," one day as I made my way to his bunker 175 feet below Riverside Park. I'd met him because the historian Laurie Gunst and reporter Sammye Chisolm both had told me about a man living underground near Ninety-Sixth Street. Although I had started writing about people living underground in the 1980s, I only found Bernard in 1989. This relationship would last more than two decades, our conversation continuing in his underground bunker, in restaurants, and in my own apartment, discussing life, politics, drug stories, children, wives, family.

We continued to talk about all these issues even after he left the underground and moved into an apartment in the Martin Luther King Jr. Houses, about a block from where I currently reside. I invited him to speak at the university, both at Princeton and the New School, as part of my "Seminar of Engagement" course. We met last at Princeton in 2011, before I heard of his death in 2014 of unknown causes.

Bernard is one of the many people who lived underground and whom I call "poor fragile people" because the world they live in, work in, love in, and made their homes in for many decades

FIGURE 1.2. Bernard resting in the fire spit area behind the Goya's *Third of May* graffiti wall.

Source: Photo by Teun Voeten.

is just that: poor, fragile. The term "fragile" also points to the sheer number of people included in this account. New York has a population of 8 million. At last count, over sixty thousand of these individuals are in "fragile" circumstances. In his book *Homelessness in New York City*, Thomas Main wrote:

The post-paternalistic features of the city's homelessness policy were broached during the early Bloomberg years. It was under Bloomberg that, with much publicity and acclaim, a five-year plan was introduced, the expressed purpose of which was to "overcome or end homelessness." Ending homelessness really meant having a disproportionate impact on the use of shelters and services by focusing on the chronically homeless, as Culhane had suggested, sending them to supportive housing, and doing so without demanding "good behavior" first, in keeping with the Housing First policy.[2]

I had come to know a place in the city underground where a group of discarded (homeless) people were living 175 feet below the sidewalks along a mile stretch of land under Riverside Park and along the West Side Highway in New York City. My main contact's real name was Bernard, but as I indicated earlier, his nom de guerre underground was "Lord of the Tunnel," a title granted by his fellow underground residents. For my field notes and for the sake of writing in the journal, I called him "Glaucon." I thought that was a perfect name for him since IRB rules state I must provide anonymity. Although I began writing "Glaucon" in my journal rather than his family name, he insisted that in this book I use his real name, Bernard, since he was not ashamed of his underground persona. As matter of fact, he was proud of his living underground as an unhoused person for so many years, in part because he had gained a certain notoriety. Nevertheless, this was one of my early ethical issues as a researcher: I wanted him to remain anonymous, as the IRB insisted and my ethical principles dictated; I also considered him to be a person who might need some protection from his own ego. In the Allegory of the Cave, Plato takes the reader through a journey, an odyssey that is both pedagogic and poetic, an adventure that pushes the person from one end of life, where they are unknowing or ignorant, to the other end, that of knowing. Here, Glaucon serves as Plato's interlocutor: Socrates describes to Glaucon, to get him to better understand what he's trying to convey to him, a group of prisoners who are trapped or chained to the walls of a cave and cannot seem to get out. All they can see are the shadows on the walls, projected by the fire directly behind them. They see these shadows as reality when in fact they are not. Bernard was the Plato to my Glaucon, basically doing the same thing for me; he was schooling me, as they say in the street, "pulling my coat" to the many underground realities; taking me as a neophyte ethnographer to school, teaching me the ropes, telling me about life underground, how people live there, what they eat, how they survive the seasons. It might have been more apposite to have called Bernard Plato, but Glaucon sounded "cooler."

In the process of writing and assembling my early field notes, this idea of living in the bowels of the city led me to the psychoanalyst Harry Stack Sullivan's notion of the "not me." Sullivan argued there are three basic ways we see ourselves: (1) the "bad me," (2) the "good me," and (3) the "not me." The "bad me" represents those aspects of the self that are considered negative and are therefore hidden from others and possibly even ourselves. The anxiety that we experience when recalling an embarrassing moment or the guilt we experience when recollecting a past action are examples of our encounters with the "bad me" parts of ourselves. The "good me" is everything we like about ourselves. It represents that part of us we share with others and that we often choose to focus on because it produces no anxiety. The "not me" is the final part of us, which represents all those things that are so anxiety provoking that we cannot even countenance them being a part of us. To do so would create overwhelming anxiety. The "not me" must be kept out of awareness; that is, it must remain unconscious.

As I walked through the underground, I saw lots of shadows and felt at times I was truly living a sociological allegory, seeing the shadows around me as emblematic of the city's unconscious. Yet never for a moment did I forget that I was experiencing anything but the stark truth of people living in the bowels of a great city and how disturbing and wrong that reality is, how *it should not be*. As my friend and fellow scholar once asked me: "Why should people care about people under the ground when they don't care about people living above the ground?"

"NO NAMES"

There is also the chance that I as ethnographer would become part of the field notes of others. I wonder what it means to have the ethnographer be a character in someone else's book.

Here is one example of this. I took the Dutch photojournalist Teun Voeten down to meet the Lord of the Tunnel, and I found myself being an informant. The photojournalist wrote this account of the situation:

> The mouth of the tunnel looms a few hundred feet wide. Broken down railroad tracts wind between a forest of steel and concrete pillars and disappear into the darkness, into the netherworld I am about to enter. Professor Terry Williams leads me inside the tunnel, into the unknown. Slowly, the daylight disappears behind our backs, until we are engulfed by a cold, damp darkness. I shiver. I don't like dark caves with hidden dens, and to make it even worse, today is Halloween. I'm not in the mood for crazy tunnel people popping out of the darkness with Dracula masks and bloody butcher knives. Quietly I curse at Williams who thought today would be the perfect day to bring me into the tunnel.[3]

A few more steps down those dark stairs and a voice says, "Watch out for the next step. Walk along the edge, grab hold of the steel pipe and jump over the next step." A tall, dark-brown complexioned man about thirty years of age comes into view, carrying a bag of cans on his back. At first, he refuses to tell his name, saying that what people call him "has no societal purpose. I don't live 'up' there. I live in this dark community. None of us has any real need for names. We are no-names. This whole space down here is the land of the unforgiven."

Then he's silent. I walk with him along the train tracks. Autumn leaves, yellow and brown hues with specks of green, fall through a grate directly in front of us. Fall is the time of descent here, too, when people begin moving from the streets, subways, and other shelter locations into undergrounds. This underground has been called an asylum with a concrete sky, but my newfound guide, Bernard, now talking freely, describes it as a private space and a sanctuary from the chaos that is life above ground.

I walk the remaining steps onto thousands of hard rocks, scattered against miles of these glistening, rust-colored tracks. Underground bunkers, beneath highway embankments, abandoned cars, and derelict buildings. Bernard speaks in a professional manner, forming words carefully, educating as we move along. He speaks intelligently about art, science, and poverty. He mentions Shaw's celibacy and Melville's fidelity. He tells me he has Robert Caro's *The Power Broker*, Kierkegaard's *Either/Or*, Kafka, and other books kept in the cartons in his bunker. And his biblical allusions are too numerous to mention. "Hezekiah," he says, "who was the thirteenth king of Judah, lived and built tunnels in 700 BC. He built them right in Jerusalem. By that alone we are in good company. We have no reason to be ashamed of our underground existence."

He also destroys the myths about the underground. He tells me he knew of no one who ate rats; in fact, he held Friday night "fish fries," spit chats, and gourmet canned dinners where a host of other "lost souls" would sit by the campfire with me and tell stories about the "topside people." He knew of no people whose skin had become translucent because of time spent without sunlight—as a matter of fact, later I would go to Yale University to discuss with a scientist there the effect that a lack of light has on people who live underground. Bernard was right: it was a myth that people's skin goes translucent from too little sunlight. But what remains true is that these people are indeed fragile: of health, of station in life, of resources. They reminded me of Cervantes's exemplary novel *Man of Glass*, about a man who felt he was so fragile that if you touched him, he would break. This sense of fragility was present in my conversations with Bernard and with the others he introduced to me.

By the time we reach what he says is Eighty-Sixth Street, the only sound is of water dripping from recent rainfall: twin puddles across the tracks, one puddle at each end of the steel rails. I do hear cars rushing above in the distance, but their racket is muffled by the silence down here. We stop for moment as he explains a passage from the Bible. The shadows of park joggers stretch across the high grate overhead as we again move up the tracks.

I do like the still, quiet, and calm down under. An intimate quietude—not hurried by the rush of people, no movement save our own, no one at all, until he points to an alcove above the tracks. There, he says, lives a reclusive fellow rarely seen coming or going. We pass an entrance that is now sealed, making traffic nonexistent.

In the shadow of the half-light, Bernard's features cast an eerie glow. The trek becomes dank and difficult; I feel uneasy on this uneven terrain. I can barely see where I'm going and have no idea of where we are except that we're moving north. Bernard is talking about the underground, but half my attention is focused on maintaining a sense of place and footing. There are few underground markers, and the space is now totally dark. I look ahead, trying to make out a fleeting image, but I am unsure if anybody or anything is really there. As a researcher, I have learned how important it is to "be there" in the physical and sociological sense to capture the moment, to record the significance of events as they unfold. But nothing in my experience has prepared me for this level of uncertainty.

Bernard mentions other residents: Bobo, Beatrice, Jason, Tin Can Tina, and Jean Pierre. These individuals are just a small part of the underground population. There are an estimated 250 neighborhoods in New York City (at least), and the populations in each neighborhood can run into the hundreds of thousands. I am reminded that, above ground, this neighborhood along Riverside Drive consists of middle-class brownstone occupants as well as multimillion-dollar skyscrapers that house the super-rich. The main identity of the neighborhood is the Hudson River, Central Park, Riverside Drive, and Riverside Church.

If we define the neighborhood as from Fifty-Seventh Street to 125th Street and from Riverside Drive to Central Park West, that is, as the Upper West Side, we would find that it has a population of roughly two hundred thousand. By contrast, Bernard thinks there are fewer than one hundred people in this underground community. He does not think highly of those who have surveyed and written about underground life thus far. "We had a woman down here once, and she wrote a book about us and told the most outrageous lies. She came down here on and off for about three months and just made stuff up. Her work was so sloppy, she didn't even spell my name correctly. I hope you do a better job." I told him I would be here for the duration and that I intended to stay as long as he did, maybe even to see him leave the underground. He smiled and said, "That may be a long time."

We continue walking. It is difficult to tell whether the image I see, or think I see, is moving away from or toward us. Four distinct sounds can be heard, and only four: water dripping from a tiny aperture about seventy-five feet above, the echo of cars passing over concrete, the gravel rocks underfoot, and my own breathing, which grows louder as I notice a figure that's *definitely* moving toward us. But when we get to the place where the figure should be, I see no one.

Bernard has said nothing about mirages in the underground, but as we walk farther, I realize this must have been a visual hallucination. Moving from light to darkness creates at first a sense of isolation, then a nervous tingling up the back of the spine as the lack of light plays tricks on the senses. This movement from light to darkness, openness and freedom to claustrophobic confinement, is unnerving, to say the least. But what truly strikes me so far are the paradoxical features of the underground: even as the underground is evoking images of burials, basements, tombs, catacombs, and coffins in me, I am with someone who lives here and considers it as home, safety, and security, more so than the city above.

How do people accommodate themselves to the life down here? How do they survive the more extreme moments, by which I mean winter, cold, noise, and dust pollution? "I never stay down here all week without getting out for an hour or two. But this is peaceful compared to what you have to contend with up there." Bernard points upward. He admits to being an avid reader, and he reads wherever he can, which sometimes is in the park but mostly by candlelight in his cinderblock room. "I guess you could say I'm a bibliophile." Like many other underground residents, he gets his reading matter from building superintendents along Riverside Drive, who in turn get them from their well-read tenants. He has opinions about many subjects. Spirituality is a favorite topic, as I will learn, and he holds forth on God and Satanism, white and black magic, totemism and Freud.

He is particularly piqued about the new "Afrocentric" view of history: "It is not new at all but was and has been the origin of knowledge destroyed in Alexandria and Timbuktu, the two depositories of ancient knowledge, along with the pyramids where white men have desecrated and continue to destroy and rewrite the wrong history of the African." He says the Egyptian government should be brought down for allowing Europeans to desecrate the ancient tombs, "because the history they are plundering belongs to all Africans and not just Egypt."

I ask whether his store of knowledge is the reason he is referred to as the Lord of the Tunnel. "People call me that, but it has nothing to do with knowledge. Let me tell you the story. When I first came here six years ago, some people I knew told me some

FIGURE 1.3. Underground.

Source: Photo by Teun Voeten.

guys at the south end were charging people as they enter the underground. I paid that no mind for a while because I came in all over the place—there were many ways to get down here then. But one day as I came in the south end, a bunch of guys, mostly Cubans, stopped me and said I had to pay a tax to enter the underground. I told them, 'Me? Pay a tax? Why, I'm the Lord of Underground! I pay no such tax. If anything, you should pay me such a fee for the mere pleasure of conversing with me.' They looked at each other and shook their heads. And from that point on I have been known as the 'Lord of the Tunnel.' The name just stuck."

Bernard's lordship might not be a serious matter, but even in this desolate setting, hierarchies develop: people are trying to establish a community of their own but still aping those "topside" with their talk of order and rank. Roughly, the highest status belongs to those who sell books (some get hundreds of books from supers during the course of a year, which they sell to booksellers along Broadway); then come the can sellers; then the plastic bottle sellers; then the squeegee men (who are considered "beggars with a high school diploma"), who rush forward to clean windshields during red lights and then ask for a handout; then beggars with a regular spot on the street, in the subway, by a cash machine. At the bottom are the mentally ill chemical abusers ("MICAs," in social services parlance). Within the underground, people make claims about where they fit, claims that reveal a sense of who is more valuable.

Of course, rank is contested. Bobo, who fought in Vietnam, feels that all veterans—no matter where they live or what they do—are superior to everybody else "because we fought and died for this country." But, he adds, "The smart people are the ones who can read and write and work. If you sell them books and read them books, people down here look up to you more than they would if you're out there washing windows or begging."

Jason said that cleaning car windows with a squeegee, which is the way he spends his working time, "is not the most prestigious job, but it's better than begging."

Kal's comment reflects a general view: "Everybody know the crazies are the ones they should be taking outta here. Not us. They're the only ones that be rolling around on the tracks and disturbing the situation for all of us." Perhaps most telling of all was the annoyed response of a man who is often seen with his palm out at the Seventy-Second Street subway station when asked how he felt about begging: "What the fuck you talking about? Everybody in America begs. You begging now. Begging for info-motherfucking-mation. Get the fuck outta my face. On my radio I hear the begging all the time. On the TV they beg, big corporations beg, the city begs too. They beg you to pay your fucking taxes. I never paid no fucking taxes. Yeah, I beg, what of it? These motherfuckers should pay me for not fucking them up. Don't ask me no fucking questions about this underground. I'm sick of motherfuckers asking me questions about this fucking place. We all in Hell down here. Ain't nobody shit down here. They want to bulldoze over us and if they did nobody would give a flying fuck."

LIFE IN THE SHADOWS

The people underground scream, whistle, speak low, and cough; some do not speak at all. Some talk clearly; others use confusing language, especially those who cannot or will not communicate with anyone. At times I must place my face close to hear what a person is saying; for others, I have to stand back to avoid their aggression. Life in the underground is full of uncertainty, and the stories of the men and women who live here reflect that uncertainty, often blending fact with fiction and drawing on some form of urban mythology. Something about underground space clearly engages the imagination: it is the ideal setting for myth and fiction—dark, vast, labyrinthine, a refuge, a hideout from defeat, but also a place of emergence, resurrection, recovery, and triumph.

I want to learn how people came to live in the underground, how they survive, and what happens when they get out. The stories they tell vary in intensity depending on how urgently the teller needs money or someone to talk to. They also vary in content: Kal offers slightly different versions of his life from day to day—and yet another version in his written journal. Is lying different from mythmaking in name only? I have no interest in catching people in lies, yet it is clear that I cannot always trust what I hear. There is so much rumor and storytelling I find myself reevaluating the "truth."

Bernard meets me at the south gate. Up the tracks, on the right, are eight concrete bunkers: one is severely burned; two others have trash piled alongside. All are damaged, except for Bernard's and Kal's. They are about fifteen feet high and nestled between four graffiti-tagged, pyramid-shaped concrete pillars. A massive overlay of steel beams criss-cross the underground ceiling like a giant spider web, and piles of ice are spread beside the tracks. It reminds me of a passage from a Jack London story:

> From the undergrowth, where high water of the previous spring had lodged a supply of seasoned twigs, he got his firewood. Working carefully from a small beginning, he soon had a roaring fire, over which he thawed the ice from his face and in the protection of which he ate his biscuits. For the moment, the cold of space was outwitted. The dog took satisfaction in the fire stretching out close enough for warmth and far enough away to escape being singed.[4]

The burned-out bunkers have soot-covered plastic wrapped around the edges of their charred front entrances. Next to this last bunker is where Bernard and Kal live. Kal is standing near a fire pit with a stick in his hand. He's animated and on edge. He wants to get high; as they say down here, "*he's thirsty*," an ironic phrase, since the person is often craving smoke, not liquid. He begins abruptly: "You know I like the attention people coming down here give us, but don't you think they oughta give something to the people they talk to?"

He was pleased I agreed. "You're a real soul brother and I like you," flashing a snaggle-toothed grin. "Hey, this guy is cool. He's all right." Friendly enough at first, Kal made it clear he liked the attention but was ambivalent about it, complaining in the next breath (since I did not immediately take out any money), "Everybody who's been down here gets something but us. They come and they go. They write their stories and make their promises, but they don't deliver. We had a *New York Times* guy. This guy comes down here and he made promises but nothing ever happened. We had a film crew from Holland come down here and nothing happened. Now we got you down here and what's gonna happen?"

As noted, Kal lives in one of the eight concrete structures. "I got a nice one. I've got a gas lantern, a gas lamp. A queen-size bed resting on railroad ties, table, chairs, wall-to-wall carpeting. I got to clean it up for you. I'll let you see it one day." When I did see it, there are no railroad ties or queen-size bed, just an extremely dirty mattress on the floor, a few disheveled milk cartons, lots of newspapers, and blood on the wall. Kal tells me he's a good short-order cook—"flipped hamburgers and fried eggs all over America"—and repeats this several times, maintaining that he is "the only cook in the underground." This seems to be his way of saying he is a skilled man in an unskilled world.

He explains how he goes about his daily duties. "The first thing I do on Monday is pick up cans from my supers. I walk from Broadway and Ninety-Sixth to the World Trade Center three days a week. That's my exercise. I get paid, too, you know. After I been done that, I get the laundry, at least part of the laundry, done and then I go and get me a cup of coffee and relax."

Kal is the oldest of three brothers, one a police officer in Chicago, the other a priest. "I think I was happier in Chicago than I am now, but that's that. The thing is right now. You know, not where you've been or what you've done or how much schooling you have—it's where you are today. Now take Bernard, he says he want to get out of the underground, yet he stays here. It's like a good front. He says these things but never does anything."

He and Bernard bicker constantly. At first, this seems a sort of contrived one-upmanship, but it is really a choreographed way to get favors from topside people. The game was to make the other look less genuine, so the one doing the bad-mouthing could seize an opportunity to take advantage of the other person. For example, Kal says, "Bernard repeats the same thing over and over all the time. When he's interviewed, I could tell you word for word exactly what he's gonna say about dealing with the man, all of this other stuff. I've heard it fifteen, sixteen times. The same exact word for word." The implication being, talk to me—and pay me—instead.

In fact, Kal and Bernard are good neighbors; they live in abutting bunkers and respect and help each other in caring ways. And whenever any crucial decisions come down, each thinks of the other first. When Amtrak police told them they had to leave the underground or be forcibly evicted, Bernard said he would not leave without seeing that Kal had a place to stay, and Kal said he would not think about leaving without helping Bernard. But in spite of Kal suggesting we could cut Bernard out of my information-for-cash deal, they actually work out issues rather cooperatively.

Around the fire one evening, Kal and Bernard talked about their families. Bernard: "My mother used to say, 'Never go any- where without washing your face.' She told us this up until high school. Believe it or not, before I graduated, my mother would always say 'come here boy.' She'd run her hands up under my shirt to see if we were wearing a T-shirt. I was home last time in '83. I said 'mom, come on, give me a break.' Our mothers never change, man, that's one thing I can say. Mothers and kids, they never change. The only thing in life that basically remain the same are moms and kids. Boy, I'll tell you. You can put a group of kids, one of each nationality in one little area with a ball and they all play harmoniously. But when you become an adult, something happens."

Kal, who had stepped away during this "speech," returns with wood and beer. "What? He telling you the same thing, right?" Kal asks. He ribs Bernard about repeating certain phrases and slogans.

"Why don't you get off of all that, Kal?" Bernard remarks. "You know ignorance is bliss. Excuse me, Terry, but he needs to check himself, that's all."

"I was just telling him what you say," Kal says.

"You don't have to tell him what I say," says Bernard. "He hears what I say. You tell him what you have to say. You be con- cerned about your story and leave mine to me. As I was saying, Terry, *before I was so rudely interrupted*, it's necessary that you remain a child at heart to a great degree. I think that keeps some men sane when they mature. People wonder why I'm down here and say something must be wrong with me because I'm here. I say, think about it, people do what I do all the time, but in dif- ferent ways. When people go on vacation, those who can afford it, they're getting away from the madness of their everyday lives. When they go to the mountains or on that retreat in the woods, they're getting away from the madness. When the poor man goes into the bar before he goes home to that wife and kids, he's getting away from the madness. Well, I'm down here to get away from the madness. But I don't have to tell you that total man has gotten away from anything spiritual.

"And," Bernard glances over at Kal, who is within earshot, "man has failed to perfect spirituality, so he must have chaos. It's one or the other. Like I've told people who come down here, this is the perfect environment to destroy oneself or to grow. And to never take too much for granted. I think in life man takes too much for granted. I think one of his greatest mistakes is he thinks he's in control of his destiny. He's not. He just puts God on hold. Money is more important. But he forgets the material plane is only temporary. But don't you forget the underground is a great teacher."

Kal: "Well, I told you I didn't want my money like a horse shit in the road. You know, here and there. Ha! And that made him pissed with me for saying that. But the truth is the light."

Bernard looks over at him and says: "Healing is often so difficult because we don't want to know the pain."

Kal, silent, reaches into a pile of kindling, places two large boards on the waning fire, and when they begin to burn pushes them under the grate.

2

GENESIS

*I smell cherry blossoms at the grate as I peer down on the tracks
before heading down under the ground. The Hudson River is
right across the highway. There is also a huge crowd of people
taking pictures of the cherry blossoms. This is cherry blossom
time, and much is in bloom; there is a low-growing, hairless
perennial flowering plant in the buttercup family (Ranuncu-
laceae) resting there, with fleshy dark green heart-shaped leaves
and distinctive flowers with bright yellow glassy petals.*
—Field note, April 1995

We are all dying to be dead.
—Man screaming near the entrance to the underground

ON THE HUDSON

I have had mixed feelings about the Hudson River over the
years—repulsed by the dark grayish color and dank odor,
hopeful at the prospects of the river regaining its past glory. It
was those bygone years I'd read about, when ships could be seen
floating from the Battery to the George Washington Bridge or

when ten-foot sturgeons made their way, in spring, up from the Atlantic to spawn, witnessed by tugboat crewmen.

Most New Yorkers are not aware of how many people still fish in the Hudson, especially at the 125th Street pier, which was once the Edgewater–125th Street pier. Edgewater, New Jersey, and Manhattan were linked by ferry at this site until 1950; it closed after the Lincoln Tunnel and the George Washington Bridge were built. The Englishman Henry Hudson, in the employ of the Dutch East India Company, believed he had discovered a quick passage to China in 1609 when he sailed into New York Bay, only realizing he had not after reaching what is now Albany. The river was named Cahohatatea by the Iroquois and Muhhek-unnetuk, the "river that flows two ways," by the Mohicans and Lenape. Early maps, sailor's journals, and correspondence from seafaring adventurers depict a powerful river surrounded by dense forests, a menagerie of wild animals, large snakes, mountain lions, thick vegetation, and an ecology too difficult to penetrate.

Around 1807, after the invention of the steamboat, the Hudson River became a key site for waterway travel and an important factor in New York and the United States' burgeoning economy. Forty-three years later, as many as 150 of these boats at a time could be seen moving millions of passengers along the river. During this period, as Americans were shaping their new national identity, the Hudson Valley became a cultural focal point, gathering stories and scenes from the Revolution and Dutch folklore of the region's early settlers.

When the Erie Canal was completed in 1825, connecting the Great Lakes to the Hudson at Troy, New York, the Hudson River became one of the nation's main channels of trade, ushering in a period of major economic and industrial expansion in the area. The New York Knickerbocker writers Washington Irving, James Fenimore Cooper, and William Cullen Bryant, to name only three of the most famous, wrote numerous articles and books about life along the Hudson. Irving, one of the country's first great writers, used the stories and scenery of the Hudson Valley as the basis for "The Legend of Sleepy Hollow" and "Rip Van Winkle."

Yet by the mid-to-late 1800s, the river had become polluted. By the turn of the century, as tuberculosis and other deadly diseases began to spread in New York City, the Hudson River became a health threat and dumping ground for aluminum processing, coffee roasting plants, sulfuric acid factories, and railroad siding manufacturing. Before the arrival of the railroads in the 1800s, the banks of the river hosted a community of squatters, vagabonds, and hobos.

In the 1930s, New York Parks Commissioner Robert Moses covered the New York Central railroad tracks, creating a two-and-a-half-mile-long underground under the promenades of Riverside Park, starting at Seventy-Second Street and ending at 125th Street. It would soon evolve into a shantytown. Eventually the underground was no longer used for rail traffic, and its current residents began moving into the space as early as 1974. While the Hudson lost its importance as a fishing enterprise, it was maintained as a shipping port until the 1970s. Up to that time, the West Side docks from Battery Park City to Manhattan's West Forty-Second Street had been a major port until a restructuring of the shipping industry caused its decline and eliminated one of New York's blue-collar economic bases.[1]

By the 1980s, the Hudson was polluted by so many PCBs (polychlorinated biphenyls) and other toxins that people had to be warned not to swim, fish, or even wade in the water. In recent

years, however, the Hudson has been making a comeback, largely
from state efforts to decontaminate and campaigns to destigma-
tize: in 1998, the American Goodwill Games used the river as a
swimming venue. But all along—even when they shouldn't
have—people have never stopped fishing in the water.

Today, a new era of life on the Hudson unfolds as developers
build on the site of the old Penn rail yards in the West Seven-
ties along the West Side Highway. This is the last large, unused
plot of developable land left in Manhattan. Meanwhile, Columbia University, the second-largest landowner in the city, has
acquired most of the property at or near the 125th Street pier and,
unless local zoning laws change, the university will convert much
of the land into university properties. The 125th Street pier is
now a sprawling space rebuilt to accommodate a large development including a Fairway supermarket. The last time the Penn
trains ran was January 3, 1956. The railroad was originally sched-
uled to run until September 1955, but a number of lawsuits post-
poned the abandonment until a year later.

Thirty years ago, if you ventured into the undergrounds, dip-
ping below the surface of New York City and moving parallel
to the beautiful boulevard of Riverside Drive as far as 125th Street,
you would have seen trains but no homeless people. Employment
was plentiful, and housing, at least in the form of cheap dives,
single room occupancies (SROs), and welfare hotels, was readily available.

Over the last thirty years, property values across major portions of New York City have soared. Every block and niche is
subject to development and redevelopment, and more and more
people have become vulnerable to eviction as they find they lack
the time, effort, and money needed to withstand the forces of
the real estate market.

"A SHELTER IS NOT A HOME"

David Dinkins made addressing homelessness a cornerstone of his 1989 mayoral campaign, and his agenda was based on the recommendations made in a report he commissioned while Manhattan borough president. Prepared in March 1987, "A Shelter Is Not a Home" set a progressive agenda that confronted "myths" regarding homelessness and, importantly, defined homelessness as an economic and housing problem. Yet Dinkins's tenure as mayor was defined by difficulties in implementing this vision.

When Dinkins assumed office in 1990, one of his first orders of business was to move homeless families from shelters to permanent housing, with the goal of increasing the city's "production of rehabilitated apartments for homeless families to 8,000 per year."[2] One of the background assumptions of this measure was that "doubling the supply of city-provided permanent housing would not stimulate demand for temporary shelter." This assumption was reflected in a section of "A Shelter Is Not a Home" that addressed what Dinkins's task force called "Myth 7," arguing that there was "little evidence that families forsake housing arrangements hoping to get an apartment through the city."

In the summer of 1990, as the Dinkins administration moved briskly to relocate homeless families from welfare hotels and shelters to permanent housing, "an average of 561 shelter families per month, or 55 percent of the shelter population, were referred to city-provided permanent housing."[3] There was evidence the measure was working: in 1988, the number of homeless families living in welfare hotels dropped dramatically from 3,306 to only 147. However, new entries into the system soon increased, rising from 530 per month in the spring of 1990 to 650 per month by July.

The issue at hand was the "perverse incentives" that were created by the possibility of receiving permanent housing, as had been promised to every family that entered the shelter system. The assumption had been that families would not enter the system just in order to "upgrade" their housing. Yet several of Dinkins's staffmembers were soon convinced that the increased supply of housing in fact was creating increased demand. Dinkins eventually, albeit reluctantly, accepted this conclusion, stating that unintentionally an incentive for people to use welfare hotels had been created. In other words, families had become homeless in order to upgrade their housing.

The increase of families into the system was termed the "Dinkins deluge" by the economists Michael Cragg and Brendan O'Flaherty. Thomas Main offers as examples a number of studies, including one of his own, that endorsed the perspective that "perverse incentives" had been created.[4] Cragg and O'Flaherty themselves acknowledge that perverse incentives had been created, yet they claim the effect was not as strong as many had thought, with "seven placements into permanent housing being required to entice one family into the system."[5]

In order to address this issue, the Dinkins administration created the Alternative Pathways to Housing Program (APP), implemented in October 1990.[6] This initiative cut the amount of available housing, increased the amount of time families had to wait for permanent housing, and offered housing to families on the basis of a lottery. These strategies were meant to reduce incentives for families to leave their current housing arrangements. The number of families entering the shelter system subsequently dropped.

Another challenge the Dinkins administration faced in transitioning the housing of homeless people, families, or individuals from armory-style housing to permanent public housing is

reflected in the report's "Myth 13": "No community wants housing for the homeless in its backyard. Fact: . . . Communities
have accepted housing for the homeless when the facilities are
small-scale and well-supervised by an accountable non-profit
organization, priority is given to homeless people from the same
area, and advance planning includes local input."[7]

This assumption, that communities are accepting of the
homeless being housed in their communities, if done properly,
was challenged from two directions. First, when homeless families were placed in public housing, it threatened the policy of
having an "economic mix" of residents in public housing, which
involved balancing the occupants of public housing to include
one-third elderly, one-third poor, and one-third families on public assistance. Residents of public housing that were waiting for
vacancies to open up in their building also resented having pref-
erential treatment given to homeless families.

Second, the city ran into trouble implementing its five-year
plan to provide 2,500 new beds in transitional housing for single
homeless individuals. This included a "fair distribution" of
twenty-four shelters throughout the city. "Fair distribution" in
this case meant using an IBM 3090 computer to assign the sites
for the construction of new shelters. The leaking of plans for
constructing a shelter in Staten Island to a local newspaper led
to a wave of caustic NIMBYism that caught Dinkins administration officials off guard. As one official put it, "After the plan
came out, we went to a lot of community meetings. . . . They
were brutal. They were really brutal."[8]

Also at issue in the placement of homeless shelters in the
city were two competing views over the causes of homelessness: structural/economic versus behavioral. The tenants of
public housing and communities objected to the placement of
homeless people, whether families or individuals, given the

stereotypes of the homeless as dysfunctional and criminal, assumptions the Dinkins administration assumed to be unfounded. Yet an influential study published by New York University's Health Research Program in September 1989 found that "homeless families have consistently higher rates of behavioral problems than their housed counterparts."[9]

A follow-up study conducted by the National Institute of Mental Health found that such problems did not prevent homeless families from achieving housing stability once receiving a housing subsidy. Nevertheless, a concerned Housing Authority, in June 1992, implemented eligibility requirements, including screening for behavioral problems such as substance abuse, for homeless families and ceased to "warehouse" empty apartments for placement of this population. They resumed placing homeless families in hotels.

The difficulties the Dinkins administration faced and its eventual admission that its approach was not working led to the formation of a committee tasked with rethinking the approach to this seemingly intractable social problem. The resulting Cuomo Commission published a paper entitled "The Way Home: A New Direction for Social Policy," which endorsed the "Dinkins Deluge Hypothesis" and questioned the unconditional right to shelter. The report states that "government should not, and cannot, be expected to provide housing to everyone that asks for it" and that "a determination of need must be made so that the governments resources may be targeted to where it's most needed."

The Cuomo Commission recommended that shelter be provided on the condition that clients acknowledge they had a problem, or that their homelessness had an "underlying cause," and enroll in some form of rehabilitative treatment as a condition for shelter. Thus, in what Main calls the "paternalistic paradigm," this involved a rewriting of the social contract between the helper and the helped, where the rights of the helped are linked to responsibilities of the helped, what the Giuliani administration would term a "mutuality of obligation."

After the Cuomo Commission report was released in February 1992, the response of the Dinkins administration was ambivalent, and the report was heavily criticized by some of his more liberal staff members. Nonetheless, in September 1992, Dinkins decided to put the commission's recommendations into action. This meant better management of the shelter system, what Thomas Main refers to as the "managerial approach" to homelessness, and the creation of the Department of Homeless Services. This approach was not entirely effective, however, and on December 8, 1993, the head of the DHS was found in contempt of a court order that prohibited homeless families from being placed overnight in the offices of Emergency Assistant Units.

Two days later, this person resigned. In what Thomas Main refers to as a "classic article" on the managerial approach, Dennis P. Culhane argues that

> the ability of shelters to serve as homeless management agencies is constrained by the structural causes of the homeless problem. Without renewed commitments from public agencies responsible for the treatment of mental illness and substance abuse, for reintegrating paroled persons in the community, and for promoting child welfare, affordable housing, and income maintenance, the shelter system will remain overburdened and unmanageable.[10]

Such a managerial approach would nonetheless remain a staple of the subsequent Giuliani and Bloomberg mayoral reigns.

CONTEXT: ECONOMIC DEPRESSION

In his second "State of the City" address, Mr. Dinkins lambasted
the federal government for withdrawing funds to cities and
states. "A turnaround in the national economy will happen only
when Washington commits itself to better lives for people—not
to better bombs for our armies and tax breaks for the privileged."
Despite dwindling federal support, Mr. Dinkins said, his administration had managed to close a combined 1990 and 1991 budget
deficit of $1.3 billion and to decrease reported crime by 6 percent
in the last year, compared with a 2 percent increase in crime
nationwide.[11]

Besides the economy, another important piece of the context
was changing public attitudes toward the homeless. On January
20, 1992, the *New York Times* published an article entitled "Apathy Is Seen Greeting Agony of the Homeless," which stated:
"The compassion that in the 1980s led to shelters, soup kitchens and other private efforts to help victims of bad economic
times has not disappeared . . . but some fear that it is being
overwhelmed."[12] The pervasive sight of homeless panhandlers
threatened to turn visible human suffering into a taken-for-
granted and unavoidable component of the environment. While
warning that resignation to the plight of the desperately poor
could have a broad impact on the nation's values in the future, a
number of spiritual leaders interviewed in the article saw the
danger as arising not from callousness but from a sense of pow-
erlessness. And on a personal level they acknowledged that they
shared some of the same ambivalence: "The daily encounters
harden many of us to some degree," said the Rev. Joan B. Campbell of New York City, executive director of the National Council
of Churches. "You do walk past. I've often said, 'What is this
doing to me?'"[13]

In 1997, a similarly entitled article appeared, "Charities Fear Climate of Cynicism Around Poor," suggesting that what had previously been described as a "perception" had crystallized into a reality, although only anecdotal evidence is given. "There is a moral imperative if we consider the concept of community," said Megan E. McLaughlin, executive director of the Federation of Protestant Welfare Agencies. "It has always been family, community and country," she said. "We are struggling now about whether it is going to be family and nation or if it's going to be family, community and nation. That's why I think it is in fact a watershed period, because we are making some critical decisions."[14] America had become a divided nation with no "common ground."

Toward the end of Dinkins's term, he received some negative press. In "A Roof for All Made of Rulings and Red Tape," which appeared in the *New York Times* on July 4, 1993, the journalist largely depicts Dinkins as having failed to resolve the city's homeless problem, highlighting how the shelter system had grown in size without an equal growth in effectiveness.[15]

"MOLE PEOPLE"

A graffiti artist named Freedom had "discovered" the underground in the late 1970s/early 1980s, when only a few underground residents were living there, and he used it as a space for his art. When a Columbia University journalism student named Jennifer Toth went into the Seventy-Second Street tunnel at that time, one of her informants was this artist. Graffiti artists are often connected to people on the edge or margins of society, and, as always, these marginal folk comprised the population in the tunnel. Though I never met Ms. Toth, her other contacts,

Bernard and Kal, were my main friends and guides to the underground for more than a decade. I learned from them that Bernard and others grew to mistrust Toth over the course of her research.

The real estate boom in the 1990s was a bust for the poor. The issue of unemployment and the state's lack of interest in those who were poor or middle class were beginning to take shape. This is when the underground became a locale for the indigent as opposed to a place for trains. When residents were discovered after almost sixteen years of occupying the space, media insensitively depicted them as "mole people," in part inspired by a large graffito on the north wall near a cluster of concrete bunkers.

This graffito reveals a gray mole descending underground, accompanied by two striking panels on the left wall consisting of a melting Daliesque clock, shaped like an oyster, and a headless male and female figure. The murals are spray-painted directly below one of the many shafts of light beaming down through the underground like a dream. Visitors can see the gray mole piece near the Joe DiMaggio and Marilyn Monroe murals on the same wall. This graffito was done by the artist Chris Pape—aka Freedom. The irony is this graffito was also a harbinger of their exploitation: Freedom purportedly "discovered" them, yet he was also responsible for a pernicious representation of these individuals, one they found abhorrent.

Kal says some residents practice what is called "Santeria" in the underground, discussed openly by a few and in hushed voices by others. Bernard dismisses it as low-level sorcery but also calls it a religion to be respected. Santeria is an underground religion in many senses, so the underground is a perfect place for its practitioners: the darkness creates a sense of mystery and fear of the unknown, and many believers say it would be misunderstood if practiced openly.

In Spanish, Santeria means "the worship of the saints." In fact, it is a mixture of the ancient African Yoruba religion and Catholic beliefs. Bernard and Jason, a man of Puerto Rican/African descent who also lived underground, had a lively conversation about a white man with a small cult-like following involved in witchcraft-related rituals who jumped to his death from the window of his Riverside Drive apartment. According to Bernard and to rumor in the street and under it, the man was possessed: he had sold his soul to the Devil, and the Devil came to claim it. Jason was more interested in why the man had attracted so many followers. The incident itself was real enough; newspaper accounts show that Oric Bovar, a "mystic healing masseur" who lived at 666 Riverside Drive and had many famous clients, died by suicide. Apparently, Bovar had been brought the body of a man dead or dying of AIDS, before the disease was widely recognized, and tried to revive him. Bernard continues the tale: "The story goes that the body of the dead guy began decomposing. The neighbors called the police, and Bovar was arrested. His friends and followers protested at the precinct, and Bovar was released until an autopsy was performed. Well, in a day or two, Bovar was dead. I kept asking: where did he get such ancient powers to raise the dead? He was dealing on the dark side, and he had no choice but to jump because he failed."

"The man had special powers," Jason says, "And he wanted to use those powers for good, that's why he was taken. He used to come to the underground because I saw him many times." Bernard was skeptical, but didn't openly dismiss Jason's account. Later, when Bernard was not present, Jason confided, "I'm known as the Wizard of Oof and Poof," he says, with a half-smile on his face. "Bernard believes I'm into magic, because

90 percent of the things I've told him was gonna happen down here with individuals and people, it's happened." This is not intuition, he says. "It's because after a while you get to know people and get to know what they're like and then you become a good judge of character and you know what they are headed for. So it's easy to say, 'in one night soon this person is gonna come down here scared out his wits, hyper, thinking people are out to get him. He'll be nutty for a week, and then he'll calm down and everything will be okay.' Well, I said this about one guy and it happened. This guy keeps coming down, thinks everyone's out to get him. I said, 'It's okay Bernard. In two days he'll be fine.'"

3

UNDERGROUND ECOLOGY

A tree grew over there last summer. The workers on the tracks cut it down. It grew up under the grate where the sky shines in. I love it when it rains or snows because it cascades down under there. It's beautiful.

—Beatrice

We are below the water lines and the sewer system," one underground dweller informs me. I have no way of knowing if he's right or not. "But," he adds, "this tunnel is part of a maze of underground byways and secret passageways that have been built near the tracks, in walls and embankments." I pace off, using the light from matches and the dim glare through the grates, measuring one alcove at forty four feet long with a thirteen-foot outside diameter.

These nooks and crannies are situated near or above the tracks, in thirty-foot niches or inside wall enclosures originally designed as emergency exits. Some of the smaller alcoves were constructed to provide drainage; these were sealed after the tracks were laid and later found by street vagabonds. This particular underground space is several miles long and seventy-five-feet

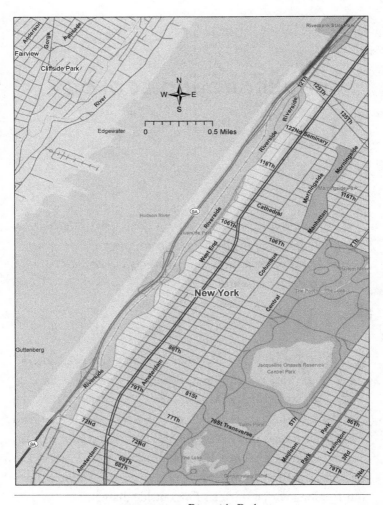

FIGURE 3.1. Riverside Park.

Source: Map by Rick Bunch.

deep, starting at Grand Central Terminal (see figure 3.1) and running through the living rooms of homeless residents from Seventy-Second Street to 125th Street and Riverside Park.

There are also more than 32 million miles of utility lines, ranging in depth from a foot below the street to more than eighty stories below ground. They transmit or transport various things and are of varying danger: orange is for electrical wires, yellow for steam, red for gas, black for television cable, and pink for telephone lines. These are the life tissues of the city: the nine million people who live here cannot eat a hot meal, drink a glass of water, or sleep in a warm bed without them.

The underground sits on a major rock formation called the Fordham Gneiss, which ambles down through Connecticut and Westchester County to form the spine of the Bronx. The gneiss then crawls under the Harlem River and is the plate on which the entire island of Manhattan rests.

The stones are hard and strong underfoot, and light flickers through the grates. I feel as if I am in a perforated grave. There is an eerie sense of freedom and surrender in these pillared passages where people live in tents and bunkers, holes in the walls, on beams and concrete ledges, hideaways, and hidden shafts. One engineer told me that underground sumps would collect the water that flowed down into and through each pair of rail tunnels. Pump chambers, directly above the sumps and between the tunnels, would push out the water.

A cross passage is built high above the pump chambers, between the walls of each pair of railroad tunnels. One bunker extends vertically about seventy-five feet below the highway and extends under parts of Riverside Park, according to the engineers I talked to. There are five such bunkers under this part of the underground, with several hundred people inhabiting the entire space, which stretches over two and a half miles.

The underground portions of Grand Central Terminal, where I first began my conversations with people living under the street, extend like a vertical spiral; this area is much harder to map than the Seventy-Second Street underground. There are few underground markers to indicate where you are in relation to the aboveground blocks at Grand Central, only a maze of dangerous looping tracks, making determining your precise location almost impossible.

TWO FIELD NOTES (MAY 1991)

I feel the world under my feet.
—Bernard

Heading up to the West Side highway along the Hudson in the spring, I see an apple tree with only one apple, partially red, partially green, hanging in the bright sunlight near Eighty-Ninth Street. Another tree, one near the walkway coming down near Ninety-Fifth Street in a stretch parallel to the highway overlooking New Jersey and the Hudson, has tiny black berries. Local horticulturalists from the Riverside Conservancy Garden tell me it is a Kwanzan cherry tree, a sight so distinct in the park and now recognizable along the embankment near the mouth of the underground gate. In the embankment, green crabapple trees sprout next to elderberry vines and Texas scarlet quinces (lesser celadine). Birds are here, too: a robin nest in the cherry tree, and sparrows everywhere. A butterfly flitters incongruously with black and yellow movements, and I cannot recall the last time I saw a butterfly in the city.

I previously called and spoke to a patrolman named Corbin at the Twentieth Precinct to alert the police that I was planning to visit the underground space between 125th Street and Seventy-Second Street. I went to several entrances along that route but found them all shut by the Parks Department, the police, or Amtrak officials. I decided to head for the Seventy-Second Street entrance. By August, the entrance had a new green fourteen-foot-high green fence, and only those who know how and want to go into this space can do so under these present conditions. You can't go over it, or under it, or cut through it.

From where I stand it seems impenetrable. I looked above the fence into the sky on this warm day; monarch butterflies are fluttering around, and even the Hudson River smells good. After seeing all the sprouting apple, cherry, and elderberry fruit trees, I made my way down to this point. I saw no homeless people sleeping under the arches near Seventy-Second Street like I usually do, as construction workers were removing most of the iron grating from the highway area down to where the folks once slept. At least six poor indigent people who once slept under these arches have moved into the underground.

The construction workers tell me they saw these same six people all going down there together. These workers are welding the grates. The lead engineer says the height of the steel beams from the grate is forty-five feet. He says people have taken to living on top of the forty-five-foot steel beams: he found a folding chair and a foam rubber bed there. I ask how they got to the point of nesting there, and he said they climb through the grate in the park. "These people are homeless, so we should not allow the state to get away with the idea that these people aren't human like the rest of us." A large number of pigeons fly near the Seventy-Second Street entrance. Oddly enough, a man is playing golf near the area playground.

The underground is a mile-long expanse of dirt, rocks, and old railroad ties with a recently reactivated rail line run by

Amtrak. There is a coldness down under that pulls at the bone; you can get pulled through the underground as if hypnotized by the gaze of graffiti on the walls, the sameness of rocks, the tracks that run people back and forth up north and down south via the Amtrak line. On the tracks underneath, the darkness starts around Eightieth Street and runs for three blocks to about Eighty-Third Street. The tracks are about fifty-three feet across.

On the wall at the far end of the underground space two blocks away from Kal and Bernard's place is what they refer to as their living room. Several graffiti pieces appear on both sides of the tracks. One is a modern Mona Lisa, and the other is of baseball icon Ted Williams. Both have been tagged by antiartists. A bright orange penis has defaced the mouth of the Mona Lisa, and a machine gun is sketched near Ted Williams. The space is near the entrance where gay men meet to consummate sexual acts. Kal and Bernard have taken to cleaning up the pieces and want to do so with the help of anybody who can give them a dollar for spray cans.

I touch the tracks after the train passes to see if it's hot. I look for signs of life other than humans; a white cat creeps by, searching for mice; a colony of ants and centipedes, rocks, steel concrete, wet, damp, but nothing green.

There are about 113 people living in various structures in this underground space, only one of many such locations in the city. The area contains a cross section of the city, with a mixture of white (5 percent), Black (80 percent), and Hispanic (15 % percent); teenagers, women, men, the mentally ill, homosexuals, and heterosexuals all call the underground home. The study of the various communities—or "encapsulated" lifestyles—that coexist in cities, in different social and cultural spaces, primarily in residential communities but not limited to them, is one of the most established traditions in North American urban sociology. It began with urban sociology itself, with the Chicago School, which between 1913 and 1940 defined theoretically and empirically the research agenda for American cities. Using the perspective of "human ecology," a group of sociologists at the University of Chicago argued that the spatial and physical organization of the city and its neighborhoods had a direct influence on how different styles of life developed within that city.[1]

The starting point for the Chicago School was a foundational article in 1915 by Robert Park, which ten years later was included in a widely influential collection entitled *The City*, edited by Park, Ernest Burgess, and Roderick McKenzie. Park and his colleagues were inspired by the idea of natural order in the fields of ecology and botany, and they sought a similar kind of order in urban sociology. They argued that modern cities were made up of physically distinct natural areas and that each area constituted a social world of its own that could be explored by researchers. Physical proximity and contact between residents were seen as the basic elements in the organization of these areas.

In Park's analysis, the combination of all these areas makes the city a mosaic of little worlds and neighborhoods, which were separate and did not interpenetrate one another. In this context, the role of sociologists was to develop case studies of these neighborhoods. Another important step in the development of the human ecology perspective was the publication of Louis Wirth's 1938 essay "Urbanism as a Way of Life," which soon become the dominant theoretical piece in the field. Wirth recognized the existence of this mosaic of social worlds in the city. Yet he went further, arguing that the new environment of the industrial city—characterized by its large size, high density, and social heterogeneity—would have a negative impact on the kind of social relationships that human beings could have with one another.

In his view, this new urban environment would lead to "the substitution of secondary for primary contacts, the weakening of bonds of kinship, the declining of social significance of the family, and the undermining of the traditional basis of mechanical solidarity. All of this would produce a fragmentation of the consensual moral order of the city as a whole, while social relations among residents would become increasingly cold, impersonal, and fragmented, ending ultimately in generalized anomie."[2] For Wirth, this fragmentation of a common moral order among city dwellers was also the principal cause of the crime and delinquency that plagued urban society.

In sum, the Chicago School was characterized by the promotion of case studies of concrete, spatially defined communities, in which ecological variables played a central role in their analysis. At the same time, these studies emphasized broader changing trends away from "traditional" (meaning rural) styles of life and toward a new and modern "urban way of life."

In subsequent years, however, this perspective was criticized by other sociologists, who argued that class, occupation, ethnicity, and gender/family cycles were more important than ecological factors in determining how and why people react in different ways to their environment. Writing in the 1950s and early 1960s, Oscar Lewis, William F. Whyte, and Herbert Gans began to refute the assumption that local solidarities and primary group social relations would decline dramatically with the continuing evolution of modern urban life.[3]

The underground is underneath Riverside Park, where kids frolic all day on swings and in playgrounds, while their parents chat together and watch from park benches; where adults play tennis, throw Frisbees and balls, work up a sweat swinging bats, sit in yoga positions along the middle parts of the park, or walk their dogs. Joggers sprint around the edges in a neat track leading up some stairs. In spring, a veritable pantheon of blossoms approaches the center of the park, tulips and roses mostly.

Down near the end of the promenade are towering apartment buildings, a skyline in shapes and colors and prices too expensive for most New Yorkers. This is real estate worth billions of dollars; meanwhile, below this rests the great unwashed, penniless, in spaces unassessed by "topside" prices. J. Paul Getty, one of the richest men in America, said: "The meek or the poor may inherit the earth but not its mineral resources." Even though they might almost literally live in the mines.

Human ecology is the study of the relationship between people and their environment. There is a spatial as well as a temporal ecological dimension to be considered. Murray Melbin offered a fine example of temporal ecology when he looked at the way people move across the metropolitan terrain as a kind of frontier of time: "night has become a new frontier . . . and that time, like space, can be occupied and is so treated by humans."[4] Other studies work with time as a key factor in our sociological understanding. The spatial and ecological view has become prominent in our sociological imagination, and Lynds and Hawley have become classics in the field.[5] Hawley's contribution is in seeing community as a temporal structure, one guided by different forms of labor. Theodorson's accounting of Hawley argues "that the main task of human ecology [is] the analysis of community structure, which he conceives primarily in terms of the division of labor. Community structure from the ecological point of view is seen as the organization of sustenance activities— the way a population organizes itself for survival in a particular habitat."[6]

Inhabiting a harsh ecology, deprived of water, natural light, food, electricity, and heat, the dwellers of the underground are in a continuous struggle to protect themselves against cold and

FIGURE 3.2. Men at work repairing bicycles underground.

Source: Photo by Teun Voeten.

dampness. Some live in cinderblock structures that can be found along sidetracks and were originally used by railroad personnel. Others live high within tunnel embankments, inside wall niches accessible only by thirty-foot ladders, or in free-standing structures they have built in the tunnel's dark recesses. Pet cats are highly valued as predators against rats. There is a communal kitchen, where meals are prepared on a spit positioned under an air-vented grate. The firewood comes from broken furniture. The claw-footed leg of a Chippendale is placed on the pile: the fire spits out a bluish flame, and a spark shoots through the air, with a trail of smoke behind, illuminating a corner of the reproduction of Goya's *Third of May* spray-painted on the rear wall.

Water, food, and firewood are gathered topside from construction sites and barges along the Hudson River. The setting is visually powerful, the horror of these living conditions lit by a cathedral-like shaft of light. Graffiti extends throughout the underground. "Home of the Queen," at the Eighty-Third Street and Riverside Drive entrance, is a reflection of the homosexual activity that takes place there. "Donnie 3–10–90 Rest in pice" records a tunnel resident's death from AIDS. At the north end of the tunnel, graffiti replicas of Dali's clock, Michelangelo's David, the Venus de Milo. Much has been vandalized, not only by teenagers but also by Amtrak workers to assert their dominance.

RATS

This is a harsh environment: in winter and fall it is cold, and in spring and summer, damp. Mary Douglas in her book *Purity and Danger* (1966) said of dirt that it "may not look nice but it is not dangerous." You could argue that the unhoused underground live in filth and dirt, and though it may not be dangerous, it is unsanitary, the dust and dirt unpleasant.

These spaces are permeated by the smell of animals, mainly rats, who threaten to overrun the underground. The rats are brown rats (*Rattus norvegicus*), also called the house or Norway rat. The Egyptian rat (*Rattus alexandrinus*), also called the ship rat, is also present, and like the other two types, they are large, with big ears, short tails, stout skulls, pointed noses, and have ten to twelve teats each. The black rat (*Rattus rattus*) "is distinguishable from the brown rat by its smaller size, longer ears and tail and glossy black color."[7] People who live here know a lot about mice, ants, and rats. A rat, they say, is nothing more than a large mouse; however, rats have more rows of scales on their tails, and their tails are as long as their bodies.

All these rats carry diseases such as Brill's disease (a type of typhus), trichinosis, and tularemia (a plague-like disease carried by rabbits and squirrels, first found in Tulare County, California). The most deadly of all the diseases transmitted by rats, particularly the brown rat, is the bubonic plague, or "black death." The rats are host to a flea called *Xenocheopsis*, which is the most frequent carrier of the plague. Recently in Switzerland, over one million mink were killed because they contracted COVID-19, a situation demonstrating the hazards when a disease carried by animals threatens to switch over to humans, or vice versa. Such cases are rarely monitored by scientists around the world. Yet it is well known that rats began to live with humans during prehistoric times, "when the agricultural revolution stimulated domestication and prompted humans to build settled places. These humans constructed houses for themselves and containers to save grain. Since the beginnings of domestication, rats and mice have adapted completely to an indoor life, along with similarly flexible insects including fleas, flies, spiders, lice, bedbugs, clothes-moths, and cockroaches."[8]

As far as rats are concerned, people respect them but hate them as well. They have no illusions and understand they cannot get rid of them, regardless of how many cats they own. Bobo and Beatrice probably have a clowder of cats, perhaps owning more than any other underground resident. "I know they bite if you get 'em [rats] mad and if they are cornered somewhere, but hell this is their world, we're just visitors in it." Bobo said this on his way topside to get milk from a dumpster on Broadway. "But I've never been bitten by one, and I don't know if anybody down here has been. And I don't know if rats are smarter than cats or not, but I do know they can read a situation pretty darn well. They know when bait is poison, and they know, maybe it's the old ones, they know how to avoid traps. I saw one push a stick onto a trap to spring it and then grabbed the food." Whether this is true or just another underground myth I leave to the reader to decide.

Most rats in the city are the common city variety, the Norwegian brown rat, which we see everywhere—parks, playgrounds, subways and other undergrounds. The exterminator I interviewed confirms rats live for four years and are wise creatures, difficult to catch. One generation may become immune to the poisons that killed their parents. Once, behind one of the old bunkers, I found a small rat den with a spoon, a rubber nipple from a baby bottle, a penny, and shredded dollar bills.

Bobo tells me one day that the rats (he calls them "track rabbits") don't worry him. "No rat ever bit me. I've seen 'em fight cats, though. But the cats definitely chill out the rats. I haven't seen rats around here in months. Now everybody's scared of rats, and I know this. But if you don't bother them, they won't bother you. I had one in my room all the time I've been here. And I didn't bother him, and he didn't bother me. But if you start trying to hit him with a stick or something, it just makes 'em mad. They're more scared of you than you are of them."

Kal says, "What bothers me is when they try to get on the bed, even though my bed is built up, mounted on railroad ties. I don't use a box spring or anything because I'm off the floor. But you got to watch out if you have a cut or something because they are attracted to blood. Once in a great while, you got one big one, and they jump, but, you know, as a rule they can't get in because it's about a foot and a half high."

In fact, as I discover later, there are no railroad ties in Kal's room: he sleeps on an extremely dirty mattress, with a few disheveled milk cartons and lots of old newspapers strewn about, a perfect environment for rats and other vermin. "Some of the people in our area did have rats. My friend Nellie had 'em, and she had no wood or nothing to block the entrance, and the rats, of course, are going to come in—you know when it's cold they want to come in to keep warm." Some of the people in our area do have rats, but they are not seen as pets.

The *New Yorker* writer Joseph Mitchell wrote the following in 1944:

> The rats of New York are quicker-witted than those on farms, and they can outthink any man who has not made a study of their habits. Even so, they spend most of their lives in a state of extreme anxiety, the black rats dreading the brown and both species dreading human beings. Away from their nest, they are usually on the edge of hysteria. They will bite babies (now and then, they bite one to death), and they will bite sleeping adults, but ordinarily they flee from people. If hemmed in, and sometimes if too suddenly come upon, they will attack. They fight savagely and blindly, in the manner of mad dogs; they bare their teeth and leap about every which way, snarling and snapping and clawing the air.[9]

Bernard tells me a dead body was found at the Seventy-Second Street end of the underground about a year ago. Rats had eaten much of the badly decomposed body, I am told. Just inside the underground to the left, I notice a man's head, barely visible under some rags, newspaper, and cardboard boxes. He's not dead, just sleeping. A few feet away, two big rats scurry up a forty-foot concrete wall, under fallen leaves, and through a grate into Riverside Park. On the right are two old lean-tos, with recently added wood, cardboard, and tin. And a few feet away but several stories above a man has lived perched precariously on a beam for several weeks now. Bobo remarks, "If he falls, the rats will get him."

A block or two further on is a green tent placed well away from others; Bobo says this location is so rat infested he doesn't understand how anybody could live there. But Green Tent, as he is called—a big, burly, friendly man—apparently disagrees.

Kal says he sees rats as big as kittens around the underground and walking under or across the tracks. Along the edge of the paths rats can be seen alone and in groups. Most are about fifteen inches long, the males larger than the females, brown, sometimes white and black in color. They weigh about half a pound. I've seen these rats eating anything people eat, leftover food, seeds, and fruit, and I'm told by one homeless man that he has seen them eat fish, birds, and bird eggs.

These rats like to live near the river, or near water, for sure, and they are very productive, breeding sixty young each year per female, with a gestation period of only twenty-four days. The young are raised communally; that is to say, any female in the group can raise a pup. The rats are not particularly afraid of people: they don't always take off running every time a human approaches. They have excellent senses of smell and hearing; most are seen at night. Since the underground is mostly dark all the time, I see the rats all the time here.

Kal claims he can smell rats and keeps his place rat free by keeping cats and, on occasion, by setting big traps. "I told Bernard I can smell them, when they've been in my place or when they are coming around, but he don't believe me." One of my worst fears is to be bitten by one of these buggers, and that's why I have turned down invitations to sleep underground by many residents. I know the rats feel the vibrations as we walk because they scatter as I walk up the tracks.

The Rat Man is an authority on rats in the underground. While his fellow residents in the underground believe rats live longer, he argues that they only live two years. The brown rat, which goes by the moniker "sewer rat," has a pug nose, small ears, and, of course, shit-brown fur. But the Rat Man says they come in other colors too, like salt-and-pepper grayish and sometimes even black. This rat has been known to be cannibalistic if

hungry and will eat other rat species too. Since they are ninety
times more plentiful than the black or Egyptian variety, this tendency probably accounts for why they are so large.

I see rats again, now and then a pigeon nesting near the top
of the girders, and I think I see a bat, too. I meet Bernard near
the Ninetieth Street entrance and walk into the darkness. I can't
see much for a few minutes. Finally, we sit down at the fire spit
and converse on topics ranging from God to Nietzsche, neither
of whom I know much about. Bernard does most of the talking.
My grandmother said once to me that I have two ears and one
mouth, so talk less and listen twice as much. I guess that's what
I'm doing today. The weather is on the cold side, but the tunnel
is quite serene. I'm beginning to enjoy coming down here. It is
less chaotic than above ground.

Bernard goes into his house, which he has not allowed me to
enter yet. I have not asked, and he has not offered. He keeps saying his place is a mess. I end up counting the insects in the
earth, looking for *Spirobolus marginatus* (millipedes) and ant colonies. I stop digging when he comes back out. He wants to talk
about the kids who have been in the tunnel for the past few days
causing problems. "I can say without hesitation that the only
ones I hate are the kids who come down here and paint on the
walls and deface the nice work that Zane and Chris have done
for us. The kids have tried to destroy all the art, and that's why
I'm going topside tomorrow and buy some paint to have it
retouched. I guess you heard about the homeless guy sleeping
down at the end of the tunnel who was burned to death by a
bunch of kids. They just poured gasoline over him and lit a
match. You know the kids are at fault, but don't it make you
wonder what kind of parents they have to do such a thing? And
I bet they will just say they were having fun. My place was set

on fire too last year. It wasn't kids that did that. I know who did it. It was jealousy that tried to burn me out. I know where the person is and everything, and when I get myself together they're going to get theirs. You mark my words.

"We had an epidemic of rats about a year ago around the grill area," I think he says. "We just couldn't get rid of them. We didn't know what it was, you know. We don't keep food around. We keep it where they can't get at it. They was just, you know, they just congregated. And of course we got some cats down here fast, and the cats took care of all that. Like I said, it's been a month now since we heard anything out of the rats."

ANTS

My main problem is not rats or cats or people or dog barking but ants. They get into all my food stuffs, and that's a real problem for me.

—Beatrice

The family to which ants belong is called *Formicidae*, of the great order *Hymenoptera*, to which bees and wasps belong as well. The insects of this order have mandibles for biting and two pairs of membranous wings. The first abdominal segment becomes closely associated with the fore body (thorax), of which it appears to form a part. In all ants, there is this first part of the insect, the abdominal segment markedly restricted at its front and hind legs, which then forms a separate node at the base of its hind body. While the queen and the male both have wings, the queen ant is larger; the worker ant is wingless and smaller. Beatrice says her ant problem is because they are so damn smart. "I could swear these ants are smart as they can be. I put food away in plastic, and I know they can't smell it, but somehow they get into it before I know it."

She is not the first to think ants have intelligence: the fact that ants have impressive senses and powers of communicating is well known to scientists.[10] But while Beatrice thinks the insects are drawn by smells, which is true, they are also guided by light, being very sensitive to ultraviolet rays, and sound. When you see an ant highway, the trail of ants moving back and forth in a line, the ants are following their own scent track, secreted by the tenth segment of the feeler. They recognize other inmates of their nest by a sense of smell that resides in the eleventh segment; are guided to the eggs, maggots, and pupae to which they have to tend by sensations felt via the eighth and ninth segments; and take in the general smell of the nest itself by means of organs in the twelfth segment.

The work and experiments of Sir J. Lubbock of inducing ants to seek objects that had been removed show that they are guided by scent rather than by sight and that any disturbance of their surroundings often causes great uncertainty in their actions. Ants invite one another to work or ask for food from one another by means of pats with their feelers, and they respond to the solic-itations of their guest beetles, or mites, who ask for food by patting the ants with their feet. Scientists after Lubbock have shown that ants possess memory and can learn by experience, demonstrating a significant degree of intelligence. Even Lub-bock asserted that ants "have the gift of reason and their mental powers differ from that of men, not so much in kind as in degree."

It seems obvious to me that ants are not automata and that their powers are real, not imagined. The ant colonies I poked around in while waiting for Bernard and Kal are usually estab-lished either by a single female or by many females in association.

The queen, or foundress, of the nest lays eggs at first, before feeding and rearing the larvae, the earliest of which develop into workers. In some species (*Lasius alienus*), in which a colony is set up by a single female, the first workers are not born but only emerge from the cocoon after a hundred days. These workers take on the labor of the colony, some collecting food, which they transfer to other workers in the nest, whose duty is to tend and feed the larvae. The foundress is then provided by the workers with all the food she needs; she does not need to do anything except lay eggs. The population of the colony expands quickly; nests grow exponentially.

CATS

You are bound to admit that it's very nice
To know that you won't be bothered by mice—
You can leave all that to the Railway Cat.
The Cat of the Railway Train!
　　　—T. S. Eliot, *Old Possum's Book of Practical Cats* (1967)

While the rats and ants in the underground can be found everywhere, what we know to be cats have a counterpart to them here, the domestic cat turned feral (*Felis catus*), which are the ones most often cared for here underground.

Near the entrance to the underground and to right of the opening are several bungalows made of assorted materials. It was here that I saw a domestic cat, a shorthair of yellowish color, as well as a black and white tomcat on the prowl. The cats move slowly near the top of the embankment; the tomcat sat perched on a ledge as if overseeing a kingdom. Every dwelling has at least one cat; some residents, like Bobo and Beatrice, have many. They had by far the most I counted underground, maybe twelve at least, plus a litter of kittens. In the case of Kal and Bernard, one cannot say they own the cats that prowl around their bunkers: these cats are more like strays that find food in the area of the compound and keep returning for it.

Since cats breed quickly—about sixty days for gestation—and produce about three litters in a year, it's a wonder I don't see even more cats around. These cats are just like wildcats in this underground environment. They show sensitivity to light, their ears rotate or twitch when they hear sounds, and they are extremely sensitive to any vibrations. Watching cats battle rats, as I did on more than one occasion, is quite a sight: the sharp, strong teeth and retractable cat claws ripping the rats apart in unbelievably quick actions. They have sharp canine teeth that stab and hold onto prey; their molars resemble shark's teeth, scissor like and razor sharp. Most of these cats are not huge animals, although they are close to thirty pounds. Unlike domestic cats, they have not lived in homes or houses before but were born and bred here underground.

THE VAGABONDS

Stop state criminalization of poverty. Everyone should have a home and free healthcare.
—Graffito on the wall

"Hobo" and "vagabond" are synonyms for "vagrant" or "loiterer," which refers to the state of wandering without any settled home. The terms today mean an idler, a disorderly person, rogue, unlicensed peddler, or beggar. "Tramp" bears a closer origin to wandering: its origin comes from "one who tramps or walks about with heavy tread." The word is also used for a "cargo steamer not running on a regular line but passing from port to port where cargo or freight may be picked up."[11] In his book *The Hobo*, Nels Anderson draws a picture of what he calls "Hobohemia," the "jungles" of hobo camps alongside the railway lines. The most prominent were the lodging houses: "Social life in the lodging house districts was part of a larger trend that saw increasing numbers of single people moving into the city from small towns and farms. Skid row offered a residential infrastructure for the diverse assortment of single men who congregated there to meet their basic needs and find companionship and support."[12] Today, those same people can be found underground, and in these passages, it becomes clear that linking ecology with ethnography and studying space and culture is particularly fruitful.[13]

The underground is a marginal space where many vagrants find themselves, especially as the seasons change from warmer to colder. They move to underground spaces that are essentially free, without immediate monetary costs. The irony is that just above the same ground, the value of the land has risen astronomically. With the recent purchase of the rights to the Penn rail yards, the largest piece of unused real estate in Manhattan, construction on which is now nearly complete, the area has taken on a value it never had before. The space has quickly been transformed from marginal to prime in only a few years. It is no wonder these same developers built fencing near the entrance to the underground.

How long before the land under the surface becomes just as valuable to those above ground, who never see, hear, or could possibly know what is occurring there?

Like the rats that scurry occasionally into the park and into apartments, the unhoused from the underground occasionally come "topside," as they refer to it, for food, water, wood, or work. An apartment above can cost one million dollars or more, whereas the underground residents live relatively free. It is inevitable that these residents will be pushed out from the underground because they are propertyless, powerless, and thus devoid of full citizenship rights. Bernard tells me, in one of his succinct comments: "Social value in our society is based primarily on property or labor, and if you have neither to offer you are so fucked."

Property and labor determine these boundaries between above or below, rich or poor. Yet an ecological perspective might find less of a hard distinction between the two. Duncan speaks to this possibility in his writing on tramps:

> The term prime and marginal refer not to a dichotomy but a continuum. It must also be noted that they are relative terms. By looking at the city as a whole and grossly dividing it into space which is prime and marginal in the eyes of the host group, I have in effect lumped all the citizens of the city into one group, which is an obvious over-simplification. Whether a place is prime or marginal depends upon the perspective from which one views the situation. The tramp is aware of the diversity of perspective within the host population. In day-to-day decisions he must see things from their perspective. He must take into consideration the fact that what one person considers prime space another considers marginal.[14]

Walking away from the ugly new high-rises that are part of the old Penn Rail lines, down the hundred steps overlooking the Hudson River, down the sideways of green grass and past the makeshift, awning-covered bar in the corner of the park, straight in front of me is a long beautiful promenade that extends out into the river, opposite of which are old skeletal remains of bent steel and wood left by longshoremen. These remains are a legacy and a form of welfare for former workers and their families.

"Take one step at a time, otherwise you can fall down. It's a nasty fall. Be careful." I'm told this by an old lady walking up, but as long as these eroding eyesores are in the water, the endangered striped bass fish will not be disturbed, and the union members' families will receive a pension.

The wooden and steel eyesores are fascinating, and I look toward them as I descend the stairs. I move over to the new park bar, order a soft drink, swallow it quickly, and enter the dark corridor of the underground, leading to the homes of people I've come to know over the years. The first place I reach is a spot called Cubano Arms, where I meet a man who calls himself Ramon. "It's my home place. It ain't much, but it's my place."

The home is six feet by ten feet, made of wood, carpet, plywood, mattress, tin, Japanese tatami mats, a gray rug that has been cut into strips, and old clothes. At one side of the home is a water canister and food stuffs. He says the place is fifteen degrees colder in the winter and fifteen degrees cooler in the summer months. The home next to his has a makeshift tent, loosely constructed and standing near two large garbage cans, which are smoking but contain no fire. This place is the very definition of a shanty: made of plastic and cardboard, wood, and a large steel plate held up by two planks with hooks around them; across the top is a grayish tarpaulin. Two big concrete pillars like the kind you might find at construction sites hold the front in place.

As I make my way, the darker the underground becomes, until after what feels like about a two-block walk, I see Beatrice and Bobo, husband and wife, in a bunker constructed about ten years ago for construction workers who lodged underground in these spaces while they worked on the highway.

4

MEN UNDERGROUND
Bernard, Kal, and Jason

New York is dying like a pretty woman in a coma.
—Bobo, underground conversation at the fire spit

BERNARD'S JOURNAL

Sitting next to the fire in the kitchen compound, Bernard reads from his journal. One function of the journal is as a repository of the "data," as he refers to it, and it is a special form of data itself, depending on the way it is used.

> My name is Bernard Monte Isaac. I am 37 years of age, and have been a resident of Riverside Park's Underground for six-and-a-half years. On May 17, 1985 I asked myself what I consider to be the ultimate question that one would ask of oneself in life, and the answer was simply that before I departed from this life that I know myself completely and totally and that I seek and make true contact with the universal mind known as GOD.

His dreadlocked hair, sometimes tucked under a cap, today flows like a Rastafarian. He stares away, then piercingly into my face, gets up and moves around the fire. He reads on:

Being one to allow logic and reasoning to govern my existence, the task seemed very simple, I must simply dare to be myself. With the understanding that I know nothing, logic would be my key to all understanding.

To know myself completely, I came to the conclusion that the best study of myself was to study another man, by allowing myself to be misled in them in terms of strengths and weakness. In making contact with the inner being one of the first things I was cautioned of was not to dwell in human nature, because being human is truly a condition that man imposes on himself to justify him being the idiot that he has become. Human beings are not what the true and living GOD created. He created beings to just be and all that man would need in this life was provided in an unlimited supply. It is truly my belief that it has become the things as they are. He seeks to change things to his liking, a most audacious act on his behalf I find.

On June 7, 1985 I descended the staircase of the underground and felt vibrations of an alien nature. Listen to the inner voice. I turned to my left and walked about 500 yards north and observed some concrete structures, eight in number. I decided that this would be home. Knowing that this level of existence was truly new—to me, the inner voice was to get to where you want to be— you must first accept where you are, and what appeared to be my lowest point was my highest. The reverse, what was high and what was low, is truly based on one's understanding of what is, and that everything is as it is without definition. And so my mission began.

He stops and reflects. Bernard had arrived at a philosophy that would justify his failings above ground and provide a rationale for living underground. His new life did not hold the possibilities of life above ground, but at least he could avoid some of the difficult decisions he had to make "up there." As I was to learn, living underground allowed him to abdicate certain responsibilities.

But Bernard is too complicated for mere roadside psychoanalysis. Take, for instance, a rather interesting dream note from his journal. He writes:

> I've often dreamt of death and actually thought about death a lot down here. But this dream had the symbolism of death and I guess life too. Because I saw pearls and other gems on my coffin in this dream. The dream started as I was standing behind a large group of people dressed in black as they went into Riverside church. Well, the dream started out with me telling Kal about "smoke-black" and how it's made. We had been smoking the night before and I guess that triggered the dream. I know the fire smoke made me think of it and I went in and wrote most of what I could remember for you in this journal. I was telling Kal that if he held a piece of paper over a flame for the lamp or from a candle or from a lighter to prevent it from burning, he'll soon see that it's covered with a thick black smoke.
>
> This is called smoke-black. I told him that lamp-black or lighter-black comes from the sooty fumes of rosin. I went outside to show him how it's made from wood, and how it's made from the stove and I told him I had to pee and wait for me at the fire. On my way to pee I met a man who showed me, in a small beaded pouch, some precious stones. Well, I should record what he said.
>
> He said, "You'll gonna need some of these for a special occasion one day. And I'm gonna help you choose the right ones just as a favor to you." Well, he sounded like a salesman, you know and full of shit, so I said "how do I know they're real?" He said, and Terry, as I write this, I swear on a stack of Bibles, and I don't

know much about stones but in this dream he said exactly what I'm recording here.

"Well I'll tell you. The most perfect diamonds are colorless. There are others of inferior value differently shaded. Precious stones may be more readily distinguishable from each other by their different degrees of hardness than by their color because I have green diamonds, sapphires, rubies, emeralds and agates— most of our most beautiful emeralds come from Peru, although I have messengers in other parts of the world that bring them to me."

At that he stopped and said he had to go to the church on the hill and that I should go because he'll show me the display of more precious stones up there. When we get to the church suddenly my clothes were different and I could see from the long lines of people dressed in black that it was a funeral.

When I got to the church steps the man disappeared and I watched people crying as they went in. I didn't recognize anybody until it was my turn to view the coffin. Oddly enough, near the front of the coffin was my youngest son and his mother sitting there and they looked up at me and you know how at funerals people see but don't see and I figured they were mad at me anyway so I just nodded and went up to the coffin. I stood there for a moment without looking in and when I did it was me.

When I talked with Bernard after this dream he said that it was "part of the story" and was quick to remind me it was he who first suggested I record the dreams of the people underground. I took "the story" to mean his reflections on his life and why he chose to live underground. He does have a reflection of himself in the underground world he inhabits. Why did he go underground in the first place? There is no single event that caused him to question his own identity but a series of things. He is certainly not a caricature of what the world thinks of him.

When he tells me he has a son (I would meet the boy a few years later), he did say his underground life had robbed him of part of his identity, his purpose as a father. But there is a slight sadness in this tone. He obviously misses the boy and is hurt by the thought of the boy seeing him as a "bum." When he begins to reminisce about his days hustling and hanging out with Rick James and pretty women—though he tries not to think about that—what he laments is not having a warm shower and hot baths. Bernard shared these thoughts with Kal after he'd recorded the dream in his journal.

I've mentioned how Kal constantly reinvents himself and what that means in the context of an ethnography. In making a distinction between words written in a journal and verbal self-reports, this suggests a distinction between what people say and what they write—not to mention what they've actually done. What follows is an example of each of these descriptions; Kal speaks about his life and writes about his life. When he wrote and spoke these words, he was not expecting that I would continue to follow him and visit the underground for years on end. This perhaps made him feel more confident that he could change his stories, switch them around, and embellish them, assuming there would be less chance of getting "caught in a lie." The reader should keep the discrepancies between the two accounts in focus as they read on.

KAL'S JOURNAL

When Kal learned Bernard had talked to me about his life, he offered to "set the record straight" about his life, too. Kal talked a lot, but much of what he said was hard to remember. I asked him to keep a journal with the same pay arrangement I had offered others (a nickel per line and/or dollar per page). He was difficult to understand because he was often high and jittery and moved around a great deal. Today he's sober and lucid and wants to get paid for his "journal work."

The following journal account is reprinted just as he wrote it.

I was raised in Chicago, Il. I am one of six children. I have two brothers, one is a cop and one is a priest. My mother went to church every day for over 50 years and my father worked at one job for more than 42 years, ever since he came to the United States. I never got along with my mother because she was always on my brother's side the priest.

And my brother the cop well we had nothing in common. He was much older. But the only good thing about my younger days is my father. He always took me to the Zoo. But my father would never go against my mother about me. They wood fight every day but they were married 52 years till my father died first. I did not know about his death till six months after he died. I don't talk at all to any one of my family.

I never talk to my mother since 1964. She is dead now. At age 19 I got married to a girl from Irland. She was something else. She was a Moma's girl. But I did not know that until it was to late. But as everything in my life it did not last very long. My wife's family had money, and she was the only child. One day she said to me that we were going to go back to Irland. But I said I did not want to go. So she took the child and went back there by herself. After that I joined the Air Force I stayed in for three years. It was there that I started drinking and doing drugs. I loved the feeling of being high. I was always one step in front of the next person.

After I got out the Air Force I started cooking. But by that time I could never hold a job very long. Because if I was high I just wanted to party. After a wile I gave up the booze but started doing pills twice a week. All I wanted to do is stay high know matter what it took. I would stay up 2–3 days at a time, sleep for 6–7 hr. and start all over again. People did not want to be around me because I could be very warm and then very cold.

After ten years of pills I started to travel from N.Y. to L.A. and S.F. every six months. I lived in every city in Calif. Drugs made me feel powerful. Know body could beet me. I lived like that for 25 years. All this led me to become homeless. I became homeless in L.A., then I found the Salvation Army. Being a cook they put me in the kitchen working. I was doing very well but always thinking about the pills. I stayed there about six months. One day the capt. came in and said he was gonna put me on the payroll. I did not want that so I left.

I started taking diet pills, I had 25 doctors to get the form, I would by in L.A. and sell in S.F., by in S.F. and sell in L.A. know one ever new where I stayed. I did not trust anyone. I never sold to kids. I only sold to gay bartenders and owners, they paid the most. Things started getting bad for me so I went to six drug programs but never finished. Maybe I did not want to stop. All I can say is drugs were my downfall. I came back to N.Y. to the 79th Band Bacon ? [boat basin] where I lived for 2 years.

But there started being to many strange people staying there so I moved. I moved to the Amtrak underground I started cooking at a soup kitchen that were I met Bernard. We became friends. We cook together for abouit 6 months and he told me that anytime I need a place to come and see him. Well one day I did.

In the winter of 1986 at 11P.M. at night. All he said was here's a bed and it is yours. A lot of things have happened. A girl got raped. But Bernard and I got the 2 men and both are in jail. Another time the Bridge and Tonel left an 50 foot ladder with us for safe keeping Bernard and I always said anything left here stayed here. Also Amtrak left 1/2 mile train with box car at our front door. Nothing ever happens from 91st to 99st in the underground That was our space. We got along with the Park Police. 24 and 20pc [precincts] police, they all know us. The Amtrak police started coming around and bothering Bernard, they have nothing to do. But try to make things bad for him and me.

They would come around 1–2 A.M. and make all kinds of noise. They would tell us to put out our cooking fire even though we keep an eye on it. One put his hand on his gun. That's when we call the papers and T.V. and CNN came down here. We were on CNN and Amtrak police were on our side just till the cameras were on. They come around 4–5 times a day and start bothering Bernard. Because I am never home. I pick up cans for a living. Every day rain or shine. Both Bernard and I have never asked anyone for anything. I worked at We-Can, a place were homeless people can take the cans without any trouble.

Because the stores give us much trouble. I pick up cans every day. Sometimes people look at me like I am doing something wrong. But as long as I don't ask them for anything then the hell with them. Back at the tonald. The park people sealed off entrance to the tonald from 72nd St. to 122 Street. But me and Bernard have a way of getting in and out without any trouble. Bernard could tak to Amtrak police. But I can't and I don't like this. Being down there for 6 years has give me a new meaning on life. Today I don't think anything for granted. I do what I can for today and what I can't do I do the next day. I try to live very simple. I get my cans, my food, and I go to sleep very early about 6 P.M. Because I get up very early about 5:30–6 A.M. every day. Aftr this is all over I think I will be a better man. I grow a lot. I respect people. I can talk to another hustling person. Writing this has helped me. Look at my life. My life is what I made it. Know body got me here. And know body will get me out but me. I won't be in the tonald very long any more. But when I do move I will be a lot more real that I was for over 45 years. By the way I am writing this with a broken hand.

FIELD NOTE (JULY 1991)

Saw Kal's place today and it was an awful sight, filled with cups and cans, broken glass, and a small table with drug paraphernalia. Bernard took me there. He was angry at Kal because he said he stole the tape recorder I gave him to record his life story. I'm not always inclined to believe people when they say these things. I guess if he stole it, he sold it for money to inch his habit along. Bernard says Kal is strongly addicted to crack, cocaine, and amphetamines. At any rate they both play such games; I wouldn't be a bit surprised if they are in cahoots with this little charade.

I gave Bernard another tape recorder after he misplaced the first. The other week Bernard called me to say they need a lock on the east entrance to counter the Amtrak officials who had sealed the entrance shut with a padlock. Kal called the next day to say they needed money for a lock and chain. The money is never too much, so I don't see the necessity of such contrivance. But the $17, which is insignificant to me, may be more to them, particularly if they are putting together many such small-scale scams.

After I received a call from Bernard, I went down with the photographer to see what it was all about. I had not been there for some three weeks and wanted to check on the flora and fauna as well. I picked three different kinds of apples, one apple tree by the Eighty-Ninth Street entrance and two along the West Side Highway. Then I walked a bit further to find an assortment of crabapples as well as elderberries and cherries. I tasted all of these fruits before walking down to Seventy-Second Street, where a huge fence—at least twelve feet high—had been erected since my last visit.

CONVERSATION WITH
KAL (AUGUST 1991)

In the next passage is an account of Kal's life in which he first reveals his role as underground hero. We can see in this anecdote his need to show himself to me in a positive light—a natural thing to do.

You got good guys and you got bad guys down here just like you got everywhere. When we first came down here, the people who were here didn't create any problems, and we in turn let some people stay down here. One person we let stay was a woman who was raped by two guys we knew but didn't know. You know what I mean? I mean we saw 'em down here, but we didn't have that much to do with them. We just met 'em once or twice. But the fucking guys come down and rape this woman and then try to get away, and we caught them, turned them over to the cops. That was our good deed for the day. Naw, for the fucking year. Those two fuckers are in jail, and we helped put them there.

FIELD NOTES (1991)

I changed my clothes twice to help battle the cold down underground. No matter what I wear, I get cold after an hour or so standing, walking, no matter what. Kal asked me to meet him topside at ten o'clock, but he is nowhere to be found. I decide to go call him through what Bernard refers to as their "intercom."

It's the grate on the West Side Highway. It's a little risky to walk out in the curving highway traffic, bend over and scream fifty feet down to someone you cannot see, but I did. I see Kal after hollering a few times, his face staring up from the face of the tunnel. I walked about two blocks along Riverside Park, parallel to the highway, to get to the entrance. The first thing he starts talking about is the rats. He is walking ahead of me, and I can't quite make out what he was saying because of the gravel underfoot and the cavernous echoing ways of the underground itself.

As he talks, I feel the cold wind burst through at us. We move closer to the outside area called the kitchen. The floor of this dirt kitchen compound extends about 130 feet by 30 feet, an environment strewn with pots, pans, and cans. The spit, a steel divider from a stove, is fitted over bricks and blackened by wood smoke.

The taming of fire by humans was a special moment some eight hundred thousand years ago. Perhaps three hundred thousand years ago, Neanderthals, *Homo erectus,* and the forefathers of *Homo sapiens* used fire on more or less a daily basis. Harari writes in his book *Sapiens: A Brief History of Mankind* that fire was already being used for a number of purposes, not only to cook food but also to prime wastelands and keep predatory animals at bay.[1]

"The train," says Kal, "is the worst thing that could have happened to us because it brings so much of the outside world into a space we considered our own for a long time. We get along with the park police from the Twenty-Fourth and the Twentieth Precinct. The police, they all know us. But the Amtrak police started coming around and bothering Bernard one day. They had nothing to do but try to make things bad for him and me. They would come around one or two PM and make all kinds of noise. One put his hand on his gun."

JOURNAL ENTRY, KAL

I know everything will come to an end within one or two years. After all of this is over I plan to go back to Chicago to live. I have not been home for thirty years. I need to find love again. But will not know what to do with it once I find it. I will have to adjust to being on top. I think I will be a better man. I grow a lot. I respect people. My life is what I made it. Nobody got me here and no one will get me out but me. When I do move I will be a lot more real than I was for over forty-five years. I hope no one will ever have to go through what I did to live. I will try to live one day at a time, do one thing at a time. Writing this has helped me look at myself in a mirror. I never hurt anyone but myself. That was big for me. I hope God will let me live a few more years so I can go back to my past instead of running from it. Writing this I feel all alone. Maybe because I am.

I am moved and disturbed by Kal's journal as I think about his self-deprecating account of his life and his taking full responsibility for his fate. While "taking responsibility" is the tenor of an argument so often heard today in our political circles, there is much evidence that can be mobilized to gainsay such claims. One example is the classic account of rootlessness in the American context, which is offered by Robert Merton. I had a conversation with him while we were both at the Russell Sage Foundation.[2] In his writing, Merton noted that our culture teaches that everyone can and should strive for the same lofty goals: failures are but way stations to ultimate success; genuine failure consists only in the lessening or withdrawal of ambition. Kal has absorbed that "lesson" of our culture—we could also call it an ideology—and cannot see how that very same culture restricts and in many cases completely shuts off poor people's access to ways of reaching those goals. When I talked with Kal about this, he said: "Rich folk feel good about putting us down." I took his words to mean that as a society, we feel confident when people fail because it reinforces in us a perverse belief in our own success.

KAL KILLS THE CAT AND TIME

Six-thirty in the morning. Kal gets to his feet from the rumpled three-tiered mattress and goes to wash his face in the basin positioned along the dirty, blood-stained wall. He pays scant attention to the dead cat in the corner. Sometime during the previous evening, in a crack-high frenzy, he killed this cat—a beating, he says, like the one he took as a child when his father accused him of stealing money and knocked out his two front teeth. Kal said he was angry and frustrated at the cat for littering his bed.

"I didn't want to hurt the cat at first. But I thought what my father said was true that cats couldn't die. You know what he'd say? 'Curiosity killed the cat, understanding brought it back, there goes the nine lives of the cat.' But when I threw that stick at him and he fell over, I just started hitting him more and more and then I picked him up by the tail and smashed his fucking head against the wall. Then I could sleep."

Bernard has this explanation: he says many of the men in the underground, including Kal, engage in acts that border on the mysterious. "There's black magic and white magic and some of the people here do white magic. Some people feel better, somehow, in the mouth of the devil. Because somehow being there, there is heat and a little juice of nourishment. So when they holler, nobody comes to help them. But there are people, and I think Kal is one of them who's in love with the Devil—he could be one of his children, his son or something. And because he loves him, he wants the Devil to take him alive. You remember that guy Abbott who stabbed that kid in the Village? Mailer helped him out of prison. He was a writer—at least that's what they say he was—but he was really the Devil's son, and as soon as he got out, he drew blood. Maybe killing that cat is a sign of the Devil."

I think perhaps he's joking and look for signs that he is, like a wink, nod, or smirk, but nothing. I conclude he's serious. Then, it comes: he purses his lips to indicate he's half-joking and maybe a little annoyed at Kal for some reason. Maybe he even wants me to think ill of him. I'm not sure.

These days, Kal spends time in the underground getting high and other times walking around picking up cans. He also collects used books and sells them—fifty cents for hardbacks, twenty-five cents for paperbacks—to street book vendors. But for the most part, Kal's a can man. He gets up now to walk from Ninety-Sixth Street to the World Trade Center collecting as many as a thousand cans before he arrives back uptown to buy crack for what I call his "toxicomania."

"I could do no right in my family, and my brother, who turned out to be a priest, could do no wrong. I was born seven days after Pearl Harbor, and one day when I was sixteen my mother told me that I was a mistake. I shouldn't have been born. It was that day I left home, and to this day I have never seen my parents alive since. They are both dead. I haven't seen my brothers, nobody. When she said that to me, it really hurt me. I came to New York on a one-week, I thought, vacation of sorts. I fell in love with the city. For a cook, the money was good. Living was kind of high, but in those days living in New York wasn't that expensive. I'm going back '69, '70. But now you know it's outrageous."

Kal may have gotten a lot wrong about things he's said to me, but he's right on target with this comment: housing prices have risen to such high levels that it is clearly becoming a city only for the rich. Three recent trends in the city should be noted. First, increases in rent are outpacing increases in household income; second, the rent-to-income ratio is increasing, or, in other words, people pay more now for rent as a percentage of their income; and third, in 2014, three out of ten households paid more than 50 percent of their income for rent, whereas it was two out of ten households in 2002.[3]

Kal talks about cooking a lot, maybe because he was a short-order cook at one time or maybe because he's hungry after his crack binges. "I make a mean stew. Believe it or not, I make good home fries. I make, scout's honor, sure-enough home fries. I do cordon bleu, I do scampi. I cut ice, do buffets and hors d'oeuvres. I like decorating. You know, you give me the right stuff to decorate, and I'll put you out some platters that you could take pictures of. Because I know how to design. Yeah, I like to be creative. I used to get a lot more creative when I was high."

He then switches to talk on the subject of drugs:

> I feel freer down here than I do up top. See, down here I don't have to deal with nothing except myself. Up top I have to deal with society. Now that the underground is ending, I'll have to learn how to deal with society twenty-four hours. Now all I have to do is maybe six or seven hours, then I go back down to the underground. It's like I'm in my own sanctuary here. I don't have to deal with nothing that I don't choose to deal with. If I want somebody to knock on my door, fine. If I don't want somebody to knock on my door, I let 'em know ahead of time don't bother me. Bernard knows if I say I'm going to sleep, don't bother Kal. See, up top I have to deal with a hotel, I have to deal with welfare, I have to deal with society, I have to deal with buses.
>
> I figured I'd be down here another summer. But now in a way it's good. I'm sort of like getting out now, doing things that I

haven't done. I was avoiding work because I still have the disease
that tells me I don't have it, which is a coke habit. I used to have
a $150–$200-a-day coke habit about four years ago. I was popping
on the average of three to four thousand milligrams of amphet-
amine a day. And coke. But you know my drug of choice is crystal meth. I divorced my wife and kids and married the drugs,
that's right.

I used to say I think I could take one hit. There is no "one" of
anything. That one hit would cost me about $900, last me about
five days. No sleep. I walked around and looked like a zombie.
But I made sure that I ate. You know, I did the stuff you are not
supposed to do when you are high. Because I stayed the same
weight. Even being a cook, I've never went over 180 pounds. I was
criss-crossing [mixing stimulants with depressants] to keep
awake. Some stuff I never told you. I was an addict. I like to say,
I was an addict. But I had twenty-seven doctors I'd go to. All for
amphetamines—I had a doctor in each drugstore. But see, I was
smart. I always used my right name. To this day I've never even
had a traffic ticket.

They were all diet doctors. See, at that time, in the 1970s, there
were a lot of diet doctors. It was all cash. No Medicaid, no nothing. I got one right now. I could go in there right now and get
amphetamines. That's another thing I gotta deal with. I mean
doing everything straight when I'm used to being up high. Down
here I don't have to worry about getting high—you know, doing
amphetamines at night. Down here, what's there to do? I want
to go to sleep.

Now I'm gonna be up top, my mind says, "well, maybe you
could do this, maybe you could do that." But I can't do everything. You know me, I try to do everything. And being down
below I haven't had the urge—once in a while I get it, and then
it goes away at seven o'clock at night when it becomes dark, it

becomes cold. That chills me right out. I don't feel like going back out again.

Kal uses the term "diet doctor" to refer to the pharmacists and doctors who specialized in providing amphetamines to people undergoing fad diets. Diet pills were in widespread use then and were prescribed without regulation, much like with oxycontin, percodan, quaaludes, and other popular trends in pharmaceutical drugs over the decades.

The use of drugs underground is part of the social life of the place. Instead of going to a bistro or bar, they party with their drugs in their tents and lean-tos, where the air is thick and the authorities far away. Someone might have a radio, or some might sing together in a quiet corner at the south end. That's where I see Jason with a dark Puerto Rican woman dancing her version of the lambada in risqué fashion, until Bobo shows up trying to tell a ribald joke about a woman cheating on her husband. Bobo's joke doesn't break up the action, but the depleted radio batteries do.

JASON

One evening, sitting, watching the fire blaze and the smoke circling toward the roof of the underground, waiting for Bernard, a tall young man with an angular face and short stubby beard comes over and introduces himself. His face is reddened and blackened at the temple, wrinkles covering the crown of the forehead. He's not disheveled and seems somehow calm in his black-gray jacket, a kind of down coat; blue jeans and old sneakers complete his attire. With slight shadows pecking away at his face, I notice no movement other than the wind topside and the train's lights moving down the line.

He takes the end of a piece of burning wood, breaks it with his foot, and puts it on the fire where two other pieces smolder. "I know you want to know how I ended up here in the underground and without a home on topside. My name is Jason, and I've been down here two years. I came to New York from North Carolina, and I been in the city for a few years. Well, I was like everybody else topside. I thought I was immune from any bad things happening to me. I had a job working in an office, and I got married to a younger woman. She was very pretty, but about a year into our relationship she started using crack and had bowls with money in it and a cigar and pebbles and all of that voodoo stuff in the house. I thought. 'Whoa! This is out.'"

Take note, this is all without prompting: I never ask Jason one question, he just starts telling me his story. I found out later that Kal had told him and everybody else he knew that I paid money for interviews. This guy was telling me his life story expecting to get paid at the end. But I was determined not to give him any money because I hadn't solicited his story. In fact, I was a bit annoyed once I realized why he was telling me all of this. But when he finished, I decided to give him the ten bucks anyway, add him to my "characters list," and perhaps at some point follow him topside. I should know by now that word always travels when an ethnographer is working. And with this group, they had experience, so to speak, with the news media and reporters, and it ultimately boils down to self-interest. Men like Jason ask, "What's in this for me?"

One day I come home, and she's getting high, and I tell her it was me or the crack. I guess I shouldn't have said that because she said she didn't need me as much as she needed the crack. So I was all fucked up. I was devastated behind that shit. I went to my job and took all my stuff out of my drawers and started walking. I walked around for days and I ended up talking to a friend who says there was people living underground here and I could go down and see what was happening.

I did that and I ended up spending the night and he says I could stay as long as I wanted, and that's how I got down here.

After I left my wife, I went to look for work, but after a while, I couldn't say I was living there anymore, and I couldn't say I was living down here, so I started selling books and the like on the street, taking odd jobs here and there.

One of the things we do down here is look after each other. You see how I came over here to check you out, because I'm also a little piqued off at the journalists.

They put my name in the paper and say I live down near Seventy-Second Street. Well, if they say that, then my friends topside will know that's me. Because how many Jasons could you have around Seventy-Second Street? You tell me.

It's very cool down here, and not what you think it is. It's not dangerous, really. You just gotta be aware. We know everybody here. I know people who come down here and get laid. I know people who come down here to get paid. You understand me? Listen, let me tell you something. I got two kids. Well, it more like they got me because I haven't been able to do much for them lately, but I gotta still find a way to take care of them.

My wife still has an apartment on Ninety-Fourth and Columbus, and she comes down to visit me. She knows where I am.

Once he finishes, there is an awkward silence, and the firewood burns lower and lower. I hear footsteps, and in a few minutes, Bernard comes up, shakes my hand, and grabs some wood from a corner behind his bunker that I can't quite see, with which he stokes the fire.

I ask Jason how he supports his kids, just to keep the conversation from fizzling out. "I get up at about twelve or something, and I go to the store to buy milk or cook for my mother. I then wait until about six, then I go out looking for odd jobs. I ask people if they want their cars washed or wiped down, and then I come back here. I open the door for people and try to see if they want any help with groceries, or if somebody is moving they might want someone to help them with heavy stuff."

How does he feel about begging? He shrugs his shoulders and says he would rather beg than do the kinds of things people do to get money. He doesn't elaborate. For reasons having less to do with any evidence to the contrary and more with intuition, Jason doesn't appear to me the window-washer or beggar type. I would like to one day have a more systematic conversation with him, and I wait for the opportune moment to ask him for a more extended interview. Is he reinventing himself? I don't know. So I ask if I can talk to him topside one day soon. But he ignores my request.

He continues telling me that when he's in the street, he will see a person leave their car, and he'll approach them for a wash. If the person says no, he will wipe the car off anyway, and when the person comes back, he will tell them he wiped it off and could they give him something for doing so. I look at him slightly askance, trying to get him to break and say he's kidding, but he doesn't. "I have not been to jail," he says without flinching or revealing anything out of kilter with his past statements. "But I have not had a real job in a long time either."

What he means by a "real job" is honest work, steady work. Among other made-up jobs, "banking," "bank standing," or "door holding" seem to be by far the most common. Jason thought about going into "bank standing," but he found it disgraceful to be begging that way. He says he could never get to the point where he had to beg. "I'd really most likely prefer to die than do that kind of begging."

Despite such avowals, Jason would run other games at ATMs. "You know the ATMs are good places to make that cash because people need a little time to get their money and think about how poor others are. But the problem with this is that they get big dollars and not many people wanna give up a dollar. Some do and that's worth the effort of staying there all day and night."

The competition for the ATMs is fierce, and there are many fights over territory. "I worked this ATM on Thirty-Fourth Street for three months before this guy comes out and says it's his spot. Because I used to live in Penn Station, I held the spot from midnight to six, which I felt was the best hours. But this guy comes back and we got into a fight, and the cops come and they know this guy, and I had to move on."

I see Jason topside a few times over the next few weeks, and he tells more of his story. I give him a few dollars, but not for talking with me, instead because he looks like he needs it. Often, we eat a meal or a quick snack.

Often sullen and occasionally with his head busted or eyes swollen as the result of some altercation, Jason tells me, "I got beat up last night." Without a trace of shame or embarrassment he explains, "I didn't get into this much trouble until I started getting high. You know my basing, free-basing. That's when I got into this conning and stuff." Jason hardly ever says more than a few sentences, rarely curses, and doesn't raise his voice, except to holler down through the intercom at Ninety-Fifth Street to get someone's attention underground.

His extended conversation today is out of character, but perhaps this is a sign of trust. He admits he one time begged and used to sing songs in the street. "But at the time I couldn't seem to get anywhere, no other way. You know I started the beg game, although I do less of that than I used to." I misunderstood what he meant by begging in this sense. Apparently the "beg game" in this instance refers to a pimping term that connotes a "soft swindle," where the man convinces the woman to give him her money. This behavior, he admits, is neither forced nor coercive in any way, since he (the man) simply asks for the money in a charming way.

> All of this happened after I left my wife. But I've tried to work.
> I tried to work at the airports, but one day something was missing
> and I was accused of taking it. I didn't take nothing, but they said
> I did. So they put me on the graveyard shift delivering lost suit-
> cases at night. And the next thing I know I'm out copping when
> I should be delivering and they had somebody follow me one
> night, and he reports me. So the supervisor follows me one night
> and he caught me smoking crack in the truck. The next day they
> make me take a drug test. I failed, was fired. No hearing, no
> explanation, no nothing, gone.

I ask what should he expect, since he'd committed a crime on the job. "I know I was caught dead to rights," he says sheepishly. He shrugs his shoulders, turns away, expecting me to be more sympathetic. But at that point I felt he was wrong and had to acknowledge some responsibility for his actions. I told him perhaps the incident could be seen as a blessing in disguise: he could have been arrested and served some time.

In trying to figure Jason out I thought about the trickster character in Native American and African mythology. Paul Radin, the anthropologist, wrote about this Native American trickster: "Trickster is one and the same time creator and destroyer, giver and negator, he who dupes others and who is always duped himself. He knows neither good nor evil yet he is responsible for both. He possesses no values, morals or social . . . yet through his actions all values come into being." "The devil is an agent of evil," Hyde argues in his masterful book *Trickster Makes the World*. "Trickster is amoral, not immoral. He embodies and enacts that large portion of our experience where good and evil are hopelessly intertwined. He represents the paradoxical category of sacred amorality."[4]

Hyde's point about Trickster's ambivalence and "devilment," or doing of "evil deeds," is well taken. Jason fits well into this category, as good and evil for him seem interlinked. It's perhaps this aspect of his personality that makes him so ambiguous as a person. He also reminds me of Harry Stack Sullivan's idea of the "not me" and Freud's "return of the repressed." In his readiness to avoid and disavow the parts of himself that are most shameful, in his inability to recognize what he has done wrong, Jason ends up invoking all of the things that he makes an effort to lock away in his unconscious.

JASON AND THE SPONSORS

I wanted to see Jason outside the underground because I'd never seen him do any of the things he said he did. My hunch about his "Trickster" character was borne out when one day we finally met up topside. Although we originally met at the beginning of my study—two days after I arrived, to be exact—Jason is rarely in the underground for long periods of time, even in the space he calls home, within a cluster of beds and lean-tos that I never see him come out of or go into. Nor do I observe him doing any housekeeping.

At first, I don't find his behavior unusual; I have known Kal and Bernard for years and have only seen their places once or twice, but I have done something with them I have not managed to do with Jason, that is, follow them on their daily rounds of can picking, book gathering, food shopping, scavenging for food, water, wood, and other kinds of daily survival work. But Jason makes me anxious because he is elusive. One reason may be time spent in jail—even though he has on occasion told me he's never been to jail—and a mistrust of social workers and reporters. Yet I feel certain he avoids me because on the occasions I've asked him for a time to talk and hang out, he either does not show up or gives me some line. Leaving the underground for the day with Jason proves to be an adventure beyond anything I had anticipated.

Jason says he's done most of the hustles New Yorkers are familiar with: the phony drug seller bit, the phone con (he never explains what that was), and beggar-robber. Since I have known real con artists for a long time, if he was lying, I would catch on. I just want to see him wash car windows or be near an ATM, but none of that transpires. After his wife left him, he decided to "go for broke" and was arrested (for what he calls "various illegal acts" in 1993 and 1994). He claims he learned "things" while he was "on vacation," meaning time spent in jail. When I finally catch up with him again, this time on Broadway, he tells me I can come with him to see his "sponsors," a rather curious lot of gay men, religious do-gooders, and others trying to save lost souls.

These topside sponsors take in destitute men and women and offer places to bathe, eat, and spend the night. Jason's sponsor is an older woman he met at the courthouse during his trial, or, rather, his plea-bargaining session, but when I get to the building she supposedly lived in, he said it would be best if I not came in: she would be afraid to have two men visiting. I waited half an hour for him to come back down, but he never did. When I tell Kal the story, he says that Jason's sponsor is a "fag" who would have loved to see two men and remarks that Jason is full of shit.

5

WORKING LIFE

We are in an age of uncertainty.
—K. Khan

This chapter concerns the misconception that unhoused people are lazy and unproductive and describes a variety of work-related jobs, from collecting cans to selling books and other discarded detritus. The sociologist Nels Anderson saw the hobo as a special category of worker and described the differences among the hobo (a migratory worker), the tramp (a migratory nonworker), and the bum (a nonmigratory nonworker). One way to see these variations in roles is to understand what accounts for people being driven onto the streets: unemployment, drug misuse, evictions, or simply economic forces are all recurring observations. As a matter of my own observations and experience, Anderson's distinction between migratory and nonmigratory is problematic: the issue of folks living and/or working on the street always involves some form of migration. This is emphasized in Kal's narrative, where you have a kind of epic migration in terms of place, from California to

Chicago and finally to New York, as well as in Jason's narrative, where you have constant physical movement—though short distances, a migration nevertheless.

All of this raises a series of questions: Where are you from? Why are you here? How did you get here? What are you doing now?

After several more attempts, I finally see Jason topside.

To be completely honest with you man, I spend most of my day walking around the city. I know this might sound funny, but if I'm not searching for food or finding some work, I'm looking for a way to spend my time, and I read a lot because I used to go to the library all the time but now since the hours are so funny I don't make it there as much as I used to. I still go to visit my friends at the shelter, now and again, but now the guards won't let me go but so far, and I have to wait for them to come out. Sometimes I visit my old friends back in the neighborhood, and then I usually have some work to do too. I'll go to the park, hang out there for a little bit, then, if I can get an extra dollar or two will go to the movies on the Deuce [Forty-Second Street], but I don't do that too often either because it way too expensive from what it was back in the day when you only needed five bucks and could stay in the theater all day.

The old bathrooms at Grand Central is cool to use, but now it's mad crazy and too many cops. Let me tell you about these cops because the number-one problem for most of us is them fucking cops who all want to bust you down for nothing. Just for sitting around. They want you to "move on." Move on where? Where the fuck do I move on to? Whether it's winter or spring I still go to the library or the park. And I ride the bus sometimes and of course I take the subway for a snooze every now and then.

Some nights are the worse because of the kids who want to torch you or burn you up or beat you if they find you sleeping under the bridge or on the subway and that's a drag. . . . But I had a friend who used to have these kids work for him. He'd get them liquor and cigarettes from the store if they gave him a buck.

But the other thing I do mostly is canning since I pick up cans on the trash days and take them to the recycling center or to the supermarket side entrance. On a good day I make around forty, sometimes fifty bucks. I do a little dumpster diving too around the school, but you can't be there on certain days, or I should say certain times, because the cops will chase you away, and anyway it's just not cool to be around the kiddies anyway. But I know a lot of good stuff can be found around there and not just food. It's amazing what kids throw away and what those lockers have in them. I mean the school dumps the content of the kids' lockers out every so often, and so I can get what those contain.

A woman told me she sells her food stamps, and some women do blow jobs. I've sold my food stamps at one time and got around sixty cents on the fuckin' dollar for them from the groceria, but these fucking guys are unreliable really. I used to get a disability check, but I'd only get less than fifty bucks from that seven-hundred-dollar check when I go to the program. My friend steals; he's a con man who fences shit, steal cell phones, will swap gift card and prescriptions. All of that kinda shit.

I give Jason a few dollars, and we go for a coffee. I'm curious why he has chosen to tell me these things now. I notice he didn't mention his wife or his drug habit or any of the things he'd told me before, and I wonder now: is any of his story true? Or did he just figure I wanted to hear a particular story and invented one for me?

THE WORKING PEOPLE UNDERGROUND

Underground residents like Kal, Bernard, and Jason work in order to survive, and they make every effort to find something that preserves their self-esteem and dignity. Often this involves finding valuables the rich have thrown away.

"Bernard and I used to clean the scrap metal at the south end one time," Kal says. "That was good money. I also made some money when I rented out my space down here to accommodate some people. I had like three couples down here at one time."

It got to be a thing where nobody wanted to help out. Nobody washed pots. Nobody did nothing. And like . . . hey. I just got bored. After two years of being on an adult's ass all the time like they're children I said the hell with this, and I let them go. Everybody had their own cubicle. But I had as many as three roommates in my old space in the underground, 'cause it was bigger, twenty by thirty. I had Indian rugs and some really great shit. It was burned out by one of the guys.

Bernard, coming out of his bunker, hears the end of the conversation. "Yeah. It was Nat that set it on fire. The guy is a pyro. One of the guys who used to live down here. He was a paint-job artist a few summers ago. Set my room on fire too, out of meanness. We've been through it down here, I'm telling you. But it's all accepted. Even though he burned the place, revenge does not repair an injury. You understand what I mean? Kal wanted to go and hurt the guy but I say no. Leave it alone. 'Forgive them father, for they know not what they do.' It's not up to us to make them suffer; they will get what's coming to them. Listen, man, I got some things for you to see." He goes back in the bunker and brings out three small glass ashtrays with silver trim. "You like those? You can have 'em for three." I buy the ashtrays and ask about other silver items.

> Now I just pick up silver, man. I work with silver only. The West Side is rich, man. I've always said that one man's trash is another man's treasure. They throw out the cream de la cream. I've sold silver-plated things. Beautiful stuff that I gave [he names a newspaper reporter], I gave her gifts, and one or two of them was silver. One was a ring. About two years ago. And her friend, the goblets in her house, silver goblets, she bought them from me. I got a silver tin there now that's worth . . . worth maybe two hundred dollars . . . engraving on the back . . . it came from a very expensive setting. I got to get that to Laurie [Gunst, a mutual friend who lives nearby].
>
> There are ways you can make money. I was redoing furniture. I found this wicker chair, and I put the chair together down here. I mean to have a cane chair done, that costs you about two hundred dollars. I was going to do this chair for Laurie because she liked wicker, and I had a hamper and everything. But painters came, and they destroyed everything.

Many people in the underground say they have skills that, under normal conditions, would bring them a decent wage. Kal claims, for example, "I paint houses, apartments. Not just paint. I move furniture. I do buffets. People have parties, I can do all kinds of buffets, decorating, stuff like that. I make designs. I can make meatloaf in the design of a fish, or I can make potato salad in the design of a swan. I mean, I like to decorate. I get a feeling of achievement. . . . Like I say, I clean as I go along. If I dirty a spoon, I wash it right away. If I'm in the kitchen, I'm the only one in the kitchen. Nobody else is allowed in the kitchen." He lights a cigarette and fidgets, agitated and nervous. "I was supposed to go down to Medical tomorrow, but I canceled out and got the appointment for Friday so I can be at the job in the morning. Five o'clock. You know, when I go out and work I make about $450–$500 a week. But I'm not at work for more than two months. I need to get out of work into a place where they'll give me a month's rent, where I can put money together. 'Cause I can work."

Most of the men can and do work, but as a resident says as he digs in a garbage can near Seventy-Ninth Street, social workers and other officials "keep asking me what job do I want, and I keep telling them I want a job I can do." What many homeless individuals on the street do is mostly day labor, and there isn't much of that around in the early 1990s.

STREET BOOKSELLING

The relationship between margin and mainstream is no more apparent than the constant movement of underground residents topside, for goods and services, foods, water, drugs, and other required and needed necessities. This relationship is seen in one of the most useful items the aboveground populace needs from those below. "People need other people to look down upon. You know what I mean, right?" Beatrice tells me one day. "They need us down here so they can feel better about themselves. And I've seen it, people think they are better than other people."

Her point is succinct and clear. A common need for people is to feel superior to others. Beatrice is referring more specifically to how people treat her and Bobo and others who go topside to work or do other things like selling books. "It's the way people look at you; they turn their nose up at me and act like I don't exist. I don't know if they know I'm homeless or not, but I think they do, but even if they don't, they look at me, they look past me, you know what I mean? They look past me. They look through me like I'm Casper the Friendly Ghost. And when I'm selling books, they turn their nose at me because I'm selling books on the street."

"Them topsiders, oh man them topsiders. They something else," Bobo sounds like Beatrice here, although he notes that while the topside crowd looks down on him, they still need what he has to offer: books. He says he and Bernard are *bibliophiles*, mocking some of his gay buyers as he says the word with a slight lisp. Curious about all of this, I go watch them one day sell their books along Broadway. When I arrive, it is only Beatrice sitting there.

How books are sold on the street is realized through an intricate process of gathering discarded used books and magazines along Riverside Drive and Broadway. In order to sell these items, Bernard, Kal, Beatrice, and Bobo retrieve them from superintendents along Riverside Drive, receive from citizens who give them their discarded books, or just take the books people have left on sidewalks and then resell them on the street. The supers have favorite homeless people to whom they give books, who then resell them to regular street vendors. Some homeless people sell the books themselves, although most do not.

The arrangement with superintendents is explained in part by Hakim Hasan, whom I interviewed for this account and who sold books on the streets for a living some time ago and became the subject of the 1999 book *Sidewalk* by Mitchell Duneier. When Duneier did his work on street booksellers in Greenwich Village, he found that one of the tactics the men used was to be lookouts for children and others in the neighborhood, thereby gaining the trust of residents, who not only allowed them access to their buildings but also gave them books and magazines to sell.

On the street, there are many "distribution" sources for books. In New York City during the 1990s, there was an explosion of booksellers throughout the city and many ways to obtain old and new books. Hakim, whose knowledge is based on past experience, describes the market for these books and the process as follows: "Books are sold by condition (new or used) as individual pieces or what one might call a 'package deal.' A package deal is when you buy the entire lot with good and what we would call 'dead books,' i.e., books that probably won't sell. A good book vendor has to know what he/she is buying and where they can make them money. For example, there might be an art book in the 'package deal' that you can sell for $25.00. Let's say you paid $25.00 for the entire package—well, the rest is pure profit."

All of this varied from market to market and, as Hakim notes, depends on the knowledge of both the buyer and seller. A lot of book vendors know what they are selling, but a lot of them have no real idea of the value of what they have. Many street sellers just place books on a table. Eventually, the logic goes, someone will buy these books.

The booksellers on Broadway (uptown) are where Bernard and Kal operate. Bernard has certain book vendors that he sells books to at an agreed-upon price, but most of the men from the underground who also sold books, like Bobo and Kal, had no such arrangements. Street bookselling is one of the few sources of income for underground residents not involving "dirty work," as Beatrice put it.

The marketing aspect of setting up a vending table is central to a book vendor making money. Hakim remarks that "competition on the street is fierce . . . quite fierce" and notes that first, a sensible book vendor has to understand pedestrian traffic flow. Which way are people walking? Second comes attention to the organization of wares and presentation. "I separated nonfiction from fiction, and there were subcategories—a Donald Goines section, a sci-fi section, a jazz section, and so on. This made it easier for prospective customers to wade through books very quickly. Also, we used comic book wrappers to cover and protect books from dirt and humidity. A dirty book is a negotiation point with a prospective buyer. A good vendor wants to remove negotiation from the equation because their presence on the street contextualizes all transactions as a negotiation." Hakim's book vending table was set up to catch a pedestrian's eye so that they would stop at the middle of the table. "This is tantamount to setting up a display window at Macy's. No one really knew this. They thought all of this was done haphazardly. In certain cases, that's true. I have thought about the following a great deal: Dinkins was still mayor when I began to sell books. And, of course, his administration ordered its share of crackdown on vendors in Harlem. However, when Giuliani became mayor and 'quality of life' enforcement became his administration's mantra, in conjunction with the Business Improvement District in Greenwich Village (Honi Klein was the director), the book vendors on Sixth Avenue were under tremendous pressure by the police."

When the Giuliani administration began its quality-of-life crackdown in 1994, it issued police guidelines offering a new interpretation of a 1969 regulation. The ban on anyone erecting an "obstruction" on city streets could now be applied to a homeless person sleeping in a cardboard box. A 1996 police manual for carrying out such sweeps, "Quality of Life Enforcement

Options: A Police Reference Guide," lists thirty-five offenses that can prompt an arrest, including camping in the park without a permit and being present after the official 1 AM closing time.

Hakim points out that the amped-up assault on the homeless was labeled "the criminalization of homelessness" by Hillary Clinton, who was then competing with Giuliani for a U.S. Senate seat. Many articles covered the outrage, for example, a November 29, 1999, news piece, "In America: Bullying the Homeless," by the columnist Bob Herbert. In it, Herbert notes the cruelty of the policy and its futility as a measure of public safety.

> Most of those arrested are back on the streets a day later, back to the cardboard box or the dark alley or the tiny corner of a park that they've turned into a wretched approximation of home. I doubt that a night in jail has made them any wiser, or the city any safer. What it does, according to homeless advocates, is make the street people a lot more frightened. Perhaps the mayor, who has bullied people throughout his public career, thinks that's just what they deserve.[1]

Since quality-of-life enforcement had been going on since 1994, seemingly under the radar, some of the outrage it triggered smacks of political opportunism. Clinton, while running for senator against Giuliani, is quoted as saying, "Breaking up families that are homeless is wrong. Criminalizing the homeless with mass arrests for those whose only offense is that they have no home is wrong."[2] Whether her criticism was genuine or opportunistic, the mayor was unrepentant and a week later was quoted as saying, "You are not allowed to live on a street in a civilized city. It is not good for you, it is not good for us," here adding a familiar refrain: "The homeless have no right to sleep on the streets."[3]

On November 15, 2000, the article "Computers to Track Quality of Life Crime" appeared in the *New York Times*, offering a summary of the previous tumultuous twelve months: "Of the 28,671 homeless questioned by the police in the last 12 months, 6,365 were transported to shelters, 532 were taken to hospitals, and another 1,317, or 4.6 percent of those questioned, were arrested on charges including outstanding warrants, urinating in public and disruptive behavior with police officers or social workers, the mayor said."[4]

Hakim is quick to elaborate on the involvement of the police in harassing booksellers. "The magazine vendors and other ad-hoc vendors (anyone could sell anything with a table as long as it was written matter), some of them would literally go crazy at night and 'just lay shit out' all over the ground. The sidewalk would be a mess. A mess! And you are talking about near condos that were probably $600,000 at the time. In fact, I am not going to say that some of this was not justified because I remember when one of the guys transported a platform bed to Sixth Avenue and sold it. They sold plate of glass. Clothes. Shoes. Records. Anything. There was a hierarchy on Sixth Avenue, and I was on the top. I was not making the most money. There was one vendor who made close to $4,000 selling books every weekend. He had a connection for new books, and they were being transported from out of state to New York."

Hakim, like Bernard, has an air of political and moral authority and uses that authority to solve disputes and problems between people in their respective cliques. While Bernard settles disputes of one kind or another underground and negotiates money from reporters, filmmakers, photographers, and writers for interviews of residents, Hakim settles various kinds of disputes topside among street booksellers. He explained one situation: "You could not just set up vending tables on subway grates. The tables had to be a certain number of feet from the subway entrance and, as I said, entrances to stores. I singlehandedly fought the Sixth Precinct police with my acute understanding of the regulations. And here is what they did. They spray painted the curbs bright yellow or orange so that the police would know walking or driving by which vending spaces were legal or not. I don't think, to my knowledge, this had been done anywhere in the city."

There is a "life cycle" to any given book—especially in the neighborhoods where universities, students and professors, and large numbers of the intelligentsia reside. In Manhattan, many neighborhoods have a college or university nearby: Harlem (City College and Columbia University), Greenwich Village (the New School and New York University), and Midtown (the City University of New York Graduate School). As students and professors are constantly on the move, books get distributed like so many seeds spread across the reading terrain. When students leave for summer and winter breaks, they sell books to street booksellers like Bobo, Beatrice, and Bernard, who offer fifty cents for good-condition softbacks and one dollar for hardbacks. "If a man can double his price for a book upon resell, then he can 'pay rent' or at least provide the means to live one meal away from starvation. But if he can triple the price, he lives high on the hog for a longer time." Bobo tells me he sells only "high-quality" books and has taken to marking prices in his books because people like to bargain otherwise. "People don't like to pay more than five or six dollars for no street book, and I would rather have the price in 'em."

College students who are traveling—Columbia, for example, has many foreign and out-of-state students who don't want to transport their books—end up placing them in the hands of street vendors like Bobo. "This is what I mean by transient lifestyle," he informs me. "This is where people move about and can't afford or don't care to take their books with them." I believe this is particularly true of students who bring their books to sell once the semester is over and again once they get ready to leave the university for the job market. Only people's most prized books are kept. One superintendent explained to me that when people move, even the most ardent reader will leave some books behind, maybe those trashy novels they think are not worth saving, or that thick chemistry book from college, or that great novel too heavy for the box. For whatever reason, every tenant will leave a book or two behind. Books are like the ubiquitous penny in the street: they are always around and not always picked up.

Additionally, college students lose money reselling books to college bookstores, and places like Strand Books, one of the oldest booksellers in New York, do not buy used textbooks. Indeed, many bookstores don't buy used books unless they are in good condition, and that depends on the type of book a person is selling. In that regard, for the residents of the underground, bookselling all depends on the "market" you are involved in, as well as other factors such as the literary quality of the books and the niche markets that book vendors engage in. The most important factor is the confidence of the book vendor.

Bookselling is a type of work few underground residents do; it is more a passion that only some wish to pursue. The books are heavy and cumbersome and require tables or stands or at least boxes to transport and to sell. And then there's the problem of storage at day's end.

MENDICANCY

I used to use the public library as my sleeping spot during the winter, but the hours got so funky and some of those places closed down altogether and they became totally unreliable as "get over spots."

—Jason

Along highways outside the city, at major and minor intersections, near food stores, or at ATMs, one often finds "begging spots," the locations where people attempt to get money from a sympathetic public.

Many of the people I've come to know underground have a street slang they use for making ends meet by "hook or by crook," and it's called "getting over," which is another way of stating the obvious: they want to gain advantage over another person and/or the system. It may be that they join a program for a day to get benefits or "borrow" money they have no intention of repaying, all with the intention of winning a momentary victory.

> In order to avoid the guardians of the host landscape, the forgotten person must adopt a low profile. Often this is not easy to accomplish because the person/tramp/hobo/vagabond wears old worn clothes that are easily recognizable. It is not easy to alter this reality, because to do so involves an outlay of resources that is usually not available. He would also severely diminish his chances to panhandle successfully because his clothes are a sign, often the only visible sign, that he needs a handout.[5]

The sociologist Brian Bartholomew notes that mendicancy is a part of the culture of the city. He considers beggary and its more specific urban form, "panhandling," as a marginal business enterprise, one closely associated with con games. "The economic rationality for the panhandler is suggested in the studies that report the panhandler/beggar makes decisions about where, how, and whom to beg from, what to wear, and what to say or not to say during the encounter." Bartholomew also suggests there's essentially a beggar's guide, an approach, including a script, to draw the potential giver to the cup.[6]

There are other factors in the beggar's world; for example, location and race play a role. Take, for instance, how difficult it is to get money as a panhandler in a poor neighborhood, or consider the psychology of a Black panhandler in an upper-class white neighborhood, which is an admixture of guilt, reified subordination, and economic supremacy.

The Black panhandler is fully aware of this and uses it to his advantage. He needs props: clothes, a way of speaking to people, facial gestures, or physical handicaps, and even that may not be enough. Many years ago in New York City, a Black beggar named George James and his dog were struck by a cab, and well-wishers sent more money for the dog than for the Black man. Or at least initially. There are times when an area or neighborhood, so to speak, will adopt a panhandler, which is to say recognize him or her as a regular.[7]

THE BEGGAR'S SCRIPT

The beggar's script, a handwritten plea usually constructed on brown cardboard, is the standard form by which people—men, women, Black, white, Latino—solicit money from the general public.

All beggar's scripts I've noticed around the country are made of cardboard, handwritten and in pencil or ballpoint pen, held up with two hands or propped on the body as the person stands, sits, or lies, stretched out on the sidewalk, resting with their back against the wall, or seated yoga style, on occasion half-asleep or with their eyes completely shut. Most stand, holding the sign against their body; others hold signs above their heads; others walk from one vehicle to another. Most people look healthy, if not fit, but they are deliberately unshaven, hair tousled, occasionally overweight. Standing near a supermarket or stoplight is the preferred approach in suburban areas, while busy vectors like subway entrances and highway stops such as the Bruckner Boulevard entrance ramp at 149th Street are common spots in the city.

Verbal begging is not heard as much today as it was a decade ago. Most beggars let the signs do the talking for them. Of course, "throwing a sign," slang for begging, is illegal in the city if the person is verbally asking for money.

"My teenager daughter's birthday is coming, and I have nothing to give her."

"I'm a vet."

"I have HIV."

"I'm hungry."

"I lost my apartment."

"I have a family, but we're homeless because of a fire."

"I'm a homeless sober vet."

The beggar is usually a man, though occasionally you might see a woman or an accompanying dog—but no children, unlike in European cities in Italy, France, and Hungary, where I have seen Roma with children and often babies in arms begging in the street.[8] Their clothes are usually soiled, and the person sits, often with their eyes closed. They are not necessarily sleeping, since they need to be aware of what is being placed in the cup or hat or cloth resting next to them or at the feet. Sometimes a sign is seen around their neck, on their lap, or right next to the person resting on a wall. The message on a sign may be humorous: "My family was kidnapped by aliens. Help me get them back," read a sign in the hands of Black male at an onramp to the Major Deegan Expressway, in the Bronx. Alternatively, it may indicate despair: "I'm homeless. Need food. Please help," said a sign from a one-legged white male, mid-fifties, at a highway underpass near the Cross Bronx Expressway.

In areas outside of New York I have visited such as Greensboro, Charlotte, and Winston-Salem in North Carolina, as well as Dallas and Houston, Texas, the signs are the same: "I'm a homeless veteran. I need food and housing"; another, "I need work. Will work. Please help," belonging to a white male, mid-forties, wearing work boots and a blue headband at a Whole Foods supermarket. This kind of personal detail asking for work may be where the person may not openly beg but will leave the cup or hat nearby, on the ground or concrete. "I will take any job."

SEASONAL BEGGING

The times of day or times of year that beggars appear on the street vary, but the most active time of year is summer, because of the warm weather. Similarly favorable is spring, especially if the weather is agreeable. Accordingly, winter is the least active time. As far as time of day is concerned, the lunch hour in the city is especially timely, because having lunch leads others to think about those who are without food. As Jason says: "When people are full or about to eat they think more about what it must be like for somebody who don't have anything to eat, and they are more than likely to give up something." Jason was one of two others I met who literally sang for their suppers. He sang a song by Oscar Brown Jr. "Somebody buy me a drink." Another favorite time to solicit is the evening rush. While most begging is for food, in the city this is usually a ruse, since many places like churches, soup kitchens, and pantries are available that make it almost impossible to go hungry. If I happen to tell the person I will take them to buy a meal, they will often refuse. Beggary in the city is often for drug money. And in the countryside, beggars appear during midday even in the hottest weather. Outside of New York, mendicancy follows a similar pattern.

In the old Grand Central Terminal area in New York, one could see and find beggars at all times of day, early morning and late at night alike. In Harlem they panhandle around favorite outdoor restaurants in the summer and straight away beg at other times. "I have birthday coming up can you help me get something?" asks one sign. Another reads: "I'm HIV positive and need food and medicines. Please help."

Another casual strategy is for the beggar to ask for a cigarette. Once received, they will ask for money or a bus ticket. This same approach is used in the city, where a subway token, or, now, a swipe of a MetroCard, replaces the bus ticket. All of this is to suggest that these begging games are uniform and, in some ways, universal. Some beggars use humor as part of the ruse to get money. "Give me a dollar to get to the point so I can get me a joint." One of the most celebrated street beggars in New York City was a tall, partially blind Scandinavian man named Moondog. During the 1950s he stood on Sixth Avenue holding a large spear and wearing a Viking hat and leather vestments, no matter how hot the weather. He also sold a book of poetry he kept in a little bag he carried. The poetry wasn't very good, but he sold it as a self-published text. Few realized that this eccentric character was also a composer and inventor of several idiosyncratic musical instruments and is considered an important forerunner of later New York City musical trends, such as minimalism. Another public character who sits near a church on Fifth Avenue near Twelfth Street and sings the chorus to "Great Balls of Fire" has been the subject of a documentary by the artist Pearl Gluck.

As we know, the vagrant has a long history. Take this excerpt from Elizabethan times. Fernand Braudel writes: "Beggars from distant provinces appeared in the fields and streets of the town of Troyes in 1573, starving, clothed in rags and covered with fleas and vermin. They were authorized to stay there for only 24 hours. Vagrants include many kinds of harmful and harmless persons, but they were hard to distinguish that they were all included [in] the one comprehensive term, Vagabond, and were legislated against in common."[9] Braudel goes on to note that vagrants were then divided into two groups: one class was referred to as "sturdy" and the other "impotent."

We can see this classification play out today. Jason, like so many of the others I talked with on this study, is a member of the new disposable class. Every system based on capitalistic principles needs a large pool of unemployed labor that can easily be tapped into. But those living *beyond* these surplus laborers, however, are not needed at all. Homeless people like Jason, Kal, and Bobo are prime examples of this situation. They are rejected and neglected with the hope that they will be forgotten, rendered invisible.

But by working and finding ways to make a living, they are not so easily disposed of. I don't think it is a stretch to say that society makes it look like most homeless have themselves to blame for the situation in which they find themselves. The concept of individual responsibility is one of the bedrocks of the American mythos, and it is hard not to believe in such balderdash, because the American Dream is tied into this myth. But if you start to examine this idea, even scratch the surface, you will find it full of holes and completely mean-spirited. Homelessness is not a conscious decision people make, and even if they did, there is something called the social contract, and the state has the responsibility to help.

After listening to these men and women in dire straits, it becomes clear that regular citizens do not understand that panhandling or begging is not haphazard. All life underground, whether a rat or a human being, is hardwired to survive—to figure out a *survival technology*. A person's needs do not diminish because of the season, especially if a drug habit is involved; panhandlers, like airlines, have routes that they regularly work at certain times. In certain areas or spots, one might encounter the same person on a regular basis. Part of it is a con game; on another level, it is an abdication from the regular work world. But this is the ruse: you are never quite sure if the person is really using the money for what you assume they are using for, and it is that ambiguity which allows the person to get a coin in the cup.

CAN-O-NOMICS

A man without money is the very picture of death [homo pecunia imago mortis].
—Giovanni Reborna, *Culture of the Fork*

We call it can-o-nomics but it is still working, it's a job no matter how you look at it.
—Bobo

The residents see the underground as having a hierarchy of misery, where some people are afforded more privileges than others. Booksellers like Bernard sell cans and make money from journalists, TV crews, photographers, and others who come to do stories on the underground every few weeks. He finds wood in the park and collects water from drinking fountains and food from soup kitchens. Bernard is up as soon as light shines through the grates—five in the morning this time of year—preparing to load, sort, and arrange cans into plastic sacks with his roughened hands and split fingers.

These he carries across muscular shoulders from the far track side to a place underneath the stairs at the west gate, placing them into a chain-locked shopping cart stationed there. Then he lifts cart and all onto his shoulder, takes it up to the steps to a short landing, opens the gate, and wheels the cart uphill through the park, with the skyline of New Jersey at his back.

Some cans he collects from building supers the night before; others he buys from homeless can men at half price. Bernard is an entrepreneur; he offers cash, five cents for two cans, and many sellers are willing to forgo the extra nickel in part to avoid the hassle of dealing with people at the local We-Can operation or at supermarkets. "I save the other nickel for a 'rainy day,'" he tells me, the day he plans to leave underground for good. He's got a housing voucher from the Department of Housing and Urban Development, after the HUD secretary visited the underground and promised to get them out. As a bookseller, however, he is more highly regarded than other can collectors. The recently discharged mental patients are at the lowest end of both the space and the social structure.

At the end of the day, he takes the cans across the park, down the sloping hill to the west gate. He unlocks the door with his special keys, snaps the lock back, and hoists the cans down the newly repaired stairs and back across the far side tracks to another storage area. He then takes two plastic containers, fills them with water from the park fountain, and places them back in the cart. Back in the underground at day's end, he's washing his hair from two big buckets, one for washing and the other rinsing. He wraps his dreadlocks in a cloth, lights up a cigarette, and waits for his hair to dry.

Kal says people underground are given a bum rap and no credit for what they do for the city. I ask what he meant by that. "I mean think about it. If it wasn't for the homeless, the city would be filthy. They clean up this city when they pick up all these cans and bottles. They are doing a service for the city that they get no credit for doing."

Now, I'm a can man. Each day of the week, from 101st maybe 110th to Ninety-Sixth on the East Side, Sunday to Monday, I do it. Sometimes I go down from 110th street to Ninety-Sixth on the West Side on Tuesday and Wednesday. And it keeps going. Crisscross, each day, you know, they put out the blue garbage barrels with the cans. So I hit each side.

One day I lucked out because I filled a whole black fifty-gallon bag in one block, up on 100th Street. I just happened to walk right in. There was nobody on the whole block and all these blue barrels had all cans and plastics in it. I said, well, here we go. So the super felt so sorry for me because I was putting them in little bags, he brought me a big fifty-gallon bag. Man, I just started filling them up. Broke 'em out, and that was it. When I got four hundred cans I got twenty dollars. And an average fifty-gallon bag, twelve-ounce cans, will hold roughly between $17 and $18 dollars' worth. That's to the top. You just gotta itemize, you know, add. I'm talking about twelve ounce, not sixteen ounce, because sixteen's take up more room.

I go up by east from Riverside to Broadway or Riverside to Amsterdam in one day. From Amsterdam to Central Park West is another. So I criss-cross, depending on what days you know you get. And you could do good. You know if you get out early and you know when they are putting the cans out and there is not a lot of guys picking up.

Sometimes there's a beef or two, if you have the crazies out there but most of the time it's OK, especially if a super likes you. You can make yourself twenty dollars in four, five hours. And for picking up cans that's a lot. But there's a trick to knowing just when to go out. 'Cause a lot of time you won't hit anything, 'cause you know they just bang and make a racket and they're all be there at one time. They are the crazies.

Not everyone would agree to his distinction: on the street, Kal is completely oblivious to the looks of people as he passes by in a ragged shirt and old worn sneakers, with his bedraggled hair and filthy appearance.

Aboveground, he walks swiftly and unevenly, darting between cars instead of waiting for the light and moving on and off the sidewalks instead of following a straight line, sifting through garbage or retrieving an object from the gutter, talking to no one in particular. He does not, however, see himself as "crazy"—being homeless, he insists, does not necessarily make one crazy, just homeless. "And everybody talks to themselves in New York. It's the people that don't who are suspect."

The area between Ninetieth to Ninety-Ninth Streets, Kal tells me, is "our turf," meaning his and Bernard's, especially at night. "In evening time," Kal says, wiping his greasy beard on his sleeve, "there's red sun rays coming from the sun setting down. Just gorgeous. I wouldn't miss that for the world." There is no such view from this vantage point in the underground; the thin rays of light that do penetrate the bunker come through best from the south.

The essence of can-o-nomics began on June 15, 1982, when New York State set up the nickel-deposit law, or "Bottle Bill," or Returnable Container Act. Environmentalists, beggars in the street, bag ladies, garbage can men, store owners, supers of buildings, and the general public all praised the law because it afforded opportunities of one kind or another. The general public endorsed the law because it would mean less litter on the street; street mendicants liked the law because it would be a way to generate income from the sale of bottles.

New York was not the first state to pass container deposit legislation. Vermont passed it in 1973 and Oregon in 1978. Today, only eleven states have beverage container deposit laws. The success of the Bottle Bill has been noticeable. The website for New York City states that it has "reduced roadside container litter by 70 percent, and recycled 90 billion containers, equal to 6 million tons of materials, at no cost to local governments; saved more than 52 million barrels of oil; and eliminated 200,000 metric tons of greenhouse gases each year."

The act established a nickel deposit on carbonated drinks, mineral water, beer, spring water, and other malt beverages. This deposit covers not only metal and plastic containers but also glass. The idea was very simple. When a consumer purchases a beverage, a five-cent deposit is paid, and when the container is returned, the deposit is given back. The five-cent deposit is meant both to reduce beverage container litter and to encourage recycling. Since the Bottle Bill was enacted, "redemption rates have been 70–80 percent."

The New York Act does not permit refunds for beverage containers purchased outside of New York, because no deposit was originally required. That limits can collection to beverage containers sold in the state of New York. One high-rise building superintendent I talked with said "at this time building superintendents did not view the law favorably because street can people cut into garbage bags and left rubbish strewn all over the place. People complained, but soon the effects were felt in a different way as homeless people began to collect the cans to get money by bringing the cans to local stores for the deposits."[10]

The act also created a commodity, and not just any commodity, but a special one. Cans are a form of what economists call "quasi-money," money equivalents or money substitutes like food stamps, vouchers, or even bitcoins, but different in the sense that a can has value inherent or embodied in it. The government imposed a tariff in the form of a deposit fee, which one can consider a measure left for the citizen with no other means to acquire something of value.

This is a kind of *default altruism* on the part of the state government: most people do not care about the small deposit and thus leave it, in the commodity form of the can, for the poorest of the poor, scrounging for a pitiful few cents. In this respect, the deposit has an economic unintended consequence: money is generated by homeless people working around the city. In the underground, several residents do the work required to get cans to the exchange centers, and as a result, there are quasi-property relations that only become manifest in this setting.

Given these economic effects, the Bottle Bill has seen revision over time to account for potential loopholes in the system. The 2013 amendments to the state's Returnable Container Act specify:

- A new provision that prohibits tampering with reverse vending machines (RVMs)
- The right for redemption centers and dealers (retailers/ stores) to refuse crushed containers in order to prevent double redemption

- Clarification that all containers must have "NY5c" permanently embossed on the containers or permanently marked
  on the container label

According to the law set up in 1994, stores can take up to 240
cans. Brand-name cans also get what is called a "two-for-oner,"
which is buying two cans for the price of one when the person
paying does so in cash. We-Can gets a penny and half on each
can when they return brand-name cans from Coca-Cola, Bud-
weiser, Pepsi, and similar companies.

Bernard says proudly: "I can sell 60 cans and get $3.00 whether
they are dented, bent, ripped or whatever. I make about $45 dol-
lars a day selling cans. One day I went out and found 1,400 cans
and made $170 dollars." In doing the math, this suggests he gets

FIGURE 5.1. Bernard and friend collecting cans for double redemption.
Source: Photo by Teun Voeten.

FIGURE 5.2. One of the underground men working to process cans.

Source: Photo by Teun Voeten.

FIGURE 5.3. At the We-Can Community Resource
Center in New York City.

Source: Photo by Teun Voeten.

a nickel per can to get the $3.00 for 60 cans, yet for the $170 for 1,400 cans means he was selling big cans at 12 cents each. He notes: "Material wealth does not have any value for me; only things that have no value to most people have value for me. Like these cans."

6

FOOD

Restaurants and Soup Kitchens

The food will be served out of pans, and in part out of two wide shallow soup plates and a small white thick platter. At the middle of the table is a mason jar of sorghum, a box of black pepper, and a tall shaker of salt whose top is green, all surrounding the unlighted lamp which stands in the bare daylight in the beauty of a young nude girl.

—James Agee and Walker Evans, *Let Us Now Praise Famous Men*

Regardless of the various spaces and conditions in which people live underground, they all have a connection between their marginal existence and mainstream society, as it were. In many ways, people go to the soup kitchen not only because they are hungry but also as a way to find community and maintain a connection to the mainstream. Although how these connections are managed has been the focus of much of this text, the matter of a particularly vital resource—food—will concern us here. Bernard, Kal, and Jason, seated before the fire pit in the underground, all have found some comfort around communal meals, and in this chapter I ask where they get their food. This leads to a discussion about the many cheap restaurants as well as soup kitchens in the city and how they evaluate both on what Kal calls a "four-star system."[1] Kal says no place gets four stars unless the meal costs under five dollars; the soup kitchen needs to have metal spoons, not plastic. I'm on my way to the soup kitchen near Grand Central Terminal, in Midtown.

FIELD NOTE (1998)

The soup kitchen is packed today: men and women, mostly Black and Latino men with a number of white men and no Asians. The tables are made of wood and metal with plastic spoons and forks and knives stacked up in a big plastic bucket; the people sop up the Thanksgiving dinner in massive strokes. The lady with a huge bag slung under her arm stands looking for a place to sit. She gazes over at the men at the tables and yells: "Ain't there no gentlemen in this place?" One man with a long white beard and Yankee baseball cap looks up at her and offers his seat as he takes a spoonful of food. A man with a Karakul-type hat argues with another man about seating, while another stares at the paintings and pictures on the wall.

The dinner is turkey, dressing, salad, peas, bread, sweet potato pie for dessert and soda and punch to wash it all down. The smell is festive with these smells wafting through the air. The staff is quite generous with the food, and it's "all you can eat" day, with seconds, thirds if you wish. Right near the head of a table near the center of the cafeteria-like room a man is standing, a tall man with no teeth wearing a brand-new suit, a big ill-fitting hat, tags and all. He is barefoot. He bows several times, then looks as if he's saying grace with hands folded in front. Then in a few seconds after appearing solemn, he smiles a broad toothless smile. This was my one time volunteering at the soup kitchen: though

I'd been in this place more than once over the years, I'd never volunteered to serve food before.

The sociologist William Difazio notes:

Soup kitchens and food pantries have special meals, give turkeys to families, and attract plenty of volunteers and media attention. By 2000 there would seem to be a lot to celebrate: the eighth year of an economic boom, unemployment rates at a 30-year low (3.9. percent). But we should remember that the Thanksgiving story is a myth and that the Native Americans who shared that first Thanksgiving meal with the Pilgrims were in general the objects of scorn and violence. Here in the "Other America" of the poor, who are also the object of America's scorn and violence (given that hunger is a form of violence to the body), there isn't a lot to be thankful for. An increasing client base is overwhelming soup kitchens and food pantries.[2]

Many homeless people reject services such as shelters (too dangerous, drug infested, and corrupt), drop-in centers, welfare offices, medical services for issues such as drug and alcohol misuse, mental health support, social worker assistance, school and job training, and veterans services (too bureaucratic). Soup kitchens are perhaps the only social service many consider a viable option.

CHEAP MEALS

New York City boasts at least twenty thousand restaurants, coffeehouses, and eateries of one kind or another. The homeless need to find cheap meals—but that doesn't mean they lack their own tastes and preferences. As a matter of fact, the men and women I talked to prefer buying rather than "bumming" a meal from soup kitchens. Although they all mentioned breakfast as their favorite meal, only the New York City Rescue Mission on the Lower East Side serves a daily breakfast seven days a week.

Bobo, Jason, Beatrice, Bernard, and Kal all suggest ways to eat cheap in this great world city, and that means eating a full meal for a few bucks. Each person had a special neighborhood and location for their meals. Bernard favors two restaurants where he says food is cheap and people pleasant. "I like to go to Sylvia's on 126th for my breakfast, and when I have a few extra dollars I go to La Cocita on 106th and Broadway. Another good spot is on Broadway between 108th and 109th Streets, where another Cuban joint, Ideal, used to be."

Bobo, whose forays into the city take him as far as Chinatown, prefers the Lower East Side because "a lot of the old Jewish delis like Katz's used to be cheap, but now you'll pay nine dollars for a pastrami sandwich in there these days. The best spot for a cheap meal down there now, especially breakfast, is B&H on Second Avenue, that's near St. Mark's Place. My friend took me to a place run by the Argentines, and that place is both a bakery and a coffee shop/café-like place. But let me tell you the fucking joint is some noisy, always crowded, and takes a while to get your food, but it's worth it. The other spot is right there on First Avenue, cheap too, and by that I mean under five bucks for a meal."

Beatrice, who's only been out twice in the past year, and that was when she was able to see her "sponsor and dress up a little bit," said her favorite place is "Ollie's on Broadway and Eighty-Sixth Street because of the scallion pancakes and noodles but especially because you can see the stoves and the way they cook the food." As she says this, she's washing clothes in an ice cooler and hanging them on a steel line.

A relatively unknown ethnic neighborhood with both cheap restaurants and inexpensive groceries is a sliver of establishments located on Ninth Avenue behind the Port Authority Bus Terminal. This tiny corridor, running from Thirty-Eighth Street to Forty-Second, is a mixture of Italian, Irish, Mexican, Guatemalan, Honduran, Haitian, Chinese, and other newer arrivals. The most notable eatery here sells a one-dollar hot dog with a free soda. Although Gray's Papaya hot dogs are fifty cents and purport to being the best and cheapest in the city, my homeless friends say the dogs on Ninth are the biggest and the freshest.

They are fresh because right next door is one of the last remnants of the old Meatpacking District houses that flourished in the area before the revitalization of Times Square. But, Beatrice suggests, "When you gotta get food to cook, go to the Sunshine Vegetable Market near the Holland Underground entrance behind Port Authority, and you can't beat the meat market for a cheap steak if you really wanna indulge yourself." Bernard, who considers himself a good cook, tells me more about this location: "If you wanna buy fresh fruit, condiments, fresh pasta, or anything like that, this is the place to go."

Jason rarely cooks, while Kal is known for his "underground stew"; they both make frequent forays into the city to eat. Their favorite "on the cheap" haunts are White Castle and Sbarro's. "Of course," Jason informs me, "White Castle on 125th Street offers cheap hamburgers, but you need a wheelbarrow of them little fuckers to get full." At the same time, Kal suggests Sbarro's on Thirty-Fourth Street "because you can get a decent breakfast, but the buffet is only five dollars, and it's all you can eat. Blimpies is another spot where you can get the two-dollar special, which is a big sandwich, juice, and coffee. But you should know this, that the few restaurants that are good in that area and below are all Spanish. As a matter of fact, in the Twenties around Nineteenth Street, there's a great Chinese restaurant where beer is one dollar, brother, soda fifty cents, and the meals are three, four dollars. Now you can't beat that with a stick."

SOUP KITCHENS

The underground resident has to find ingenious ways of obtaining life's essentials (food, water, wood, work, shelter) and manage getting by without causing too many problems with either people (as in patrons of the establishment) or the police. In our discussion about food, the conversation shifts to soup kitchens and the ones with the best food, the best service, the best desserts, the all-around best in the city. The vast majority of all meal programs in the city are operated by communities of faith.

When I begin to formulate my questions, the first people I ask are Bernard, Kal, and Bobo. "Most of them suck," Kal reports, "because they make you feel like a schmuck, and them workers there would rather piss on you if they could. But there are places that are better than others. The ones I like best are the ones nearest me. Right there on Broadway at Riverside Church I fell in love with them places because of the way they treat you and the way the food is served and how good it is. I like St. Barnabas in the Bronx too because I used to have a girl who lived around there, and she took me to a basement kitchen in or near that church, and the food was fantastic. They served on real plates and real forks until people kept stealing them and they had to go back to plastics. Then there is Holy Apostles. They start serving around nine in the morning to around two and their food is good, but the people who work there have been there for years, and so you get some looks sometimes, but overall, I'd say they are nice most of the time."

Bobo, who has done his share of "dumpster diving," does not like soup kitchens at all. "I used to go to these places and just decided I would rather gather my own food. I liked a coupl'a places early on, especially the Moravian Church down on Lex, which was the best for a while until they started that psychiatric shit." (The church instituted a policy of only feeding homeless with psychiatric problems, and before people could be served, they had go through an interview process.) "I also liked Murray Hill for breakfast. You could eat back then all you wanted from 8:30 to 9:30 Monday through Friday. But I tell you what finally got to me was the people coming in who weren't homeless at all," Bobo continues. "I saw guys coming in with suits and ties on, and you know they weren't fucking homeless. They were just taking advantage and saving their money while the real homeless had to scramble to survive. It made me sick, so whenever I saw one, I spoke on it until I was asked not to come back no more. I'm a vet, and I know how to take care of myself, but I didn't wanna go to jail, so I just decided to stay away from those kitchens."

Bernard doesn't visit soup kitchens as often, but when he does, he finds Murray Hill the best for him because "the staff is so nice to people, they don't have you filling out questionnaires and asking a lot of dumb questions, and that makes all the difference because people don't need to feel any more dejected by society than they already are, and when places have caring staff, you really enjoy eating there even if the food is not the greatest.

Don't get me wrong, the food there was very good as far as soup kitchens go. I should say I also liked the community lunch program near Columbia."

The Broadway Presbyterian church, a Gothic structure nestled between a restaurant and a bookstore, sits across from Columbia University on 114th Street and Broadway. On a side door, a red-lettered sign reads: "Community Lunch Program. Mon, Tues, Wed, Sun. Tickets distributed on Saturday." A line of sixty to eighty men, mostly Black and Latino, stand two deep along the sidewalk halfway down the block. A shortish white male about fifty, with a curled mustache and well-worn jacket, shouts "wait your turn" to several men near him.

One woman, well dressed in a short-sleeved shirt and tie, holds one pant leg up with her hands. There are no teenagers in this line and only two women, one in her late twenties, the other in the suit, about sixty. It is hard to tell the age of homeless people; their faces hold years in abeyance, but their hands, usually harsh and rough because of the hard work associated with scrap gathering and difficult living, tell another story. Most of those in line today pay no attention to the goings-on around them but wait expressionlessly for the queue to move so they can eat.

Others talk casually to one another about where to go for lunch on other days. "Ninth Avenue is good every day, but I don't like the food there," one says. "Plus they have fights all the time. Sixty-Sixth Street is good if you like sermons before you eat," offers another man standing next to him. "I go to the kitchen on Sixty-Sixth Street on Tuesday and Thursdays to get my food," says another. "I have a Social Security check coming in now, and I get my digit [money] from cans every day I work the supers." The line is a sorry sight. Kids trail by from a local school, holding their faces in mock horror, pointing and calling out "beggars" and "bums," but there's nothing threatening about this group. They're hungry for a meal and a place to stay.

Aggression has been struck from them long ago. They are now at survival stage: the dole is the way and quiescence the order of the day. By three in the afternoon the line is gone; a busy chorus of Columbia students pass the church, ignoring the lone woman left sitting on the steps.

In 1999, there were 751 soup kitchens and shelters in New York City, all supplied by an independent food bank.[3] The soup kitchens in particular are dependent on government funding and private foundations, and they in turn order their supplies from the Food for Survival Food Bank in the Hunts Point Market in the Bronx, whose funding is derived from corporate and federal sources.

Some underground residents seek out these places for food as last resort; most prefer fending for themselves and avoiding what Kal calls "those begging lines." "You know me and Bernard," Kal says. "We both worked as short-order cooks at Our Lady of the Angels Church down on Eighty-Sixth Street, but I wouldn't go there to eat no more because I'd rather cook my own underground stew than eat there. A beg is a beg is a beg no matter how you cut it."

Jean-Pierre, on the other hand, doesn't have such reservations and goes to the Harlem Community Kitchen near Eighth Avenue for some of his meals. Jean-Pierre, who has been living on the edge of the underground in his rabbit hole, reminds me of this location, since it is only a block from my apartment. A volunteer there told me: "We serve about seven hundred meals a day here. And we've seen an increase in people coming here for meals since 1994. We get mostly Black, unemployed men, which is not unusual for this area. After all, we are in Harlem. I tell you what is not normal for us, though, and that's the number of mothers with children or the number of entire families who come here to eat. We expect this pattern to increase as the new welfare restrictions sink into place." Jean-Pierre said the Harlem spot was his second choice after, as he said, "my favorite place on Ninth Avenue burned down." He's referring to Holy Apostle Soup Kitchen, which did not burn down: only the roof was destroyed by fire. The soup kitchen reopened a few years later.

The "welfare restrictions" the volunteer referred to was P. l. 104-193, the Personal Responsibility and Work Opportunity Reconciliation Act of 1996, which passed in Congress and was signed into law by President Bill Clinton on August 22, 1996. This law cut assistance for children and families in a broad range of safety-net programs. It abolished Aid to Families with Dependent Children (AFDC), the primary cash-aid program; the Work and Training Program for welfare recipients (JOBS); and the Emergency Assistance to Families with Children (EAFC), a program providing emergency help to families with children for a maximum of one month per year.

The programs were replaced with a block grant of federal funds given to the states. Effective October 1996, no individual or family is entitled by federal law to receive welfare help. In 1996, New York agencies feeding the homeless served more than one hundred thousand meals a day, with about 35,000 of those meals going to children. Throughout the early 1990s, soup kitchens had been turning away people by the thousands each year, and then by 1998–1999, New York State had lost at least a quarter of the federal money it had been receiving and about 40 percent of its state money. This meant many food pantries and soup kitchens had to close or reduce their operations.

DIGITALIZATION OF SERVICES

Current health crises have shown that the relationships between technology and the community play vital roles in the survival of the local economy and the community overall. The pandemic crisis has altered the fabric of communities, including their support and communication systems in New York City.

The 2011 Bloomberg administration report titled "Road Map for the Digital City: Achieving New York City's Digital Future," presented a comprehensive plan suggesting the ways the city intended to develop a digital future. The report detailed how the New York City government's commitment to technology in the public sector could work. An idea was that the digitalization of public service would further expand access and bring more transparency and efficiency to the government, by helping connect "high-needs individuals" to funded city initiatives and programs.

During the current crisis, it became apparent that the entanglement of technology and the community was not completely understood. Questions whether the technological transformation of public services that started in 2011 under the Bloomberg administration was able to provide sufficient support to those "high-needs individuals" and mitigate the use of public resources in a more equitable way have to be approached in a critical manner. But the question I would explore here is whether this digital system of public services has been developed for the use of only a particular social group.

Social scientists know people learn things. People living in a particular community learn about their community, and that knowledge becomes localized. Different communities have different systems of local knowledge. I believe it is important to know that in poor communities, social and economic interactions are not only largely shaped through and influenced by this local knowledge but also to a great extent resistant to the use of technology, because the common bonds and social interactions that sustain poor communities tend to have been built on traditional forms of communication.

I have been studying poor communities for decades, and one focus of my work has been the links between new technology and social and economic disparities in poor communities. Generally I have been guided by two questions: (1) What social and economic factors affect the level of new technology penetration in poor communities, thus perpetuating the digital divide? (2) How did low levels of technology penetration affect those most vulnerable during times of crisis? In 2003, my colleague William Kornblum, in his ethnographic study "Digital Divide and Disadvantaged Youth," examined the links between the technological skill/literacy of teenagers and their socioeconomic conditions; he detailed how poor technological skills were affecting their future successes in life. In my recent work *Harlem Supers: The Social Life of a Community in Transition*,[4] I examined how the use of technology was changing the way building superintendents do their job, the role technology played in redefining their job duties and responsibilities, and how their increased reliance on the use of technology affected productivity and efficiency. My research showed that new technology has been eliminating not only people but also manual tasks and has become a major obstacle and deterrent, a kind of discriminatory device to keep minority groups from entering well-paying jobs.

For the past two decades, poor communities have been irresponsive to the forces of many technological innovations. Recent economic research shows that for over several decades the U.S.

economy has been growing at a slower rate; the slower rate of growth has suppressed the demand for labor. My observations of poor communities in New York City led me to believe that throughout the city digitalization has been uneven and that many poor communities have been left behind, lacking access to the internet and not acquiring the computer skills needed to adapt to a new, more technologically driven reality. Since 2000, in brief, the digital divide between the poor and affluent has been growing.

Existing studies including those by Kornblum point out the importance of having internet access and digital devices like computers or mobile phones in poor communities to address adequately the issue of this digital divide. Since many educational and employment resources are online, having access to the internet can provide members of the community with the opportunity to learn new skills and search and apply for better-paying jobs. These are necessary conditions to bring vibrancy and well-being to poor communities because they bring more opportunities; our main concern is that if left behind in the aftermath of the current crisis, these communities will never be revitalized. However, it seems that no matter how hard the city government tries to provide access to public services for all New Yorkers, one social group is bound to be left behind: unsheltered individuals living on the streets and underground, and this is the poorest, neediest, and most vulnerable social group. This group cannot benefit from public services and information available on the NYC.gov website because it lacks internet-capable devices. An individual with a mobile phone can easily locate a nearest soup kitchen or find a shelter bed available to spend a night, but most individuals living on the streets do not own cell phones or other devices that can help them access public services. This means that the digitalization of public services will not be a benefit for them.

FOODSTUFFS AND SUPPLIES

The underground is not easy. Every day to get water you had to go half a mile to get it and half a mile to bring it back. Bernard and me used to get five to seven days' worth of water at a time because you did not know when it was gonna rain. Another thing is food. We had a school back three blocks away that gave us the food at the end of the day that the kids did not want, but summer was the worse.

—Entry in Kal's journal

In regard to food supplies, several tactics are used, each resident managing their own approach. Bobo was dumpster diving long before it became a fashionable hipster tactic, Kal sold cans, and Bernard sold books and cans and worked as an occasional laborer for supers along Riverside Drive.

As for keeping warm in winter, Kal mentioned before he came underground that he slept at local churches, including St. John the Divine. "Behind the church is a good spot in the spring, and Central Park has some good areas too if you ain't afraid of rats." On my tour under Grand Central Terminal with Sergeant Henry, he showed me a warm grate he said had been very popular with the homeless before he came along. Other locations included building niches, train stations, the subway, the back alleys of soup kitchens, the Forty-Second Street Library, the Thirty-Fourth Street Post Office, the base of the Brooklyn Bridge, and though more dangerous than most spots, high on small, three-foot ledges above the railroad tracks, also referred to as "nests."

"THE KITCHEN"

There is little stimulation and even less movement in the wide expanse of the underground today. Sometimes, the only sound is the thumping of car wheels on steel bars across the concrete along the West Side Highway above me. One troubling aspect of life in the underground is the absence of plant life and nature. There is no real sense of seasonal change except what comes through the grate—a sprinkling of snow or rain or leaves—or the cold and hot weather.

Today, as Kal talked, a cold wind blew through the passage. The kitchen has been improved: a steel divider from a stove, blackened from wood smoke, fits over piles of bricks; the cabinets alongside and directly behind the fire pit are filled with tea, cornmeal, salt, pepper, and other spices on the top shelves, plates and forks and pots on the shelves below—and three shoes at the bottom of one rack of foodstuffs. Above the fire, a miniature airplane fashioned from a can twirls in the half-light of the grate.

Six chairs are placed around the steel divider. This is called "the kitchen," but it is more a communal resting space than a cooking compound. It is about thirty feet wide and half the length of a football field. The floor is strewn with cans, cups, eggshells, a scrub board to wash clothes near a bucket filled with dirty water, rocks and pebbles, thousands of nails, and twenty-five or more pots and pans.

The fire crackles against a wire-mesh screen held in place by two thick bricks; the sharp broken snaps of the fire, the bristling sounds of paper, thick log, wood chips, and kindling transform into a blue- and amber-colored smoke spiraling into the air. Behind the fire spit is a medium-sized, once-white cabinet topped by a long board holding salt, pepper, coffee, teas, flour, and other condiments. Three dusty chairs are arranged around

the fire; on one, a copy of the *New Yorker* magazine is open to a
page with a piece by Calvin Trillin. The sooty foodstuffs are
lined neatly atop a smaller cabinet. The background to this scene
is a twenty-by-twenty-foot Goya's *Third of May* mural on the
rear wall. In the foreground, the tracks and a column of sixteen
spiral-like rays of street light beam down through the grates.

"A lot of good meals come out of that fire. A lot of good
meals." Kal is an interestingly ugly man, his face etched with a
thousand white wrinkles—not from old age, he says, but from
stress—and two deep lines, curving down from both nostrils and
hooking into the lips. His salt-and-pepper hair recedes unevenly,
so that it bunches up in the middle of his head and flows down
both sides of his face. His hands with short fingers and dirty
nails are sandpaper rough; shaking hands with him is like grip-
ping the end of a fireplace brick. He has several teeth missing
from the left side of his mouth, and innumerable scars decorate
his arms, hands, and neck. A light shone through the space, and
in an instant the train roared through, heading south and blasting dust all over us. Kal squinted, held up his middle finger, and
said, "There goes my dignity, man. There goes my dignity. I'll
get up and get wood."

When he returns, he continues: "We already brought down
newspapers. I make sure we got water, you know. And we have
enough left over, I'll stop at the supermarket for food and make
sure I get a large jar of coffee, it's $2.99 right now. That'll last us
a whole week, the large jar. It's the best coffee. I'm going to have
to cut this short. I don't know, I'm getting cold. I mean, if it's
warm enough today, I may pick up enough cans to do the laundry. Each machine is $2, and I need three machines plus the
dryer just so we got enough clothes to last. Because you don't
know who is going to come down here. We got a few people
coming down here Monday. The *New York Times* reporter and

Dutch film maker, you know, is coming, and Bernard wants to make sure he's at his best, and the laundry will have to be done." He interrupts himself and blurts out, "I'm going to go to my room for a minute." When he returns in a few minutes, he's high, eyes bulging, and agitated. "I can't . . . I'm not used to people staring at me. You know?" He walks a few steps, looks around, says people are following him. "Today, I saw a man walking through the underground with a bag. He looked gay. I know young boys are brought down here for servicing."

Kal pulls at his hair and then his beard. He stokes the fire. "I know these tricks cause nothing but trouble. And I notice there is a graffiti piece over there that says something about gays down here too. Listen, let me tell you something, Professor. To lose everything is one thing. But to accept it, you know, to accept losing everything . . . that's something else. I don't feel bad being in the underground. Number one because, you know, if you look the part, let your beard grow, then you mentally can't handle it. But if you keep yourself halfway clean and you deal with the people topside respectfully, then it's like, okay, you're here. It's only a temporary situation. You know nothing is permanent in life." I think what Kal means here is that looking homeless is being homeless (psychologically), but if one can avoid looking homeless, then one can more resist the descent into a hopeless state.

Apparently, and for Kal at least, this resistance is a key factor in avoiding the psychological label of "homeless," which leads to a certain kind of self-defeatist attitude. "But the kids nowadays," he continues, "I'd like to get to talk at some of these schools, you know, and I did one talk up at Bronxville. You can't tell a kid 'don't do drugs.' You've got to show them . . . take 'em in a bus and show 'em what it will do to you. Let me tell you something else. The guy who makes it is not always the smartest. It's the guy who was smart enough to stay smart. The guy with all the scars is not the toughest. It's the guy who put the scars there. The baddest guy is not the one who has been to jail twenty times. It's the guy who stayed out of jail. Listen. I'm forty-nine years old, and to this day I've never even had a traffic ticket. And at one time I dealt drugs for close to twenty years. Yeah. San Francisco to Los Angeles. But I always respected the Man."

Bernard, who has been listening to this, squats near the fire to spit, as he is wont to do. He stays in that position for a long time, never getting on all fours or bending over. He squats to talk, squats to cook, squats to mingle, squats to retrieve stuff from the dirt floor, squats to pick up items from the cans that hold his condiments and eating utensils. Kal is more of a walker: he walks constantly, moving around in and out of camp as well as up and down the extended passage. Even when he's resting he's still moving. The movement is clearly related to his crack use, which he admits is part of his daily life. He heads topside to buy drugs from a dealer he despises.

Kal says: "If I was a tough guy I'd slit this motherfucker's throat, because I can't tell you how many times he's shafted me. He's given me bullshit, fake shit so many times I can't even remember. Why do I go back to him? Well, I tell you, a lot of these guys out here are snitches and cop pussies, so if you ain't careful they will turn you over like a flapjack. They will sell you out in a minute, so it's best to stick with someone you know, or at least cool in that regard. Now, this guy sells shit sometimes but he also sells some righteous shit more times than not. He's lucky I'm druggin not thuggin."

On Ninety-Sixth Street near Amsterdam Avenue, he cops a gram of crack. After the purchase he goes into a head shop on 110th Broadway and buys two screens for fifty cents, two Bic lighters for a dollar, and a can of beer for thirty cents. He walks back underground, entering near Ninety-Fifth Street, where the road turns onto the southbound lanes of the West Side Highway. When he gets back down under, he prepares the crack in a small shaker bottle and spins the tiny vial until a white film covers the bottom of the glass. He uses a spoon he took from a soup kitchen when he doesn't have a bottle.

He adds more fire to the solution, which has only a tiny bit of water left. After the bottle cools, a rock forms at the bottom, and he slaps the open mouth of the bottle into his palm. With his roughened fingers he shows me the off-color, jagged pebble. His fingernails are dirty and choppy. He doesn't use the razor blade that he takes from his pocket and instead pinches off a piece of the rock. It is still a bit soft, so he lets it cool, then places it in his stem and smokes. In a few minutes all is calm: he settles back, closes his eyes, and lets the cool breeze of the underground pass over him.

After these solemn few moments, he's up again walking around the edge of the campfire, talking in riddles. He says he's going for a walk topside and asks if I want to go with him. We stop and sit on the bench near the river, the water, calm and cool, the scene pleasant. Skaters drift by. One is slipping and sliding, staying upright with help from a veteran skater. Young lovers sit kissing on a bench. Kal says words to the effect of "look at that, there can be joy in unsuspecting happiness." Or maybe "there can be joy when you don't expect happiness." I wanted to ask him again what he said but decided to just wait and gaze out at the river. There are occasions when it is best not to say anything. Every now and again, he says something about God or Man or something in the philosophical realm: death, life, cosmological stuff that he's heard Bernard repeat many times, but that last statement seems genuinely his own reflection.

THE DUMPSTER STORY

We called ourselves, or I should say I, called us the three
dumpsterteers whenever me, Kal, and Bernard went out to
the dumpsters to get food.

—Bobo

When Bobo, Kal, Bernard, and other underground residents
went "dumpster diving," they were not part of any anticonsumer
movement but were in fact the precursor to what is now called
"freeganism." This is a kind of organized countercultural movement where mainstream conventional consumption is looked
down upon. As Claudia Horn, a young worker for a social welfare agency wrote: "The philosophy is to live and sustain in an
autonomous way and without purchasing and supporting the
industrial and exploitative capitalist production of goods."

Bobo asks if I know about the dumpsters where some of the
homeless get food. He says everybody in the underground has a
dumpster story.

They used to have a dumpster near Grand Union on 100th Street,
and this is how I got with the [police] precinct, because they were
right up the block. Now this is going back, like '79. So, I got into
the dumpster because I knew the manager, right? Well, he told
me they were gonna throw a lot of food out one day and I should
take as much as I wanted. So I'm in the dumpster and I got a
wagon on the side, see and I'm dumping the shit out and it's hitting the wagon, but it's also hitting the ground. While I'm in
there, I didn't know some cops had pulled up and one of them
walked over to the dumpster.

He thinks I'm stealing this stuff. So as I dumped these bags
of flour, one of them opened the lid, and the flour hit him right
in the face.

Bobo smiles slightly at this, but Beatrice is grinning from ear to ear. "And so I said, 'Hey, can't you catch?' And he says, 'Yeah. Come down here pal.' He was completely covered."

> It went all over him, right? And I said, "Oh shit . . ." And he brings the manager out and he says, "You know this guy?" And he says, "Oh yeah, he comes up here all the time, he's all right." The cop says, "Who's gonna clean up this mess?"
>
> I said, "Hey, didn't I tell you to catch it?" He got mad as hell and goes to get his book, you know, the one to write the tickets, and tells me get in the car.

Bobo knows about food dumpsters all over town. "There's another one over on Eleventh Avenue and Forty-Fifth. And it's all boxes of cans with most of the labels off, like the cans have dates and the stores can't sell the food after a certain date, so they have to get rid of it. They could feed it to the homeless, really. Give it to a poor kitchen. But they got these you know forty-yard trailers and they leave it there. And you can go take anything you want. After a while, I mean, you know the tuna cans from the cat food. You know different sizes. And they put cases and cases of this stuff out there. All of which they gonna just throw away." The men did not know until the cans were opened what dinner would consist of that night. Bobo reports that he would often go alone to the local school and retrieve left-over milk from the cafeteria as well.

There is a saying: "America can feed the world out of its garbage cans." The dumpster is a symbol of wastefulness, of capitalism's intrinsic spiritual depravity, but, of course, it is also a source of sustenance and even abundance. However, not many people even underground went so far as to pick food out from garbage cans; this was considered unclean. Even in the underground there is what they themselves refer to as a "hierarchy of misery." Only the lowest of the low would actually go into garbage cans for food.

Bobo tells me: "Well, I might as well bring it to a kitchen because that was a way to make money. Now on some of the stuff the labels would be partially off and they'd have the numbers and I'd look at the numbers and take 'em over to a guy that's got a restaurant and get three dollars a can. Those big cans sell for five dollars in the grocery store. You know, you get half. And if the guy is willing to take it then that's some money he can save." Bobo relates how he used to worry about what other people thought of him, but remarks, "Now I don't care if I go out and pick up cans, I'm not asking nothing from nobody. If I go out and pick up books, I'm not asking nobody for nothing. And people down here respect us. And that's all we need. They never ask for anything. Well, except Kal, he's always asking." He grins. "Too much pride can kill you," by which he means that the person who refuses to accept anything could starve to death or lose out on an opportunity that could be lifesaving.

Bobo does not feel that he can't accept help from people but likes to choose from whom he will accept handouts. "I once got $1,800 from Uncle Sam. That was all I ever got. I got busted so many times. I went over the hill. I spent four years in combat. Right? Did four tours. Right. Forty-eight months. Right. And I got shot up, you know, whatever . . . so they gave me $1,800, it went to my kid. Now I gotta go back to the VA. I gotta file there. But you know after a while people get used to living down here. You still have your self-image. I used to have a heavy self-image. I used to think long and hard about my self-image, and then one day it just didn't matter what people thought of me. I'm still a decent human being. Last Tuesday I found a purse in a garbage can. I took it to the Twentieth Precinct. It had a woman's ID, wallet, credit cards, and all that stuff. That's the third purse I've found and taken since January first. It had papers, insurance, and all this. But to get money from the government I almost died for, it takes a long time to wait. So I gotta go over there every day, same as going to welfare. It took me five weeks to get welfare that I told you about. And I was very desperate. One day I was so tired of all of this, I just said I was going to find work. I said 'I can't take this no more.' I had a little money on the side, you know, to help me out. So I said well, the hell with this."

The social service system is humiliating, and most people who apply for resources are aware of this situation. The Veterans Administration is just now trying to cope with massive mismanagement. After a time, Bobo felt the underground was a better alternative than trying to live off welfare. He knew it was safer than shelters. "They can see you going down in the underground. People see you coming up early in the morning with a bag of cans. Where is the work? *That* is the work. Bringing their garbage to the redemption center, that's the fucking work. You know, and they think you don't wanna work, but that ain't true. Not only do we wanna work, we *do* work."

7

WOMEN UNDERGROUND
Tin Can Tina

You are a Cool or a GooD con man. I am Puerto Rican woman,
28 years old, 5'6, 130 weight, 2 children, dancer. My name is
Doreen. My real name of Ada Lus Roman
—Underground resident "Nature Girl," note to Terry Williams, May 1992

FIELD NOTE: TIN CAN TINA

Moving away from the sour stench behind the twisted shadows
of the tunnel, squinting at the unseen eyes of danger, out of the
way of screaming lunatics looking at me like I'm a stranger, I
overhear whistling voices in this darkness, coughs of unknown
origin belching in the nights. I'm not quite convinced I'm free
of the fear of this place, so I move on slowly as if the rocks are
quicksand, walking the edge of the tracks now, slipping, slightly
on the left-footed rail, sliding across muddy cardboard, sloshing
in the watery parts, stumbling on broken glass; there are warts
of lumpy earth moving over the rocky middle-of-the-track terrain, jerkily and stiffly I reach the lighted south end. The time is
half past seven in the evening. I see the fire spit starting to blaze
and the men standing around waiting to tell me their stories.

Kal called her "Tin Can Tina"; she called herself Ada, Mary, Doreen, and M&M. She was one of the few women in the underground at the time, and though hard to approach, I finally got to meet her. She was living right near the compound where I was told the deinstitutionalized, newly released mentally ill patients live, at one of the two main entrances to the underground. At first I thought she was a "crazy," too, part of the "lunatic fringe," as other residents refer to that group.

As soon as I jump down the embankment, a clutch of people, both women and men—perhaps they are couples—appear, screaming and throwing stuff. They yell, curse, all in a kind of gibberish, a cacophony of noise as if they are singing; this goes on for a few minutes, and then, just as it started, it stops.

It is only after I pass this group that I can look back to see who they are. A huge barrel filled with wood burns in a concave, oval-shaped embankment against the wall; about six or seven people are gathered in this space. How they took over this spot is a mystery, but the rumor is that they took over from two guys who used to charge people money for coming underground at that entrance. These men would threaten people and demand a toll, and if they didn't pay, they would attack them.

At first I am startled and a bit apprehensive, but then I pay it no mind. One notices how only a select few of this "crazy chorus" of people are actually making all the racket. After the "crazies," you reach a small group as quiet as the others are noisy, a location of twin structures reminiscent of an early Frank Gehry–type house construction: cardboard, tin, canvas, plywood, paper, cloth, and carpet, a place called Cubano Arms, because the inhabitants are mostly Cuban refugees. Some say they came over from the Mariel Boatlift back in the day; others say they are just Latin criminals hiding out. Whatever the case, they make up the second group as one moves further north.

JOURNAL: TIN CAN TINA

I'm living here under the ground as if I'm here with my mother.
She lived here too and I should tell you about her because when
you talk about homeless people, homeless women, well, she is the
embodiment, you might say, of a homeless person.

She is standing right outside the gate one day and, noticing the
journal in my hand, asks if I am a reporter. She's drinking beer,
and I offer the journal to her, since I'm taking the journals to
give out anyway. I find out in our brief conversation that her
mother had lived underground, too. I ask if I could record her
story. She says "yes" and mentions how she found her mother
after an exhaustive search through city agencies, private inves-
tigators, social workers, and the police. She eventually found her
suffering the same (homeless) fate. I had given her the journal
with the promise of a nickel a line or a dollar per page, but I only
got to see her on rare occasions. She told me that her mother
ended up underground but shared little about how she got to be
here herself. I asked Bernard who she was, but it was Kal who
said they call her "Tin Can Tina." They call her that because
she's never without a beer can.

Her mother was born in the 1930s in a small town west of the
Rockies, she tells me. Her first memories were of her father having sex with her sister.

I didn't know what they were doing at first, only that my sister would cry sometimes and then she would be giddy. When
she was giddy she would tell me what my father was doing. My
mother was about thirteen or so when her brothers got put in
jail for raping a high school girl they barely knew. Then my

grandmother suddenly got real sick and six months later died of cancer. My mother had been taking care of her and right after my grandma died, about two years after, my mother got married; she was only fifteen at that time, but by the time she was twenty-four, she had four kids. I was the middle child.

After being married for twenty-seven years, my father, who was a no-good son-of-a-bitch in the first place, divorced my mother and left. Now this situation really struck my mother in the middle of her head; here was a woman who had no visible means of support, had been a housewife all her life, and suddenly she was left alone. She became a displaced homemaker because she had devoted her life to caring for her family and home. She possessed no marketable skills, and since my father was the type of man who wanted and needed to have total control over every-thing and everybody, he did not allow my mother to work, except at home. He wouldn't dare let her get a job and be around other men or other people.

I think he felt they would influence her or tell her he was a bastard, you know, this sorta thing. But after he left, she had to find a job, and she went from one job that was OK to another that was pretty shitty. But felt she could do better, so she took another job and then another. By this time the years were pass-ing her by, and she couldn't do these low-paying jobs anymore and decided to work in people's homes as a domestic. In this way she could eat, sleep, get driven back and forth to supermar-kets, and sometimes get perks not found in factory work or sec-retarial work.

But domestic work was not always that easy either, but she stayed in that type of work for a long time. By that time we had all grown up, and I was making a good salary, and my two broth-ers were too, so we asked her to come and live with us, but she said no, and two years later my brothers moved away, but I stayed.

My mother was barely making enough money to live on now and was still living in single rooms, and I bought a place and asked her to move in with me.

It was clear that the divorce had destroyed her because she was drained emotionally, she had no friends to speak of, so socially she was uprooted and economically she was in a mess. Yet she refused to move in with me, I think because she saw herself as a possible burden and didn't want that. You know, when we talk about dreams, I mean specifically the so-called American Dream, we think about the men getting rich and famous or at least getting a job and supporting a family with a nice house and a white picket fence with the 2.2 kids running around it, but women had a dream too, and part of that dream was to be a good wife, good mother, while the husband was the breadwinner and you had a happy family. But this dream was broken to pieces, and my mother had nowhere to go really, because the social programs at that time didn't exist for her, at her age, social class, and particular situation.

Tina is outlining the 1950s idea of male and female roles within the context of American family life, but this conceptualization is also rooted in "machismo," which has deep roots in Hispanic culture. But I am suddenly unclear why generally among the residents of the underground there is this characterization of her "being crazy": she is lucid and articulate in telling her story. Perhaps they saw or heard her acting out "crazy" behavior when I was not around.

Tina goes on to explain how she witnessed her mother spiraling into an increasingly traumatized state:

Now, about two years after the divorce, my mother became a bit unglued, but where most people rebound and get better she

162 🔊 WOMEN UNDERGROUND

got worse. If you had seen our house when we were kids, my mother was a neat freak, if you will; she was extremely neat, organized, every thing in its place kind of person. But now she started accumulating a large amount of stuff and carrying it around in her car, and then she would pile up stuff on the floor in her room, just one pile after another.

After a while you couldn't get through the place without having piles of clothes, furniture, books, all kinds of stuff, shoulder high, even head high in the apartment. She rented storage space at one time to keep stuff, even though she was living basically from hand to mouth. I think she moved at least twice a year, and I'd help her load up stuff, and if I suggested she throw some of what was clearly just junk away, she would yell and scream to high heavens. I later understood that all this "junk" as we would call it had memories attached to it and represented a past she no longer had any connection to except through this seemingly worthless object.

Hoarding has a purpose. The sociologist Elliot Liebow offers an explanation: "Someone whose sense of self is shaky to begin with and whose hold on private space and personal belongings in the material world is perpetually insecure is likely to feel exposed."[1]

Tina said her mother became what was called a "bag lady" back in the day. As a graduate student in the 1970s, I did a study of street life in Times Square; I found a group of bag ladies. They did not identify as such, but because many of them grouped together in public squares and locations around the city, I called them a group, albeit a disorganized one: women who screamed and cursed at passersby, women who I later learned from reading Oliver Sacks may have had Tourette's syndrome, a condition characterized by an uncontrollable movement of the voice box that triggers sounds that are often curse words.

I watched them as they lay in bus terminals, in corner spots in the subways, curled up in bank buildings, and closeted in niches and doorways at all times of the day and night. I felt cold watching them during the winter months, cowering under bridges and on frigid park benches or hunched over "hostile architecture," with unnecessary spiked sections preventing their wretched bodies from sleeping. I felt smothered watching them during the brutal heat of summer, wrapped in heavy overcoats weighing them down with perspiration, lugging shopping carts filled with all their possessions: books, toys, photographs, canned food, and rags.

Tina's mother was one of those women, lost, forgotten, and homeless.

These were the years of promise, the 1980s and 1990s Reagan-Bush years, the decades of trickle-down economics that only produced trickle-down poverty, the years of the shrinking "safety net," which didn't catch anyone; these were the decades of despair for millions of people in this country and the many more who came to live as wretches in the modern day "povertyville" that is life underground.

These women are victims of povertyvilles, much like the Hoovervilles of the great Depression. Although pretty much similar with respect to material circumstances, today these povertyvilles are concealed by the shelter system or pushed deep and deeper underground. When I observed them in the 1970s, these "bag ladies" were mostly white women who toted their belongings in shopping bags or carts wrapped with coarse cords, roped round in intricate knots too Gordian to untie. They liked to talk to themselves and were often bundled from head to toe in multiple layers of clothes, wrapped up tight regardless of weather. I wondered as I watched these invisible women there, "but by the grace of God go I." What crisis in my own life would it take to end up out on the street? A lost job, a house fire, a catastrophic illness, an eviction, a broken heart?

There they huddled in shadows of huge skyscrapers in the greatest city in the world, making cardboard homes, squatting, sleeping, shitting, urinating in spaces planners never envisioned. By the mid-1980s, the population of people in the street was increasingly male, Black, and dual diagnosed: social and political scientists focused on the issues of unemployment and racism, arguing how many people were vulnerable and could not cope with failure, even if it was predetermined by both global and domestic forces. The sociologist Kai Erikson, in a chapter titled "Furniture of the Self," explains further: "To lose a home or the sum of one's belongings is to lose evidence as to who one is and where one belongs in the world."[2]

By the 1990s, these individuals were then demonized and called "mentally-ill chemical abusers"; people were afraid of them. People would shy away more than they did the "bag ladies" of the 1970s, as the streets were suddenly flooded with the unhoused—not mild-mannered women talking to themselves but robust, angry Black men, striking back, attacking occasionally, all emerging now from the deinstitutionalized locations upstate, a phenomenon of the late 1970s and early 1980s that reverberated into the new millennium.[3]

This was also happening mainly because of the revolution in drug technology and an economy that had no place for unskilled poor workers. Many of these men and women turned their rage inward, some losing their way; newer drug therapies utilizing the latest drug technology, such as Percodan, Prozac, Thorazine, and other mind-boggling tranquilizers made it possible for those previously confined inside mental hospitals to be given prescriptions and then set "free" onto the streets. It was a time when mental health libertarians argued that mental patients too had rights and therefore the right not to be kept in institutions against their will.

These changes and the concomitant loss of federal funds to house mental patients made the community-based health care approach the logical alternative. But community-based mental health care never materialized. Some of these mental patients, now homeless people, ended up underground in the city. This is where my story of Tina begins and ends, the only single woman living underground, as I was doing my count today, starting at the entrance of what was to be called the "Dumb Fence": a newly constructed, though not completed, fence put up by a New York developer who will remain nameless. At the time, this developer was building a multistory complex along the Penn Rail Lines, which ran into the underground space where the 113 people I counted were living, a space from which the population I had spent the latter part of three years researching were about to be evicted.

I know it is not unusual to meet people only one or two times in this setting, since they are transient like Tina. She wrote only the brief excerpt that appears in this chapter in the journal that I gave her, which I collected as I came back out around nine o'clock. She was still in the same place I left her, holding a can of beer, talking to a man with a camera.

8

BEATRICE AND BOBO

Look at me well: I am indeed, I am indeed, Beatrice. How hast thou deigned to approach the mountain? Didst thou not know that here man is happy?

—Dante, *The Divine Comedy*

No matter how many times I come down here, I can never get used to the damp, the darkness, the eerie quiet, the space where there is no light at all for a few interminable blocks. On days like this, the underground resembles a prison, a kind of self-imposed encampment where the guards are the invisible sounds and stark images marching through my head every few seconds. These images are spectral shadows at one moment and, in the next, human figures slowly approaching in the distance.

This underground reminds me of Jeremy Bentham's panopticon—in reverse: tiny cells all in a row, the elusive recluses hiding in the concrete holes thirty feet above tracks, where they can see you in the center but you can't see them. As you walk the tracks, you feel someone is watching you, following behind, overlooking from the dark corners—and at any minute they will jump out from out of nowhere.

They are like—as Bernard told me one day when in a sour mood, which wasn't often—"drug addicts and street scum, not people," those convicted and sentenced for being poor, shiftless, and lazy, derelict in their duties of reaching for the American Dream.

Leaving the underground to go out is a special privilege, Beatrice once told me. "It's like a stolen moment because you know you'll have to come back down here."

Two weeks later, I visited Beatrice and Bobo at their new bunker near Eighty-Ninth Street. I arrived in the middle of the day, hollered out to them, and waited. This is where Beatrice, her companion Bobo, their dog Butch, and their clowder of cats reside. They come out to greet me and invite me in for a soda.

The concrete bunker resembles a cellblock. The white walls are decorated with pictures: Disneyland, a calendar, a map of the United States, and some posters; the walls are also dotted with tiny holes, from which smoking sticks of incense protrude. Beatrice tells me the incense neutralizes the foul smell of cats. The cats (at least twenty) are resting, standing, stalking, playing atop a Queensboro milk crate that contains layers of soiled gray blankets, next to three yellowish pillows and some candles.

The windowless bunker has few amenities and is decorated with found objects. It's about forty feet wide and twenty feet long. One cramped section in the back is used for a bed, with standard milk crates partially covered with cloth assisting as night tables. Near one corner of the bed stands a large trunk, with a box of books pressing against it.

A wooden stand at the foot of the bed at another corner holds candles, and an empty gin bottle is the receptacle for a handful of artificial flowers. There are candles, old clothes, bottles, and more milk crates near the door. The place smells of cats and damp. Beatrice offers me a cat. "We have plenty of 'em, so you can have any three of her kittens." In one corner of the room, where one might expect a window, is a wicker chair like the one Huey Newton was photographed sitting in.

Bobo is surprisingly open. "It took me a couple of years to adapt to living in the underground. But once I realized it, and once I accepted being down here, then it got a lot easier. I knew I had to fix my place up though. I have to do what I have to do for the length of time I'm gonna be here."

Bobo wears a floppy gray cap with camouflage pants and boots. We step outside the bunker and stand underneath the doorway, over which hangs a large U.S. flag so dirty it's almost un-American. We watch for a moment a steady stream of rain sprinkling through the grate above the tracks in front of us. The water flows down in sparkling silver sheets, with long arrow-like lines shining in the light. Puddles form in hidden crevices against the rails, but between these patches, the ground—or is it a floor? Are we inside or outside? In these underground spaces one is never sure—is as dry as a bone.

Beatrice comes out wearing a blue floral-print dress with muddy shoes, holding a beer can in one hand and a newspaper in the other. Chubby in face and fingers, pleasant and looking remarkably unconcerned, it seems, about her surroundings, she hands a cigarette and the beer to Bobo. Her face is clean, but her hands and fingernails are caked with dirt. She says hello but nothing else.

Standing now away from the bunker, seeing the American flag above the door, Butch barking in the background, the 12:30 train rumbling by, there whole scene feels surreal—a suburban uncanny. The train reminds Bobo of a 1949 Lionel electric train

he won as a kid for guessing how many beans were in a jar. "I
wish I had that train right now," he says. "It used to go *choo-choo*
with the switch going. It was great. I know it's a collector's item
by now."

Beatrice is about thirty but looks younger. She has an inno-
cent face, speaks calmly, and has a biting sense of humor—
though she seems reluctant to speak to other men unless Bobo
gives his approval. "I met Bobo up in Riverside Park," she says.
"He used to help my mom." Beatrice's mother had a leg ampu-
tated, and Bobo, who sold books, would come by the park where
she sat every day and let her choose books to read. He would
get her food and drink from vendors. "Didn't see a lot of mom
at that time," Beatrice says. "I would come by occasionally, but
she had diabetes, and I had my problems, but we had started
to work things out and I was coming by more often. One day she
was going to the park up here on Eighty-Fifth Street, and I came
with her. We were there maybe an hour when Bobo came by,
and he and I started talking. My mother told me he was a nice
man who helped her out." Two months later her mother died,
and one month after that she was down in the underground living with Bobo.

Her mother's death made it difficult for her to live alone. "I
was in love, and he was down here, and I wanted to be with him."
Beatrice is not a reader of fine literature like Bernard or some of
the other booksellers living underground—she preferred Danielle Steel and Terry McMillan to the classics—and so did not
catch what I meant when I compared her to Persephone, who
herself was not exactly an angel. Though she sells books, her real
interest is cooking: she says she longs for a good stove to "just
cook a good meal on."

At the moment, Beatrice's stove is a small grate placed on top
of a large brown iron barrel. A few pots and old pans hang

underneath a long metal stand. Just then, Bobo asks Beatrice to go inside and get something. Before she goes, she looks over at me, half-smiling. "You know, I'm really a woman trapped between light and darkness. There is so little light but plenty of darkness. I can't live in the light, and the darkness frightens me. I'm really a twilight woman," she laughs. "That's why I live near the grate, so I always have some light and never without some darkness, you know."

Beatrice has managed to get electricity in their place, and one of the two lamps on the wall is lit. She convinced Bobo to ask a teenager living near the south end to do it for them. Bobo met the kid in the park. "He says he could hook up electricity anywhere," she tells me. "All Bobo had to do was ask the boy." The new arrival is one of several white teenagers now living underground. This boy owed Bobo a favor, Beatrice says, "so he did it for us."

As we speak, a call from outside the bunker comes echoing in, and a small-framed white woman enters. Beatrice tells me she's a photographer for a magazine and wants to take pictures. The woman informs us that Bernard has sent her. The photographer poses Beatrice standing, half smiling, somewhat dazed, in the corner. She grimaces toward me, her anxiety palpable. Her face makes it clear she wishes the photographer would leave. The cats are eerily immobile, staring at the camera as if they are used to being photographed.

In the meantime, Bobo comes to take the cats out, his hair pulled to one side. He is wearing a soiled sweatshirt, nails dirt-filled and gnawed. The musty cats file out into what could be described as their mess hall, an alley filled with old cans of fetid foodstuffs, milk crates, broken glass, rocks, and dirt. A long iron pipe about three feet high runs the length of the concrete bunker in front, once perhaps a banister; now this pipe has a rope tied tightly around it.

There are several milk crates at the end of the walkway. Beatrice says these are filled with her belongings; she has more in the room under the bed. In Elliot Liebow's ethnography of homeless women *Tell Them Who I Am*, he states: "The women carried their life histories with them. To lose one's stuff, or to have to jettison some of it, was to lose connection to one's past if not the past itself." Liebow further argues that "past and future, then, and even one's self, were embedded in one's belongings. . . . And the ever-present threat of losing them was a major source of anxiety and stress."[1]

The photographer leaves as quickly as she came, just as rain begins to drizzle through the grate. Bobo pokes his head in, then sits down to talk. "I drink, I don't do drugs. What I do when I go to work is sell some magazines, sell some books and sell some cans. I leave my cans and books over there." He points to a large clear plastic bag of cans and two large opaque green bags. "But I sell a little bit of everything, scrap metal, copper, whatever. When I get through work, I have a few beers like everybody else. I eat steak and potatoes, you know. I go to work and make my money."

Bobo says his family locked him out and instead of trying to help, pushed him away. "So I just went to the only people who I knew couldn't do me no harm, first other vets, then on the street. I was on active duty in a lot of places in the service, including Santo Domingo. Went there to help keep their army from killing their people. Oh yeah, back in '64, when Johnson sent troops down there. Yeah. Another time we went to Turkey. We went right into the Turkish embassy."

He stops abruptly and decides to talk about the underground again. "I go for water once a day. I only got on welfare once when I lived in Brooklyn. After that I got out of the business of asking for handouts. Down here I do for myself. In winter I go for wood four times a week to get stuff like this." He points to a large pile of wood next to a seventy-foot-high concrete pillar, one of the many supports for the West Side Highway.

With one hand in his pocket, the other holding a cigarette, he stares across the tracks, appearing uninterested at first. Then, suddenly, he becomes more animated and engaged. "When it's raining like this, I only go a few times a week. I just get the wood and throw it down through the grates over there." He points to a section where a grate high above the tracks is partially open. "You know if I don't wanna keep lugging it all the way down from Seventy-Second Street. It's easier, don't you think, to just dump it through there?" He tries to hide two missing teeth by closing his lip with a quick smile.

Bobo's routine is similar to that of others in the underground. He's out early, "like about seven o'clock in the morning," and gets most of his cans from the supers. He claims he was one of the first guys to sell books and magazines on Broadway, but now "I got a guy that buys 'em downtown—he'll give me 10 percent of the publisher's price. It beats standing up in the wintertime freezing your butt off. You know what I mean?" He thumps the bottom of the cigarette pack and lifts one out with his teeth. "So if I make forty dollars down there, I could make a hundred up here, but I'm not freezing my ass off. Getting out of the wind. Make sure the hawk [wind] ain't biting my ass."

Most of Bobo's family is dead—he says this without a bit of reflection. "My kids are dead, too. Well, I got one kid left who's twenty-seven. Three years younger than she is," pointing to Beatrice. "And I'm fifty-one."

Beatrice comes out of their bunker just as he says this. "Yeah, he's a dirty old man. I think that's what makes him strong. He gets out there and works every day, staying out in the cold, and if it won't kill 'em, it'll sure make him strong." She laughs and holds up her arm to flex her bicep.

Before he came to the underground, Bobo lived on one of the rotting Hudson River barges between Sixtieth and Seventy-Second Streets. Those barges have been there for years, partly because of a clause in a 1950s contract between the longshoremen's union and the city that stated that as long as the barges remain standing, certain monetary benefits would be provided for workers and their families.

Although the barges are considered dangerous, people often sunbathe on them, and Bobo and other homeless people lived there for a time. The site was once fought over by local community leaders and developers, who wanted to build a housing complex on the old Pennsylvania Railroad lines directly across from the barges. "You had to crouch down in order to get out there because so much of the structure was broken and bent." Bobo holds his hands down by his knees to indicate the height of the space, from ceiling to floor, which he occupied on the barge. "Maybe the size of my bed back then was about four and a half feet wide. You had to jump across from one section to the other to get to your spot because whole sections would be either rotted away or just fell off during the day. And if anybody came up looking for you and they didn't know about the floor, they were in a lot of trouble. Straight down, right into the Hudson. It wasn't bad. It was only barges. But now that I'm living here, I gotta provide. I gotta haul my water; other than that all I need is light. And since I can't buy any electricity, the kerosene candles are really the way we light up the rooms. And you know if the cats jump and knock 'em over, this place is gone. I got my clothes in the trunk over there, you know, forms, pictures, and so forth. Fuck these candles." He throws his arms up and walks around to the edge of the bed. The electricity, Beatrice explains, "Comes and goes. One day it's on, another day it's off. One day it's gonna go out and never come back on."

"I had a generator," Bobo tells me, "But somebody stole it from me. You gotta make sure you got water, you gotta make sure you got food, you gotta make sure you got your drink. Make sure I got a full jug. B's got asthma, you know, so I gotta make sure she gets her medicine. Had it since she was a kid."

Beatrice pokes her tongue out. "What you know?"

"Well, it's true, ain't it?" Bobo responds.

"Now, I was young, that's all. My mom made such a big deal outta my coughing and breathing problems. It was part asthma and part emphysema. I outgrew most of that stuff. He go up every day," she says. "But I don't. Stay here most of the time." Bobo goes to open the large padlocked and chained door. "Whenever I go out to do the books and the magazines, I usually play the lotto game. I take the stuff in the store, go around and collect it. I come back up here for my water, pay for it, bring it down. I eat and I go to bed. I listen to the radio and talk shows whatever."

"It gets to you sometimes. The holidays get you." Both agree that the only time they miss topside is around the holidays. "I start thinking about the holidays," says Beatrice, looking at the picture of a relative she holds near the light. "Some stuff like that. I really don't know how to put it." She steps over to a trunk and starts rummaging through it, putting some stuff into a box. "It smells so musty because we had a lot of litter in here."

A fat gray cat rubs against my leg, and Bobo says she's the leader of the night pack. "She's the track rabbit [rat] queen down here. She's a great fighter." Bobo picks up a candle and says out of the blue, "That's one thing about being in the fucking army, I missed all the holidays. I was never home. I never saw my kids. I never came home, not even on their birthdays. Well, that's not true, I'd come home once in awhile for a birthday . . ." His voice trails off. "I'd shoot up, then go back again . . . I'd go back to training, go in. I really didn't miss it then as much as I do now,

but it was, just, you know, certain days. It was just a way of catching up. A way of making money staying all those days in the
service. And then you get tired of working for somebody else. I
started working for myself. And I was making more money by
myself than I was working for somebody else. That's why I don't
put 'em [books] on the sidewalk. I take 'em down to the guy in
the store. I used to sell 'em by ABC on Broadway. I had *Life*
magazines. All of 'em. I had like two copies of the whole thing,
all the way through. I had ten thousand pieces on movie actors
and the actresses. I had the Eisenhower series, all that kind of
stuff. It's good stuff."

Beatrice starts to tell me about the night two men tried to take
Bobo's shoes while he was sleeping on a park bench. Bobo takes
over: "They took all of us and put us in the same room. The cops
come and say, well, who did it? And I said, I don't know. 'Do
you know these guys?' I never saw 'em before. I thought why
should I rat 'em out? Because if I catch 'em next time, I'll get
'em. They had a little help, that's all."

"Yeah," Beatrice says, "Two guys with a baseball bat."

"What if next time he don't have a baseball bat?" Bobo says.
"They come up behind you and you can't see 'em, what are you
gonna do? You can't keep your eyes open all the time. It's impossible. You have to be on guard at all times when you sleep topside or you're go nuts. It's like being in the service, it's like being
in 'Nam. You have to be on guard all the time."

"Talk about nuts," Beatrice smirks, turning her eye skyward.
"Did you see Kovacs's place next door?" Kovacs is the "mad Hungarian" who hates minorities but fell in love with a Thai woman.
He moved to a farm upstate that helps homeless men regain a
sense of self-worth. While there, he left his bunker in the care
of Bobo and Beatrice. Rumor has it he's on his way back to the
underground.

"When Kovacs went to go upstate to the farm, he left most of his place intact. He asked me to look after it," Bobo says. We walk over to the bunker, which has a large chain and padlock at the entrance door. We enter, and as Bobo explains the layout, I see posters on the wall: *Close Encounters of the Third Kind*, *Streetwise*, and one printed with the words "Tiger on the Wall." Christmas lights hang across the ceiling; there are several tables, a mattress on the floor, and a large scratching post for the cats near the door. "This was his kitchen. He had his bookcase here, and his records, and he had a lot of books over there. He kept the dishes in there. He had a slight case of TB [tuberculosis], you know, and didn't allow no cats in his place until the rats got bad around here," Bobo tells me. "All he had was his dog. You know what he really liked was chalices and statues. Now that looks like a Buddha over there. And that looks like a Christmas card. He had this place decorated real nice."

As we leave and stand near the edge of the tracks, Bobo takes out a cigarette and talks about the row of bunkers facing us. "Now, you know how this was built originally? I'll tell you. This was the headquarters for the railroad guys." Pointing to the first bunker. "Our house was the bathroom. And the house next to that, right there, was the kitchen, and where that is, well, that was like where the dispatch guy worked when he tapped out radio signals. So they really had regular living quarters because all this stuff—lockers, beds. The guy next door, his house is like a telephone office, they have the lines for telephones. And then the other house is just a utility house, you know, paint cans, oil cans, and all that kind of materials is still in there."

Bobo whispers, "Listen, did I tell you the one about Johnny Long Nut?" And before I can say anything, he's into the story: "There was this guy who was called Johnny Long Nut because his nuts hung way down to his knees. One year around Christmas time, he's out fucking this other man's wife, and the guy comes home. The wife tells Johnny 'Quick! Get up in the loft—my husband is coming.' So Johnny goes up into the loft buck naked and squats in the ceiling, and there are the usual Christmas bells hanging from the ceiling there too. So the husband comes in and right away smells something fishy. He's just a sniffing cause he can smell fucking in the room. He's a-sniffing. He say, 'What's that I smell?' The wife says, 'Nothing, dear.' He looks at her and asks, 'Why you all sweaty?' She says, 'nothing, dear.' He say, 'Something is wrong here.' And he looks up to the ceiling and sees the bells hanging and one set of bells looks a little odd colored so he decides to test it with a stick. He hits one with the stick, 'ding,' and then another one, 'dong,' and another one, 'duh.' No sound. So he hits it again, 'duh.' No sound. So he pulls back as hard as he can and . . . bam hits them nuts again, and Johnny jumps down, screaming to the top of his lungs, 'ding-dong, motherfucker, ding-dong!' And hauls ass."

Bobo tells me to leave my number so he can keep in touch.

Three weeks later, I get a call from him saying Kovacs was back living in his old place. I decided to go try to meet him.

After mentioning some fieldwork I was doing, a colleague asks if he could come with me underground. At that time, 1993, the city had recently closed a homeless encampment on the West Side Highway directly above the tracks, and some people from that group had moved into the underground. When I got there, I noticed four new lean-tos built in recent weeks, despite the rat-infested garbage adjacent to it.

One of the first of these new structures was built by a Cuban named Miguel, Bobo informed me, who came to the United States on the Mariel boatlift from Cuba in the 1980s. He'd built what looked at first glance like a lean-to near the underground entrance, which was inhabited by a man nobody knows, though Bobo tells me he has been seen with a woman who screams at anybody coming near the entrance at Seventy-Second Street. He and the woman soon left the underground, but others joined the family of homeless men and women occupying that particular structure. On further investigation, it was not a lean-to in the strict sense of the term, since it had no upper edge abutting a wall or building; it was more like a free-standing hut.

After another block or so, a fire is visible in the distance to the left, at the far end: it seems to be at or near Beatrice and Bobo's place, but as there are so few markers underground, one can only guess the location. As I walk up to their place, I see Beatrice. She is rumored to be several months pregnant but to my eyes does not seem to be. She greets me with a warm hello. She insists on getting Bobo. "He's here. He's right inside."

Beatrice builds up the fire as cats creep about, one, then two, then six; they are all around the place. She wears a dingy white hooded shirt, and Bobo comes out attired in a similar shirt, though blue, his unshaven face and eyes barely visible under his hood. Both their hands are dirty with soot and wood grime. "This cat is hurt," Bobo tells me, pointing to a black cat with stripes on her head and tail. "I got to make her stay in here until she's well."

We talk of recent underground events. "I haven't been doing very much since I saw you last. I been staying close to home and living off the fat of the land." He laughs oddly, then talks about the cats. Referring to a cat-shooting incident where teenagers were shooting cats with BB guns, he adds, "You know I caught three of the four guys who shot the cats down here a few weeks back. Yeah, some guys came down here with those guns and started shooting all the cats. So I caught three of them, and I'll get the other one too one of these days." Bobo doesn't say what happened to the three he caught.

The main reason I came today, however, was to see Kovacs. In an article called "The Forgotten American," Peter Schrag wrote about Kovacs, or those like him: "There is hardly a language to describe him, or even a set of social statistics. Just names: racist-bigot-redneck-Irish-Italian-Pole-Hunkie-Yahoo. The lower middle class. A blank. The man under whose hat lies the great American Desert. Who watches the tube, plays the horses, and keeps the niggers out of his union and his neighborhood."[2]

This was the man I was now hoping to meet. Over the phone, Bobo told me Kovacs said he had been misquoted in the newspaper and wanted to get the record straight. He'd told Kovacs I was a "straight shooter" and would tell his story the way it should be told.

9

THE TAGALONG

Let's separate the facts from the fluff.
—Kovacs

When I went to meet Kovacs, I brought along a fellow sociologist who wanted to accompany me on one of my ethnographic outings. My colleague admitted he did not think much of ethnographic research: he was a "real theorist" and thought qualitative fieldwork was easy to do. Together we headed out toward the northern end of the underground.

Once we enter, Bobo tells me and my friend that he will introduce us to Kovacs, who lives in one the adjoining bunkers, about two blocks north of where Bobo, Beatrice, and Bernard reside. Kovacs has a reputation for being uncooperative, abrasive, willing to talk to women but not men, and not liking Blacks at all. As we start to walk toward his place, we find him standing near the entrance. I extend my hand. He shakes my hand limply, then looks at my friend and asks brusquely, "What you doing down here?"

At first I thought he was talking to me, but he's speaking to my friend. I notice his eyes are crossed, so it's difficult to tell where he's looking. "Who the fuck are you?" he says.

"He's the boss," Beatrice says, trying to defuse the situation.

"I ain't talking about him," he corrects her, "I'm talking about him," pointing again to my friend. Looking over toward me but shifting his stance toward Beatrice, he says, "What the fuck does he want down here?"

Kovacs is a small, frail man with a rugged appearance, his teeth yellow, stained probably from too much tobacco; blue jeans, cowboy boots, and an off-white jacket over a red workingman's calico shirt make the attire frontier-like. He's unshaven, but his full face is hard to see in the dim light, as he stands slightly to my left away from the fire.

Just then Bernard arrives and has a word with Kovacs while Bobo fills me in on the situation. "He's acting like an asshole now because he and his girlfriend aren't getting along. He's an OK guy really. He's been walking around with his machete lately, but I don't think he's capable of using it. He's more bark than bite." I didn't find this information reassuring; my friend is visibly nervous. "I'm not sure if this guy has all his wagons in one circle," Beatrice says out of the side of her mouth.

Kovacs acts and looks angry, and I don't want to provoke him. But as we approach the door to his place, everything settles down. Bernard must have told Kovacs something about us, because his manner has changed. We are soon in Kovacs's bunker.

The entire space, bookshelves and all, is clean and well kept. We sit on one of two sofas in the room; there is table between them. The one opposite is slightly darker brown than the one we sit on. "This place had shit all over it when I got back," he explains.

"The place reeked. I swear to God. I had to bring all this stuff back here and redo the place. I had to redo the place."

A dog barks and comes up from behind the second couch. A great deal has been written about Kovacs since he left the underground last March. John Tierney, a *New York Times* reporter, wrote a story about him, and other media people followed. After he appeared on the *Sally Jessy Raphael Show*, Kovacs was invited to an upstate New York farm to work on a program raising vegetables, but he returned after a dispute about his dog.

"The program [upstate] was run by this—excuse me—this nigger. Okay, this nigger was running the program, and I had to give up all the profits I made over to him. Then he tells me I can't sleep with my dog. I'm not prejudiced now. But why can't a white man, an American white man, get a fucking job in this country? You can get a job if you got a goddamn green card. You can get a job if you on fucking welfare. All the fucking green card holders can get a fucking job right away. They can get a fucking apartment right away. They can get fucking welfare right away. But be a white man in America and try to get a fucking job." Kovacs, sweating, is clearly upset, and as he talks, my friend begins to fidget. "I went to this Greek restaurant the other month, and I said I wanted a job because the sign said they were hiring. So, after a few days I go back like the jerk tells me, and he says they just hired somebody and that they don't hire Americans because they don't fucking trust 'em. They don't trust Americans? What kinda shit is that? Get the fuck outta America if you don't trust 'em. Americans are the ones who pay you. You fucking jerk. Americans are the ones who's buying them fucking sandwiches. All I want to do is feed my cats and my dog. My Mama here [the dog's name is Mama] will be fed no matter what. No matter fucking what. I go to this school down the street and get food, milk, juice from these kids' lunches. I know America waste more than they can eat. Do you want something to drink?" We both say no.

Kovacs sits for a minute stroking the dog, looking into its mouth, rubbing it down. My friend, who has been quiet until now, gets the nerve to ask a question. "What kind of dog is that?"

What kinda dog is that? What fucking difference does it fucking make? What kinda fucking dog is that? What kinda dog is you, white boy? Do you mind if I say "white boy"? Do you mind if I say "white boy"? I know the truth hurts. I know the truth hurts. But it's true. Listen, do you want my story or don't you? I went to this place and applied for a job and the guy tells me to come back the next day and then I go back the next day and the guy says come back the next day and I come back the next fucking day and then he tells me he's got people in training.

The guy didn't wanna hire me. But the least he coulda done was tell me up front that he didn't. I can't find a fucking job. I'll do anything. I work good with my hands. As long as I been here I have never been without some kinda work.

I was born right here at Kings County Hospital, and when I went to that farm I worked and was the only one who had a garden of crops or anything. I had to eat from what I made in the garden. This place was 250 acres big. I was the only one who worked. I was the only white man there, and that oughta tell you something.

I don't like to say this, but it was your people [he points to me] that run the place, and they wanted to take all the fucking little money we made. I only took a little cash with me, but they wanted to take all of that money too plus what I made while I was there. Fucking niggers and flies.

He calls and the dog, old and shaggy, walks over toward the sofa. "A mutt really," he finally gets around to answering the question. "But she's all I got. This dog is my favorite human being. I sleep with this dog, and I'll feed this dog before I feed myself. I bought two big bags of feed for Mama, and they [the people on the farm] didn't give her anything to eat. I wonder if they were going to feed her at all." He strokes the dog as he talks. He pauses for a moment before taking a cigarette from his pocket. "You don't mind if I smoke, do you?"

The bookshelf holds few books. They look overused and moist. Kovacs say he's read them. The six books include, fittingly enough, Gorky's *Lower Depths*, a novel by Danielle Steel, an Italian pasta cookbook, a dictionary, and two titles I can't make out. "I have a novel or two I read, but that's about it," he tells me, glancing over at the neatly arranged bookshelf. "This place used to look really great." He pauses. "The dog won't hurt you," he tells us, but my friend is wary and moves his leg away uneasily. This upsets Kovacs: he furrows his brow, squints, curls his lip—a tormented look. "The dog won't fucking hurt you, I said. This dog don't like people who move around in here."

The kerosene lamp gives enough light to see Kovacs's face, but not much of it, and it has gotten dimmer since we have been here. A few seconds later, he says, "I always carry my knife. I've had it for a long time." He reaches into the table drawer in front of us and takes out a greenish-brown, twelve-inch-long scabbard with a top snap button. Military origin. Inside is a long folded knife. We are both a bit nervous now. He tells me to press the button handle. I press and the blade pops out. We both jump. Sweat pops off the side of my colleague's face. The blade, razor sharp, twice as thick, is placed in my hand.

"Feel the weight of that baby. This knife is as old as you," Kovacs says, looking at one of us with his crooked eye. "I never leave here without that knife. I have some juice for you if you want some." He's mentioned the juice before, which was from school leftovers. Although we'd declined before, we decide to take it this time.

Outside, we hear Beatrice and Bobo. I mention going further north, but Kovacs warns me there are bad people at the north end of the underground and that we should stay away. "They ain't quite as friendly as we are down here. Don't like visitors much." My friend is relieved and tells me later he was glad we didn't venture further north.

Kovacs announces his decision to go topside. He is suggesting he wants to join us to go topside, but I wait to hear more. "You know, I've been here for sixteen years," Kovacs says as he walks south. "And Bobo has been here for almost as long. We've been living here longer than anybody. We remember when there was a recreational center at the end of the park down here for old Conrail workers. We remember when this place was just full of rats down on this end. Now they got a few crazies down here, and people ain't what they used to be." He's referring to the ex-mental patients who inhabit the mouth of the underground near Seventy-Second Street.

Just then, Bobo comes back over while Kovacs goes into his house to get his knife. He says Kovacs is the "last angry white man in America." "He used to be religious, he used to go to church. He used to pay his taxes, he used to obey the law. He used to do the right thing, but like so many of us, including us vets, the time to do right is wrong and gone. We did right, and where did it get us? Nowhere. Yes, down here is nowhere. When I talked to people topside, white people, white men they all say the same thing. They have to work three jobs to make ends meet. Now they can't find one job. They mad at the welfare cheats, they mad at the taxes they have to pay. Everybody concerned about what the Black man, the Latin man has to say. What about the white working—or nonworking, now—man, has to say? You the only one interested in what the white man down here has to say. Pretty soon there won't be no white man around because the world will be taken over by everybody else and you'll see how this place will be then."

At that, Kovacs comes over, inspecting his knife before replacing it in its scabbard. My friend is standing a bit ahead, looking at the graffiti on the walls. I join him, and we head back topside.

10

THE RABBIT HOLE

The rabbit hole went straight on like a tunnel for some way,
and then dipped suddenly down, so suddenly that Alice had not
a moment to think about herself before she found herself falling
down a very deep well.

—Lewis Carroll, *Alice's Adventures in Wonderland*

Jean Pierre, a twenty-something Haitian man, is the last person
I met underground. He constructed a hole to escape from when
Amtrak police would come after him. He called it "the rabbit
hole," and it led out to the West Side Highway. The rabbit hole
is how I was once able to get out from underground without
being arrested: every morning, when the 5:20 AM Amtrak train
approaches from Grand Central Terminal, the conductor calls
the Amtrak police if anyone is seen on the tracks. If this happens,
Amtrak police come in an ORV and arrest anyone they catch
underground. Unlike Lewis Carroll's *Alice in Wonderland*, where
she goes down the rabbit hole, here you travel up it, through the
dirt and muck, and you end up on the West Side Highway near
Ninety-Sixth Street.

—Field note, April 2010

GOING TOPSIDE

I am left with an oppressive, claustrophobic feeling after this last visit to the underground. I pass familiar signs: the adobe structures, the hidden bunkers near Eighty-Third, the former waterspout near Seventy-Ninth, and finally, even though it is an overused cliché, the light at the end of the tunnel. As the glimmer of light appears, I quicken my pace. To make the time go faster, I imagine this is the last time I will be in the underground. I note every crevice, every sharp edge visible, every brick, every jagged point highlighted by a shadowed gleam that makes the rocks look like diamonds, brilliant effervescence layered over rough surfaces.

In order to avoid walking the forty blocks back out, having walked from 125th Street earlier that day, I remember being told by Jean-Pierre of his "rabbit hole" exit route. I stop for a moment, now familiar with the underground geography; I get to the spot, the only exit left in the underground between Seventy-Second and 125th (see appendix B, figures B.1 and B.2), and I can see it's nothing but a hole dug out from underground into the park.

Standing at the spot, I look to see if anyone is behind me. I climb up ten steps of an emergency stairway that extends along a twelve-foot steel brick pillar, hold on to a steel girder above me, then move along the girder, inching my way to the center, about fifteen feet above the tracks. I then jump down half that distance inside an eight-by-four-foot walled space, then squeeze under the concrete and broken earth.

I climb up some rocks, wiggle my way out of the hole headfirst, my shoulders pinched against the falling dirt, lifting myself from a depth of perhaps four feet as my body squeezes past jagged concrete splinters with small steel wires extending through unevenly carved earth, until I reach the top, where specially placed cardboard and wood planks hide much of the outside light from view. I slowly remove two green-colored planks, which blend well into the grass surroundings, camouflaging the hole, and I push up into the park. About ten to twelve feet from the hole is a winding U-shaped extension of the West Side Highway, which curls around and under the highway and where the Hudson River offers a scenic view. This area is also a favorite rest stop for cabs and thrill-seeking lovers.

The dew, damp and shining, covers the floor of the park and seeps into the underground. At this location, white snakeroot, lesser celadine, buttercups, and Floribunda roses can be found, the latter draped over the steel wire fence and the snakeroot carefully arrested at the base, where underground residents usually crawl over fallen brown and yellow leaves. Brushing dirt and grass from my head and face, I walk out into Riverside Park, heading for home.

I have received a call from Bernard, who now has voicemail, set up by a friend so people can leave him messages. I told him several media people wanted interviews and asked if I could bring them down to see him. He agreed, and I entered the underground at Seventy-Second Street with a young British film director, a reporter for *Vibe* magazine, and a cinematographer for the Discovery Channel. Not soon after our visit, Amtrak will force the residents out of the underground. Bernard predicts May (1996) will be the month. We make our way down to find workers near Bernard's bunker and call out to him. He takes one look at the assembly and asks, "Where's the fire, my friends?" I explain who everybody is and what they want from him. Bernard talks for a moment or two before he says he'll allow himself to be filmed making his daily rounds; the reporter can start as soon as she is ready. He is now media savvy, handling himself with calm and resolve.

He says he picks up cans now on Tuesday and Saturdays and that the rest of his life is "an open book." As he says this, he is squinting and looking down the tracks. I leave the northern end of the underground to go see Beatrice in the southern section. I catch Bobo walking his dog near the bunker. He says he'll fill out his housing vouchers with Bernard's help and will probably be gone the next time I come to see him. He tells me Beatrice is topside, near Tower Records, selling books. I go there, and she sells me three books for a dollar each. She says she can't talk, so I leave. There is some tension between her and the man selling the books, whom I gather is the owner of the stand.

Early one morning, late in the research for this book, I go to the underground to see Bernard again. It has become more than a ritual, my coming and going through the gate. I have given Bernard a few dollars because he said he wanted to buy keys to change the locks, but for a while I'm not sure that he has ever bought the locks with the money. He shows me the keys one day, and I am satisfied.

This whole enterprise has become more than a book about unhoused people, even though he and others have asked how the book is coming along or have asked if I have seen or heard about some of the others from the underground. Over the years, we have bonded as friends; the residents, especially the men, felt this more than I did at first. All of this grew from research questions into longer discussions about their lives, the neighborhood, women, jobs—but mostly discussions about themselves. They sincerely wanted to talk about themselves. "I wanna tell you the real story of my life," Beatrice says, once it is clear to me, after all this time, that they trust me and want to talk about being women and men, real people. The problems, the trials and tribulations, the heartache, the disappointments—all that life brought them, they are taking head-on, good, bad, indifferent. They really want to talk about themselves, and since our initial meeting some years ago was based on their personal accounts, everything—our meeting in the underground, at my apartment, the diners, the pub, and on the street selling books or recycling cans—can be seen as an extension of these discussions.

I arrange for Bernard and Kal to be part of a film; many of the other underground residents I have come to know have departed for destinations unknown. Bernard appeared on a television show and has gotten some additional media attention. I am surprised to find out that he'd talked to "Hollywood" and that a deal was in the works. "I was offered $100,000 and 12 percent of the gross from a woman who flew in from Hollywood," he tells me. "But that's too little money for a movie, right?" I told him if they give him a check to take it. "I can't really buy a decent condo on the East Side for that money." We laugh.

I go to see who's left underground, if anyone at all, and the day is quite beautiful. A pole flies three flags: one POW-MIA, another the stars and stripes, and the last emblazoned with the Central Park Conservancy logo. The Hudson River breeze wafts across the area, and the park is vibrant with all kinds of activities: basketball players, kids throwing Frisbees, skateboarders, cyclists, joggers, dog walkers, sunbathers, walkers, sightseers, tourists. The entrance to the underground is now a dog run, though the infamous "Trump fence" still stands, unblemished, now for more than a decade. Starlings perch on it, and I make my way over to peek through and see what I could see. Not much, but I notice a structure near the end of the track. Though no train rolls through anymore, it would be a perfect place for homeless to live these days, but I see no one. No signs of life underground.

At the old Seventy-Second Street entrance, where the Cubano Arms once stood, the former homes of the underground residents, many whom I have now lost connection with, are now rubble. The bunker apartments of Bernard, Kal, and Beatrice and Bobo have been razed. The tents and lean-tos are gone; the underground is more desolate than ever.

The only way in or out of the underground these days is either by walking forty-odd blocks from 125th off the West Side Highway or through Jean-Pierre's rabbit hole. He is certainly the last tenant of the underground. Bernard tells me the head of Amtrak Police knows Jean-Pierre is still there, but since his presence poses no threat—he's completely out of sight and situated in such a secluded place that no one can see him—they leave him alone.

Amtrak has sealed off all the entrances (and thus, all the exits), double-bolted the locks with iron boxes, fortified the steel gates, and has posted guards around the "Trump fence" near the Seventy-Second Street entrance, where a new Costas Kondylis construction is near completion. Jean-Pierre had to find a more expeditious exit route; his hole is now his escape hatch. "I'm basically a crackhead," he tells me. "I've been on crack for as long as I've been in the underground. It's my pride and joy. It's my friend and my comfort."

Jean-Pierre leaves the underground after collecting his can money to buy crack from a location near Ninety-Fifth Street. He speaks as if a frog is in his throat, deep and guttural, and says the only way he can cope with being both homeless and living in the underground is by using drugs. "These drugs do serve a function for me at least, even though I know it's bad and everything. I do it because it gives me some relief from all the shit I gotta go through every day."

BERNARD, MARCH 2010

Today I went to visit Bernard at Dunbar Houses, his new home on 149th Street. I walked through a slow but steady drizzle to his apartment complex. As I make my way to Bernard's flat, I'm reminded of where I met him and wonder how he now feels about living above ground, in the chaos he once so proudly and often denounced.

He lives in a small, crowded, one-bedroom flat on the fourth floor in the center of Harlem. The bachelor kitchen to the left of the door is tiny, the living room full of used furniture; one piece I recognize from the underground: the large Huey New-ton rattan chair. The room is cluttered in part because a leak in the ceiling (he's waiting for management to repair it) forced him to push his furniture together, away from the dripping water.

The mattress on the bedroom floor, the furniture, the clut-tered look is eerily similar to his bunker underground, even to the point where a mouse comes running past, headed for his hole in the kitchen. Bernard tells me he left the underground on June 12, 1996, and moved here after completing his housing voucher and interview.

Here is a man who had lived as a homeless person for eleven years and who is now living in an apartment for the first time. "You know, Terry, a lot of people see us like so many wounded animals when we went into those undergrounds. You know that story about animals going to caves to heal or die? Well, some of the people that went to the underground did go there to die.

Remember we had a couple of AIDS cases that came down there abandoned by their families, abandoned by everybody. Some were hurt people, hurt by lost loves, or a failed economy, poor judgment about drugs, and chronic mental pain."

He's in one of his self-deprecating moments today. He says that he and his fellow travelers underground were treated like they were drug addicts and street urchins because they didn't have a home to live in. "It's as if we are convicted of a crime, that being of being poor, shiftless, and lazy, punished for not reaching the American Dream. Well, guess what, America? News flash: the American Dream ain't never been reachable for poor folk, but it's only been talked about being reachable. That's right, talked about being reachable because they know if they talk about it long enough you will some day believe that its real but it's not. Not really real."

I see Bernard as a person who consistently refuses to say he was hurt by past relationships (especially with his young son's mother), but I also see him as a courageous man, and one with a remarkable intellect. I ask him a series of questions I think will bring closure to this research project. It's been years since I started, and now that it's ending, I want investigate trajectories of escape—in other words, what accounts for people getting out from underground.

"What kind of adjustment has it been for me?" he asks, repeating my question back to me. "Well, I haven't had any overhead. I haven't had the problem of coming up with rent every month. I wasn't ready to come back topside and do a regular job after being underground all that time. My body wasn't ready for it. I went through an ordeal just going back and forth from Baltimore, and my body went through a lot of changes. It took about six months for my body to get adjusted to topside temperatures because as you know the temperature downside was never higher than 29 degrees in the winter, although it's like an air conditioner in the summer. I was worried I had gotten some kind of arthritis because my body was sore. I was scared for awhile, but the sun from my window helped me get the aches out of my bones. The other thing I've done is to keep in contact with my old supers who gave me books and cans. Now they give me work in their buildings doing painting and plastering."

One burning question I ask him is: What should be done for the homeless, and how should it be done? "Affordable housing is the problem," Bernard answered. "People can't afford an apartment in the city even if they got mediocre jobs. On the West Side right now, even if you found an apartment, it would cost about seven hundred dollars a month. I think the approach most of these outreach programs take is incorrect. Take, for example, people who have dwelled in undergrounds—to try to get them out. Well, there are some who are willing to go to a shelter, but on the average those who have been that free, even if it's freedom with a price, feel shelters are like prisons. I saw a lot of those fears in Beatrice and Bobo.

"They didn't want to go to no shelter no matter what. Michael Johnson and Doug Weismann at Project Renewal basically did the paperwork on the housing vouchers to get us out, and HPD was in charge of the vouchers, and Project Renewal was basically the agency that did the paperwork and the outreach. My voucher is worth $670 a month, which covers all my basic bills: rent, light, gas, electric. And I have this for four years."

11

REFLECTIONS ON LIFE UNDER THE STREET

Dr. Duke is a member of a disappearing school of folk magic. He spends days and nights out in the woods and swamps and is therefore known as a "swamper." A swamper is a root-and-conjure doctor who goes to the swamps and gathers his own herbs and roots.

—Zora Neale Hurston, *Mules and Men*

The underground became for me both the start of an ethnographic field station and a unique locale from which to reflect on the life of homeless people in the city. There are many ways of analyzing the phenomenon of homelessness: unemployment, personal responsibility, deindustrialization, a tight labor market, the demise of the family structure, loss of social programs, and drug misuse, to name only a few. All these issues play a part in the ongoing drama of homelessness in the city. But the field station approach to longitudinal urban research requires that resources be made available to scholars and younger social scientists, talented individuals who wish to conduct research in hard-to-reach places, be they undergrounds, drug dens, or secret organizations, and who may benefit from the experience of other scholars with similar interests. Their access to research sites, with key contacts into specific local communities or organizations, may need support from both prior and ongoing contacts with local scholars.

The older model of the "lone ranger" researcher venturing into uncharted urban environments to develop a research project is not altogether outmoded, but it is not always the best way to do high-quality research, either, although it may often be the only way some research can be accomplished.

None of my sociological training prepared me for this research underground. It was both a psychological and emotional adventure and a reality to which I still feel connected. The underground offers a tense, dense, and profound world, and its symbolism points to universal themes—the problem of human existence and quest for identity prominent among them.

One of my original intentions was to look at the "resilient factors" present in New York City's homeless population. In other words, what are the material, social, and psychological survival strategies used by people who are homeless, and at what points in their lives do they use such strategies? Is there a process of adjustment to homeless life? How do interpersonal relations and material adaptations change over time? What, if any, are their trajectories of escape? I wanted to hear these answers directly from the mouths of those trapped underground, through their stories and experiences.

I usually spend two years or more doing the research I do and observing the groups I am investigating—in this case, a tiny community of homeless people living in the Amtrak train tunnels on the West Side of Manhattan. The question of what happens when they emerge out of their shelterless situation seemed like a logical and important research idea for a project. Another set of questions emerged from that primary question: What accounts for them getting out? Intelligence? Contacts? Luck? A job? Resilience? And if they do get out, where do they go and what do they do?

After locating the underground through a journalist contact, I initially thought I would focus exclusively on one woman or one man. I thought the project would ultimately become a piece on self-reflection, where she would confide in me or he would perhaps seek my understanding and empathy. It wasn't long after meeting the people there, though, Beatrice and Bernard in particular, that I saw things differently. I came to understand Beatrice as a kind of protagonist. By that I mean I began to see her as an *agent*, as a *subject*, as engaging in conscious acts. She provided me with her most intimate thoughts, she reasoned out loud with me, she reflected in my presence, and she displayed her sorrows and joys. I was witness to her suffering, her naked emotions. And what I tried to do was experience some of those same feelings and reactions to a difficult, often harrowing everyday life.

My visits to the underground always evoked a rather somber, almost mystical mood. Beatrice and Bernard would often tell me their dreams. "I had a strange dream last night: I quickly lit the fire with the Goya mural as a backdrop," Bernard told me. "The mural was like a movie screen, and just as I raised up, my son appeared on the screen with his mother singing on this theater-like stage. She was smiling at the end of the song, and the applause was loud, and my son stood up and clapped so loudly everyone stopped applauding to stare at him."

One of Bernard's most striking aspects was his firm belief in spiritual logic. I suppose this could also be called folk wisdom, or common sense, or maybe magical thinking. Once we were discussing the subject of suffering: he mentioned in tandem James Joyce and a shaman named Igjugar-juk, a member of a Caribou Eskimo tribe in northern Canada. Joseph Campbell once noted: "The secret cause of all suffering is mortality itself. It cannot be denied if life is to be affirmed. The one true wisdom lives far from mankind, out in the great loneliness, and can be reached only through suffering. Privation and suffering alone open the mind to all that is hidden to others."[1] Bernard constantly rationalized, made deductions, and sought explanations for all his experiences and actions. In short, Bernard knew his mortality, knew mortality itself.

It is clear that the main theme in this book is the isolation of the individual, both the researcher and the researched, and such isolation makes the world seem as if it is being seen from an absolute subjectivity. People in the underground spoke often about solitude and of their inability to communicate with other people on the outside or topside. In fact, this is the reason most of them chose to tell me their stories. As Beatrice said to me: "The thing is, how can people come to understand me? How can a single person see me as somebody that Amtrak shouldn't bulldoze over? I need to try and tell them about me through you. The media always lies about everything. I hope your book will tell the truth."

As the years passed by, occasionally I would find myself driving along the West Side Highway, which would remind me that the book I'd been planning to write about the people that had lived underneath it had stalled. I'd reflect on what Beatrice had said and felt like I was disappointing her and the others whom I'd promised to tell what life was like underground. I also thought about the differences between these two people I'd originally thought I'd write exclusively about. Where Beatrice wanted to have anybody, a single person, understand her plight and give a fuck about her situation, Bernard wanted the *whole world* to understand him. As he looks at the graffiti reproduction of

Goya's *Third of May*, which adorned a wall of his home, he sees not his loneliness and isolation but his freedom.

"This painting transcends the underground, you see. It goes beyond this place, this fire spit, and this reality. It takes me to broader issues and worlds away." His need for flight was pushing him to consider leaving the underground, and that need was so strong that his dreams at that time were only about flight: becoming an airplane, riding on a bird, piloting a spaceship, or changing into a pigeon. "I would hear the cooing at various times as I walked down the tracks, and I guess it just came into my subconscious. The dream was very real. I started cursing as loud as I could, but I know you've had these dreams where nobody seems to hear you, and my screaming was basically a kind of cooing like the pigeons, a screech-type sound turned into a cooing. And down here you find yourself talking to yourself because there is no one to talk back to you. And you can scream, too, but the scream will just get lost in the space."

In the dream, Bernard says all the screaming he did was not noticed by others in the underground. People just thought of him as doing his normal talking, but his body was shaped like a pigeon's—and nobody seemed to notice that, either. When he finally stopped screaming and talking, it was Plako [a mentally ill homeless man who once lived in the underground] who noticed his change in appearance, understood his pigeon language, and asked what had happened. The dream ended with Bernard and this man going topside and into the street.

A second important theme of the book is trouble with communication. The trouble was not exclusive to Bernard and Beatrice but was an issue for all the others—Kovacs, Bobo, Jason, and Kal. No one ever quite came to terms with one another, even though they talked all the time. Jason's marital problems stemmed from this same failure of communication. It was not until his wife became lost in smoking crack that he found the words to communicate with her, but by then it was too late.

In other words, no one in the physical underground seemed to succeed in breaking out of the psychological underground and in making their real self (desires, frustrations, wants) known to the others in any consistent way. But this same lack of understanding occurs between those in the mainstream as well. Topside society does not want to recognize the below-ground resident except as pariah. Some conservative critics see Bernard as a "contaminated, uncontrolled individual" who could lift himself up if only he tried hard enough; such critics refuse to see homelessness as a structural creation and not an individual's fault.

Bernard is, in a way, an exaggerated example of a great number of Americans: antisocial, antitraditional, and, in the end, anticapital. As a culture, we have elevated pure market values like money and power to the center of our culture and pushed nonmarket values such as compassion, love, and caring to the edge—seemingly to a point of no return, as the philosopher Cornel West so aptly put it.[2]

It became increasingly clear that breaking out of the underground was a matter of communication and of forming connections. For instance, as much as Kovacs was disliked by all, he was the only one so far to seek communications with the outside world through love. "Love is the most powerful thing," he told me at our last interview. "That's why they call me 'the Mad Hungarian' because I know the importance of love. I might not love niggers, but I do love." Kovacs felt only through some complete relationship with another person—in his case, ironically enough, an immigrant, nonwhite, Thai woman—could he or any of his underground neighbors really get out of the underground, or out of themselves.

But inevitably, it was Bernard who felt that only by discovering oneself could you hope to escape solitude, loneliness, and madness. In the end, he wanted to surrender, because surrendering meant that he was freeing himself from the feeling of loneliness. In this way, Bernard unites with God and maybe, in a way, becomes God. He has broken with the past—as have all the residents. Some have torn away their roots, abandoned any attempt at a future, and see the future as now.

These residents find themselves completely isolated in the underground, a space in which they only temporarily reside, until they decide to come out. But for the few there is a drive for survival that does not allow them to give up completely. Clearly, Bernard is divided in his mind's eye: on the one hand, he's escaping persecution from topside and feelings of inadequacy; on the other, he is the superior "Lord of the Underground," who distrusts topsiders and whom no one truly understands—or intentionally misunderstand.

Bernard, Kal, Beatrice, and all the others down under don't really have a place. They don't belong topside but can only live so long underground. They are more or less a kind of social curiosity, an incarnation of a metaphysical problem, because the larger society sees them as nonexistent untouchables. Perhaps they are what increasingly larger and larger groups of poor citizens in the twenty-first century are destined to be: broken from the past, snatched up by the roots, and devoid of a future. In this sense, they all find themselves totally isolated, alone, in a darkened underground. And while they are not completely faithless—God provides solace as a larger, believable thing—the spirit is acceptable only as a real person or as symbol, not as something supernatural.

Yet none of the group of the eight to ten I wrote most about were quite like Bernard in this respect because, in some ways,

Bernard saw himself as a God: "How can one truly find himself without the solitude?" he says. "This solitude doesn't scare me, it awakens me, gives me strength to truly overcome." While Beatrice, Kal, Bobo, and even Jason believe they owe their existence to no one, Bernard feels he owes his to a God, but at the same time, he does not accept very many of the rules or norms of mere mortals. It is clear that he does not have much interest in the past or the future but lives for the here and now. While the others all seem lost in time, Bernard seems to open himself to the present.

He once said as much. "There was a time when I cared more about the world than I do now. But so much of what we as human beings have fought for is now lost. There are lost oceans (pollution), lost trees (rain forest), lost animals (endangered species), and lost people (poor). We are born in a careless world, and we die in a careless world. The few people that care are eaten up by the system and eventually have to fend for themselves."

But Beatrice, Bobo, Kal, Bernard, and the others eventually had to make decisions, decisions for which they simply didn't know the outcome and certainly lacking any assurance that the decision would be the right one. Bernard had logic and faith to guide him, and if that didn't work, he said he'd leave the underground and go it alone again. In exchange for the freedom to decide, he had to pay a price, as did all the others. That price is anguish, loneliness, abandonment, destitution. To what extent were Bernard and others in the underground products of twenty-first-century America, a century where, although religion is everywhere, there is nothing to believe in, and where disrespect for the sufferings of others is now the message from the state?

ENDNOTE

He had a habit of flipping a coin and checking if it was head or tails—obviously a sign of impatience or just a habit he could not break. "Heads I win tails you lose," he'd say, and laugh out loud.

—Field note, describing Bobo

The people in this book were once part of mainstream American society, but for reasons here discussed, they dropped out, became drugged out, or were pushed out at some point in their lives. But even though the gap between marginality and respectability is paper thin, it is treated as a sturdy wall separating "them" from "us."

When Americans think of the homeless, they immediately think of people unlike themselves: the poor, the minority, the other. The American middle class has an iron-clad conservative ethic at its core, a belief system that can only blame the individual for failure. To a majority of Americans, vagabonds are dysfunctional, disabled, and disaffected people who are only in the predicament they are in because they want to be and are too shiftless to do anything about it. Surely, they have had their opportunities. The assumption here is that what happened to "those people" happened because of what *they* themselves did, not what society did to *them*. In other words: there is nothing structurally culpable for their dispossession, nor has a social contract been breached. There is without doubt personal responsibility to account for here. The men and women in this book who did not take advantage of the few chances held out to them do share fault. But to assume that the system has a place for every American regardless of class, color, and condition is wrong.

The overriding belief in this country is that people are homeless because they didn't work hard enough, not because, for example, there were no jobs. This overarching belief is linked to another myth about the unhoused: people are homeless because they were born into a culture that breeds homelessness. Christopher Jencks's 1994 study *The Homeless* argues that the reason for homelessness in the 1980s was the growth of poverty among a particular group of unmarried men—between the ages of twenty-one and sixty-four—who had no jobs and little money. Most of these men were Black or minority and were vulnerable to a slack economy, particularly as it affected day labor. Today, in 2023, so many years later, we have a postpandemic situation, a tightening labor market, and unprecedented potential growth, yet homelessness abounds.

We are aware that poverty and lack of work is exacerbated when the economy has a surplus of low- and unskilled male workers who have little or no resources; recessions and economic downturns reduce demand for those workers. Economic adjustments and structural changes in the labor market impact most the individuals who have the fewest skills. As American capital moved abroad in the 1990s in search of higher rates of return, new arrivals were welcomed here because they were "willing" to do any kind of work at lower wages than the least-skilled

American. And the vulnerable, unskilled Black male, poverty stricken, one bank withdrawal away from homelessness, and facing a declining demand for the one job that keeps him afloat—day labor—once he sees that last raft disappear, he is indeed homeless.

There is no overarching theory of homelessness in this; homelessness is such a complex issue that any one theory cannot fully address that complexity. Most of the people who make up this book hold on to and indeed cherish these uniquely American and middle class values. From the oldest resident (Kovacs) to the youngest (Jean-Pierre), the consistent beliefs that America still works, that opportunities still exist, and that meritocracy is alive and well persisted in spite of all evidence to the contrary. Kovacs believes the opportunities are there if only the "green card holders" will desist from taking jobs away from white American men. Jean-Pierre believed he "blew his chances at making it" when he left his job and his former wife. Kal and Beatrice say they did not appreciate how good life was until they lost everything and moved underground. None of the underground residents linked their plight to the larger structural forces of capitalism. Homeless people are set up as examples of what might happen to any of us if we do not toe the line.

Oddly enough, when underground residents do see the underside of the meritocratic paradigm, that is, when they realize or begin to suspect that other forces may be at work, that the reasons for their social immobility may lie primarily outside of themselves, they often seek an explanation in metaphysical factors such as fortuitousness and fate. Bernard was quick to admit that maybe he ended up underground because of fate; this was an unconscious effort to justify his life in the underground.

Beatrice, Jean-Pierre, and Bobo were just as eager to explain why I should not see them as homeless drifters unworthy of society's empathy. They all said in their own way, "I'm down here, I live here, but I'm not a bum, I deserve respect and I coulda made it if . . ." The strong component of self-denial concomitant with the below-ground residents' acceptance of fairness in the American system places them in the position of self-labeling losers. By accepting such a designation, they are prevented from formulating any demands that may help them better their condition.

THE DESERVING AND
THE UNDESERVING POOR

This book follows on the heels of another piece of work my colleague Bill Kornblum and I did on teenagers in public housing projects.[1] There, our attention focused on how projects (as good places to raise children) produced good human beings who, despite all odds, achieved various successes in their lives, even when many around them failed. From that work, I became increasingly interested in the process by which human beings manage to cope with adversity, muster courage, improve their mind, and develop the perseverance to do what others cannot or will not do to survive.

Nowhere is resilience more pronounced than in the strange universe of New York City's undergrounds. Of the 113 people I came to know during these exhausting years of study, only a handful have emerged from the underground to find a different life above ground, and the reasons for that change revolve around the following findings.

First, they all entered the underground in various stages of utter despair and depression, leaving jobs, broken marriages, broken homes, or other adversity. Second, they all tried to establish some communication with people outside the undergrounds, with varying degrees of success. In this way, they were never alone, even while living underground. They knew there was someone to call on. Third, they all maintained some relationship to the outside world in other ways, either by working (selling cans or books) or through their need to acquire food, water, and wood. On some occasions they would have contact with a city agency, be it related to a shelter or a human welfare resources entity. Fourth, they all received help from outside sources in spite of themselves.

In a lecture some years ago at the Russell Sage Foundation, I heard Michael Katz speak about his upcoming work on poverty.[2] His treatise was exciting because he was tackling a controversial issue relating to what he referred to as the "deserving" versus the "undeserving" poor. He argued that "historic preoccupations" with "considerations of productivity, cost, and eligibility have channeled discourse about need, entitlement, and justice" and "have shaped and confined ideas about poor people and distributive justice in recent American history." According to Katz, the major issues dominating poverty discourse in the United States since the nineteenth century are essentially the categorization of the poor; the impact of welfare on work, motivation, labor supply, and the family; and the limits of social obligation.

Katz's central concern is with the consequences that poverty discourse has for the poor: "By mistaking socially constructed categories for natural distinctions, we re-enforce inequality and stigmatize even those we set out to help." This suggests that eliminating poverty is not simply about redistributing wealth; it is also a matter of, as a first step in having a discussion about poverty, redefining "the poor" as human beings.

Katz is highly critical of the dominant "supply-side" view of poverty, where one's well-being is framed in individual terms as a matter of personal responsibility and poverty thereby is seen as a result of the failures of the individual; this is a way of attributing moral failure to poverty-stricken individuals. This also tends to create divisiveness among the poor, who become isolated from one another. Katz is also critical of categories coming from social scientists such as "homeless" versus "underclass," which for Katz is just another way of dividing the poor into "deserving" and "undeserving," respectively. "The very poor evoked two different images among affluent Americans. When they appeared pathetic, they were the homeless; when they seemed menacing, they became the underclass." But regardless how you look at it, the homeless are seen as an indecent and uncontrolled population. Such categories at least partially arise from the dominance of quantitative methods, which make categorization inevitable, and are an effect of the "capture of poverty issues by economists and public policy analysts." Katz dismisses this approach: "Because poverty defies scientific measurement, all measures inevitably reflect political judgments." He is much more sympathetic to ethnographic approaches to understanding poverty because by focusing on the "lived experience" of the poor, "ethnographies highlight the arbitrary and partial nature of the conventional categories used to discuss poverty."[3]

Since I first began this work, the conversation has shifted. A brief literature review published in 2010 by Tyler, Lee, and Wright, "The New Homelessness Revisited," focuses on scholarly work on homelessness done since the 1980s, noting that "while scholarship on homelessness had waned since the 1990s, the current economic downturn and housing crisis are once again bringing the issue to the fore."[4] They begin from the position that "our knowledge of homelessness remains tentative," as they focus on (1) conceptual questions surrounding homelessness; (2) homeless population size, composition, and distribution; (3) homeless people's life chances; (4) coping strategies employed to meet basic needs; (5) explanations for homelessness; (6) public views and media coverage; and (7) actions taken to address homelessness.

In their "Conceptualizing Homelessness" section, the authors note that "homelessness" ordinarily involves "not having customary and regular access to a conventional dwelling" because of "extreme poverty," what the authors refer to as the "housing orientated approach." This is distinct from the "disaffiliation" approach favored during the "tramp and skid row eras," which focused on "indicators of disaffiliation such as alcoholism and living in single room occupancy housing." The authors note that

> an important recent insight is that patterns of time spent outside of conventional housing vary significantly. Three major types of homelessness have been documented based on these patterns: (a) transitional or temporary, describing individuals who are in transition between stable housing situations and whose brief homeless spells often amount to once-in-a-lifetime events; (b) episodic, which entails cycling in and out of homelessness over short periods; and (c) chronic, which approximates a permanent condition.

The authors add that it is difficult to distinguish between the first and second types of homelessness.

In the "Homeless Demography" section, the authors point out that "clearly, the homeless are not a monolithic or homogenous group," also noting that given in part its transitory nature, counting the homeless is often difficult and that such measures disproportionately capture the chronically homeless who reside in specific niches, what Mitch Duneier called a "sustaining habitat."[5] The authors go on to note that "the relegation of the homeless to a limited number of niches is a spatial manifestation of their more general marginality. This marginality in turn reflects life chances, the ability to benefit from the opportunities while avoiding the pitfalls offered by society," where the condition of being homeless is particularly detrimental to material well-being, physical and mental health, and safety. Here it is difficult to differentiate between "deficits" produced by homelessness and the "antecedents" of homelessness.

COUNTING THE POOR

In considering the sources of the poverty discourse Katz describes, we can return once more to the officials behind the policies that shaped homelessness in the period I spent with the residents of the underground and to the legacies they have left. At the time of writing, David Dinkins has recently died, and Giuliani is in the throes of a slow and gruesome political death. Both mayors approached the issue of crime and homeless sleeping on the streets and in "shantytowns" differently. Yet Bloomberg and his administration is particularly salient here for how the poverty discourse has changed.

A 2004 report from the Coalition for the Homeless addresses the flawed methodology of the Bloomberg administration's 2003 and 2004 homeless counts.[6] It was difficult to find any information about the methodology about how the homeless were counted during the Giuliani administration, but it appears that some form of a rather standard method, the "stratified sample methodology" utilized in the Chicago street survey in 1986, was used. Kim Hopper describes how this method was used during a Census Bureau count of homeless during the Dinkins years in 1992.[7] Then, as now, efforts to count the homeless are flawed, and the political stakes of the results, for example, how the results may affect city budgets, give city governments incentives to undercount the number of homeless.

What is stated in the report is that the Bloomberg administration claimed that in the second year of their administration the number of homeless sleeping on the streets declined, "despite abundant evidence" to the contrary. The city said that there had been a 5 percent decrease in the number of homeless, from 1,560 in 2003 to 1,482 in 2004. These results were contradicted by outreach teams contracted by the Department of Homeless Services, which had reported "an average 6.9 percent increase in the number of street homeless individuals contacted during the months preceding the survey."

Other sources, such as statistics on the shelter population for single adults, also indicated a rise in the homeless population. The Coalition for the Homeless report states on its first page that an increase in the shelter population "historically correlates strongly with changes in the street homeless population," leading them to conclude that the Bloomberg administration intentionally meant to "mislead" the public.

The report goes on to criticize the methodology used during the count. First, the "point-in-time" count commonly used, which relies on only one night of effort, will not arrive at a "right number," because "the mobility and characteristics of the street homeless population and the complexity and vastness of New York City's terrain make it impossible to arrive at a 'point-in-time' count of street homelessness." The "stratified sample methodology" also was at fault. This is a method that divides the city into blocks, each of which comprises four to six city blocks.

The blocks were then classified according to density of homeless people: high, medium, and low. The same was done for subway stations. In order to determine the classifications, the NYPD and Bowery Residents Committee were consulted. In this manner, during the 2003 count, Manhattan was divided into 899 "superblocks," with fifty-four put into the high category, 139 into the medium, and 706 into the low category. Subway stations were also categorized. The 143 subway stations in Manhattan were divided into twenty-nine "high," sixty-nine "medium," and seventy "low."

The 2004 count, which included Manhattan, Brooklyn, and Staten Island, followed the same methodology, with an important difference: only the "high" and "low" categories were used. High-density districts were considered to be blocks where two or more people were expected to be sleeping, while low-density blocks were where one or none were sleeping. In Brooklyn and Staten Island, high density was considered to be places where one or more were expected to be sleeping. Per the coalition, all the high-density blocks were surveyed, while only a small fraction of the low-density blocks were surveyed. All in all, only 14.3 percent of all blocks in the three boroughs were actually surveyed. The coalition notes that, as in 2003, the survey failed take into account areas such as subway trains, abandoned buildings, vehicles, and "other semi-enclosed places." In general, survey volunteers tend to avoid bridges and roadways, a phenomenon referred to as "inconsistent performance of volunteers," which potentially affects any survey. This was also something Hopper noted as occurring in the 1990 Census Bureau count.

A better way to count the homeless, argued the coalition report, would be by what is referred to as "prevalence counts," or "assessments of how many different individuals experience homelessness in a period of time."[8] Such a measure incorporates the "enormous" turnover in the homeless population and gives city governments a wider-angle lens through which to view the extent of the homeless problem, as it suggests the "prevalence" of the problem in a deeper manner.

The "Coping Strategies" section of Tyler, Lee, and Wright's review paper stated that

> recent research—primarily ethnographic in nature—portrays many homeless as active decision-makers who weigh the benefits and costs of alternative strategies for meeting basic needs. . . . Their decisions, like those of their domiciled counterparts, may not always be perfect, but even seemingly peculiar courses of action prove understandable once the limited options available are recognized. Because they face such serious constraints, the homeless must excel at improvisation, coping through creative, opportunistic, and varied means.[9]

One particular strategy is taking advantage of shelters, what has been called "the shelterization thesis." The argument here is that shelter residence encourages passivity and dependency, weakening clients' drive to escape homelessness as shelter-dwelling peers become their reference group. Critics contend that the shelterization thesis neglects the permeability of boundaries: "Individuals spend time outside as well as inside shelters, and their stays are usually short."[10] Other coping strategies include making a living, using personal networks, and managing stigma. The authors conclude this section by saying that

> the long-term implications of these coping mechanisms are a matter of debate. To the extent that the mechanisms render street and shelter life both bearable and meaningful, they could facilitate an adaptation to homelessness that reduces the odds of escape. Pressures to satisfy immediate needs might further work against the kind of goal-setting critical to such escape. Remember, though, that the vast majority of homeless people avoid becoming chronically homeless. Most are quite motivated to exit,

given their housed backgrounds and socialization into a dominant culture that equates shelter with worth.[11]

In "The Causes of Homelessness" section, the authors of the
review paper state that "among researchers, rough agreement
now exists on a conceptual model that integrates macro- and
micro-level antecedents," where "the macro portion of the model
emphasizes structural forces that generate a population of poor
people at risk of homelessness. The micro portion considers how
certain members of that at-risk population become homeless
because of their personal vulnerabilities, institutional experiences, and inadequate buffers." Thus, homelessness is not said
to have a single cause but tends to be, quoting O'Flaherty, "a
conjunction of unfortunate circumstance." They conclude by
saying: "The general lesson here is that our causal thinking
requires greater sensitivity to homeless dynamics and to the
micro and macro influences that shape pathways not only into
but through and out of homelessness."[12]

In their conclusion, the authors state that there is an emerging consensus that "homelessness is fundamentally a structural
problem rooted in the larger political economy." They also allude
to the growing preponderance of both preventative and housing-
oriented policy. They note that future research could learn much
by focusing on the transitional homeless and that research looking at prevention effects could take the form of cross-national
comparison and

> require the use of quasi-experimental designs, panel surveys,
> team ethnographies, and other methodological strategies that
> yield representative longitudinal data and that offer greater trac-
> tion for disentangling outcomes from antecedents. If the political

will to fund these expensive methods is forthcoming, sociologists could play a key role in the movement to prevent and, hopefully, eliminate the most serious types of homelessness.[13]

HISTORY REPEATS

Vico describes history as things circling back: those who do not learn from history are doomed to repeat it.

The characteristics of homeless/unhoused populations in the United States have altered considerably since the 1960s. As a group, today's homeless are significantly younger than previous cohorts of skid row populations, which were dominated by males in their fifties and sixties. On a national level, 65 percent of the homeless are believed to be in their twenties and thirties, and the median age for homeless adults is thirty-six.[14] In comparison to the "old homeless," the majority of whom were white, today's homeless are disproportionately drawn from racial/ethnic minorities.

In previous eras, women constituted only about 5 percent of the homeless population; today, they represent at least 20 percent, and homeless families comprise one of the fastest growing groups in the shelterless population. Studies also point to a high prevalence of mental illness and drug use among the "new homeless." Although estimates of the prevalence of mental illness range as high as 66 percent, a recent review of twenty-five studies found that 26.8 percent of homeless persons had a previous mental hospital experience, compared to less than 5 percent among the general population. While few studies have been able to satisfactorily measure the incidence of drug misuse among the homeless, some surveys indicate that as many as 90 percent of center-city homeless shelters may have drug or alcohol problems. In a review of the research findings, Rossi estimates that almost one-third of the homeless are alcoholics.[15]

In personal communication with the sociologist Alisse Waterston, she mentioned that individuals who have or develop drug addictions might become more vulnerable to housing displacement. Although a considerable proportion of the homeless population is entitled to state benefits including Medicaid, many homeless people encounter problems in establishing eligibility, and only a minority participates in welfare programs. For example, it is extremely difficult to receive welfare benefits or even receive official forms of ID without a mailing address.

Even when eligibility has been established, state entitlements are easily lost because of stringent requirements for recertification. In fact, according to Rossi, among the homeless in Chicago eligible for AFDC benefits, 96 percent had applied but only 7 percent were actually receiving benefits. In examining for terminations, Rossi found a high rate of "technical" violations for things such as failure to appear at interviews. Women drug users with children in particular may be loath to seek state assistance for fear that they will lose custody.[16]

Since the 1960s, New York City, like many large urban centers, has experienced a massive decline in the availability of low-income housing. Abandonment, arson, and gentrification have resulted in a drastic decrease in the overall number of low-income housing units. This loss, combined with the effects of unemployment and rising numbers of female-headed households in low-income minority communities, has led to crowding and the emergence of households characterized by frequent changes in composition and by drug use and sales activity.[17]

By the first decade of the twenty-first century, the New York City Department of Homeless Services conducted a census and found that on average six thousand homeless (single) men and two thousand homeless (single) women live in the city but that the total number living on the street was considerably higher, by 2,600, for a total of 8,612 men and women. The vast majority, about 90 percent, were African American or Hispanic.

Many households in poor communities have been forced to "double up" or in some cases "triple up" in order to accommodate housing demands. As early as 1986, estimates suggested that as many as 235,000 families were "doubling up" in apartments in New York City, and a study found that 52 percent of families in the city's shelter system reported living in "doubled up" accommodations before becoming "officially" homeless. At the end of 2022, in New York City the number of homeless individuals sleeping each night in municipal shelters exceeded 68,000; 86 percent of the shelter population is Black or Hispanic. Blacks comprise the most overrepresented minority group and the single largest group among this population.[18]

Ethnic minorities are also overrepresented among female-headed families, the fastest-growing segment of the city's homeless population. By 1988, the number of homeless families was estimated at five thousand, and almost all of the homeless families housed in welfare hotels were female-headed Black and Hispanic families. For many people, homelessness is the end result of a gradual and "piecemeal" shift from a tenuous existence that encompasses economic and social marginality, substandard housing, and family breakdown.[19]

Among the socially and economically isolated and those who are "precariously housed," the experiences of most of the people in this book appear to fit the model of homelessness as "the last stage in the downward spiral of poverty and abandonment."[20] People's choices in the underground were limited from the time they lost their jobs or were separated from or rejected by spouses or kin relationships. They could go to city shelters; live on the street; get help from city agencies, family, or strangers; get work; or engage in criminal activities.

FINAL COMMENTARY: SOCIOLOGICAL SIGNIFICANCE OF THE SHELTERLESS IN THE UNDERGROUND

Is homelessness a problem or a condition? We know homelessness will not disappear overnight, and we know a great deal has been written about it. But this does not mean we should push it to the back burner of our social consciousness. We should instead write about it until it no longer deserves to be written about. Homelessness is still very much with us, still present in our daily lives. And while there are people still living in holes under the ground, or freezing to death on park benches, or being put in cages because they can't afford to live in decent apartments, our democracy is not very democratic, our free enterprise not so free.

Here is where we start to hear about personal responsibility, but this horse has been beaten to death already, and we know the argument does not hold. Yet there are connections to be made between poverty and homelessness, poverty and private problems, and the betrayal of the social contract. We know people are lost in the city for many reasons, not just because they cannot pay rent.

Rather than viewing the unhoused as a potential danger to the public order, city governments and advocacy groups should recognize the resources and ingenuity that indigent individuals bring to their life situations. The unhoused produce an organic method of social control, manage to maintain a sense of belonging, create places to call home, and mobilize an ethic of self-help.

Their viewpoints and capacities are valuable and should be taken seriously when crafting urban policy.

This is something missing from previous work, like Thomas Main's, that investigates the economic and political conditions behind homelessness. Since Main's argument is primarily about policy developments, this should not be surprising; the voices of the homeless appear to have had little impact on New York City policy, whether the mayor has been liberal or conservative.[21] A policy-consequential approach to homelessness that takes the voices of the homeless seriously is Sam Tsemberis's "Housing First" model, where outreach groups ask the homeless straightforwardly what they think they need and do their best to meet these requirements; more typically, policy makers assume that they know what's best for the homeless and impose a concept of self and a model of reality upon the homeless that they often actively resist. Repeatedly throughout Main's book, the homeless stress their disdain for both shelters and psychological interventions. Through examining what the homeless themselves have to say about the virtues of homeless encampments, it should be evident what homeless communities can and do provide that shelter or therapy cannot.

Through building shantytowns or other forms of homeless encampments, homeless people form communities that offer safety, mutual support, enforcement, and accountability to often strict codes of conduct, if not a place to call home. In addition, these places offer what program shelters, therapy, or work programs cannot easily provide—a sense of belonging, a fundamental human need.[22] In this sense, the tunnel people were not nearly as "isolated" or "living a fantasy" as one might think. They formed a society as real as any other and with surprising similarities to "official" society. They created a place in the world where they could fit in with others like themselves.[23] Many news

articles in which homeless people have been interviewed dem-
onstrate this. Homeless communities provide a form of social
control that they feel is legitimate and not imposed from without, a rather Durkheimian moral order based in group life.

One journalist reports: "They lived without conflict, respect-
ing The Rules: No yelling at night, while people slept. No Bru-
tality. No entering the space of another person. No borrowing. If
you caused problems, you had to leave." Norms of reciprocity are
also fostered. In another article, a homeless man states, "When
I first went down I didn't care about anybody but myself . . . I
learned to care about other people." About unhoused communities, the article goes on to state, "It can provide a place to
commune with others in dignity on holidays such as Thanksgiving: 'This is the first Thanksgiving dinner you and I have
had together in 10 years. I'm thankful for that. This is a day you
should be with your close friends and family, not at some dinner in a church. When I go to one of those church dinners, I
feel like an inmate getting fed. I'd rather go back to jail.'"[24]

They sometimes don't even consider themselves homeless,
because communities offer a place to call home. In the first
article the *New York Times* published on the tunnel people, a
man, reportedly the first to move into the tunnel, describes
their community like so: "But mostly it's peaceful. It's all how
you play it in your mind. If you don't make it today, you can
make it tomorrow. I'd like to move out of here if I could get the
money together, but I'm not homeless. A cardboard box, that's
homeless. A park bench, that's homeless. Down here, it's not
too bad."[25]

During both the Giuliani and Dinkins administrations,
homeless communities were removed, dispersing the homeless
throughout the city or forcing them into more remote and more
difficult-to-find areas. I would not advocate simply leaving

homeless communities be without some kind of outreach. They need to be shown that the outside world cares. Yet the forms of dispersal that we often find, even when meant to encourage the homeless to move into shelters, are perhaps not the kind of care they really need.

Rather than imposing on them a model of rehabilitation and, moreover, disrupting the social relations that currently anchor them in reality, a new mode of dealing with the homeless problem should be developed—*homeless communities, in whatever forms they take, should be encouraged and maintained, rather than obliterated.* While serious problems can emerge in these places, for example, sanitation issues or fire hazards, advocacy groups can try to work with such communities to try to remedy such problems, especially when the number-one factor that is used as justification for razing such communities is public safety.

One such approach comes from the concept of "participatory design," which provides the inclusion of all stakeholders in the design process, providing a sense of ownership concerning outcomes. This has been tried in Chile, during efforts to transplant families from shantytowns into permanent housing. The homes were only partially finished, and it was left to the families themselves to determine the direction further development will take. Such an approach is both more cost effective and democratic—and arguably more humane.[26]

How could such an approach be applied to homeless communities in the United States? I propose that rather than uprooting homeless people from their quasi-homes, city governments work with them to help remedy the problems that frequently beset these communities: fire hazards, sanitation and waste disposal, or problems that may stem from their lack of knowhow. Volunteers with this knowledge could be used to assist in remedying these problems but also work with them to implement other improvements, as well as help provide resources and even training.

First aid as well as psychiatric outreach, similar to Sam Tsemberis's model, could also be used, and underutilized urban spaces could be designated as areas for homeless communities to establish themselves and organize. It should be noted that there would be, of course, in the city of New York, ardent opposition to such an arrangement for multiple reasons. Shantytowns are, after all, considered to be a Third World problem. But such concentrations of society's outcasts could also be a stark reminder that the "greatest city in the world" needs to be better.

The benefits of such an arrangement could outweigh the costs. It avoids the paternalism of the shelter system, which the unhoused often resist, and provides something that shelters, therapy, or medication cannot: a sense of belonging and a place to call home. Dominant models of assistance to the homeless follow the atomizing paradigm of modernity. While fostering the supposed "reform" of the individual, they may also disintegrate communities. Being "housed" and receiving therapy, while no small achievement, is not the only standard on which policy should be based. Community and belonging are also essential to well-being. The sociological significance of the underground people appears to be that society, wherever we may find it, must be taken seriously.

EPILOGUE

I work as a super in a couple of buildings uptown these days. And you can see how the community of Harlem is changing rapidly. In a few years we won't recognize this place. You already have a location that's only a short trip to the airports and everything so this place will not be the same in no time.

—Bernard

B ernard came by the house today to talk about his situation, his dreads gone, wearing jeans, light coat with black knapsack—seven months since he was last living under the streets. I had tried finding out about Kal, Beatrice and Bobo, Jason, and the others: Beatrice and Bobo moved into an apartment on 108th Street after living in a hotel for a time. Jason moved out of the city altogether for the South. As for Kal and the others, I was unable to find them, but I have news that they are still around.

Although Bernard doesn't have a regular job, he does painting and plastering, picking up a dollar or two from media companies. I referred one film company to him, and he made two hundred dollars. He says he's doing superintendent work in a building uptown. Through it all, he remains philosophical.

We talked for an hour, beginning with his sons and ending with his definition of resilience. He said he'd seen his older son (Robert) but not the fifteen-year-old (Avatar). He said the boy berated his grandmother for giving Bernard their home telephone number. The boy did not think Bernard should call because he felt it would upset his mother. Bernard is convinced the boy will communicate with him soon.

He looked fine, but he needed money; he was trying to negotiate with a producer for *The Jerry Springer Show* to get an appearance fee. Apparently, he was to be a guest on the show and wanted to help produce another show about Kal and his brothers—the priest and the cop. They had not seen one another for thirty years, and Bernard thought this would make a great reunion on television. He said he only wanted $1,500 and a computer out of the deal. Bernard might be the most well-known and publicized former homeless man in America, yet he's just as exploited now as he was before. I asked about life above ground, but he only talked about underground.

I survived the underground, but you know, a lot of people didn't. Will, Shorty, and Fran are all dead from AIDS. Ramon, Plako, and a lot of others are either dead or missing. Kal left Jeter's Place and is staying in Holland House near Port Authority. Holland House is more like a hospital than a residence because you got these SSI people there, mental patients, and folks with tuberculosis.

But you know, Terry, I helped seventeen people get their [housing] vouchers filled out when Project Renewal came around, and I was the last to leave. You know things got rough with Amtrak at the end because the animal rights people started to pressure Amtrak because we had all them cats down there. It took me two weeks to get all my stuff out of that bunker. I took dishes and that foam bed, boxes of stuff. After I was officially out, I heard rumors about people being bulldozed as they slept, so I went back down to see what that was all about. But you got to remember that many people used that underground, from high school kids, to artists, novelists, writers, filmmakers, photographers, teachers, you name it. A few Riverside residents all seeking some kind of special purpose would be down in there too. Amtrak was getting rid of the homeless—they were ridding the space of all kinds of activity.

I walked into the darkness from the light again, and I got this eerie feeling all over my body and as I approached the place where I had spent the last twelve years of my life. I stood there reminiscing about adolescent stuff. Like the time I used to melt the stalactite for water to bathe and to use for drinking water. Or when I heard this voice of a woman who was calling me at the grate, and it must have been maybe twelve midnight and it was a full moon out, and it was Tina, a woman friend I knew. I met her at the gate [Ninety-Fifth Street under Riverside Park], and she comes to my bunker, and I say what's up, and she was high and asked me if I wanted some sex, and I said yes, and before we knew it we getting down. It was a great surprise.

The place was completely destroyed except for the mural on that back wall that read "America is guilty of intellectual terrorism," and I just lost it, man. The tears came rolling down my face, and I knew those tears symbolized my final separation from the underground. The destruction of my place, my solitude, my existence after so many years was now complete, and I realized what that feeling was that I had when I first walked in there eleven years ago.

Talking about the bunker now seemed to bring more wet eyes for him, but he held back as long as he could. He changed the subject to talk about his parents and others in his family.

I have had a pretty hard time adjusting to my family because many of them see me as something of a pariah who has brought the family name down by my living in the underground. But I told them they have no right to judge me. Who among them have the right to judge me? When I said that, then well uh, you know, they all looked and shook their heads. My father has asked me to stay with him several times, but I'd rather stay in my own place and only pay two dollars a week rent.

So I can't complain about anything. You asked me if there is anything special that I have that separates me from the rest of the people in the underground and if I had it all to do over again what life would I choose. First of all, it is the most unusual of us humans who are able to live a dream twice. I wish I had been there for my youngest boy and helped him, but I know he will be a great man because his mother and his stepfather have done good by him, plus he's my seed, and that says a lot about what he is and will be.

But I don't think anything is special about us when you talk about this resilience thing. I do know that after all is said and done and after talking to everybody in that underground at one time or another, it's clear that man's first instinct is to survive. The first instinct is to look out for number one at all costs.

I asked about Kal, and he paused for a second before answering. A look of sadness covers his face.

Kal is in bad shape right now. I tell you that because he won't stop smoking. The guy has had two operations and he still does the same old thing. You know there's another book out about us by this Belgian writer, Teun Voeten, and Margaret Morton is doing something for Yale [University] Press. I think she [Margaret] forgot that it was you who introduced us when you brought her down here to meet me. Anyway, but she got mad at me because of something Bobo told her, and I think that's why she won't return my phone calls. Anyway, Margaret has gotten her priorities wrong and won't give up any of her photos, and that's too bad since she's chronicled all of New York and she'll probably die with those photos unpublished. Anyway, I think the thing is, you can't change people if they don't want to change. Anyway, I moved over here to 115th Street and Malcolm X right near you. I moved out of Dunbar Houses, and I'm here now. We should meet up and talk.

Bernard and I did meet up in quite an unusual way. I got a visiting professorship at Princeton (2011–2012) and decided to do a course on the ghetto as part of the Seminar of Engagement series I was doing at the New School. And in that regard, I had the opportunity to bring in guests from the city who had been part of my research. Mitch Duneier had set this whole thing up by doing a course in Rome on the ghetto, and we agreed that the same course on the American side would work out fine at Princeton. Lectures on the city underground included the sex lives of dominatrixes, gay boy prostitution, and homelessness. I invited Bernard to speak to the students about his life underground for the past two decades.

A limousine picked Bernard up at his new apartment in Harlem, drove him the forty-five minutes to Princeton, New Jersey, to the Nassau Hotel, and parked in front. Out stepped Bernard with a small bag in his hand. He registered at the hotel and was told to go to room 334. The next hour we spent discussing his talk, which was to be given to ninety students in Wallace Hall. He does have a tendency to repeat his same old lines, but I wasn't bothered by that. We had a nice dinner at a local restaurant. One of the students, Jocelyn Chuang, a photographer, took pictures

FIGURE E.1. Bernard and the author at Princeton,
Wallace Hall lecture, circa 2012.

Source: Photo by Jocelyn Chuang.

of us on campus. I also used her photos from the underground
she'd taken a year earlier. It was good to catch up on the latest
news from the underground, and I wanted to get his take on life
topside again. I talked to him when he first moved to the Dunbar Houses, after the implementation of the housing voucher
program set up by J. Cisneros, the secretary of housing and urban
development during the Clinton administration. At that time,
he was more in shock at being out of the tunnel, but now it seems
like old hat.

MEDIATING THE UNDERGROUND:
BERNARD'S EXIT

I had met Bernard's youngest son Avatar by chance, and I told
Bernard about an incident in which his son played a part. I was

working on a scene for the film *Harlem Diary*, with the director Jonathan Stack, about kids in a project I had sponsored called the Harlem Writers Crew Project, and Avatar was one of the seven kids highlighted in the film. I had no idea he was Bernard's son. I knew there was a connection because the incident involved a conversation where the boy used the words "the keys to the underground." Bernard had needed money to purchase keys to place locks on the gates of the tunnel.

I thought the comment was revealing. I asked him how he knew about the keys to the underground beneath Riverside Park, and he said his mother had told him his father was the "Lord of the Tunnel," the man who lived underground who had recently been featured on television. I had a few photocopied pictures of his father. I showed them to him, and he said he hadn't seen his father since he was a little boy. Upon seeing the photographs, he started to cry.

The camera crew began filming this story as it unfolded, and the next day his mother called to ask if that sequence with her son could be excised from the documentary. We agreed that it would. I told Bernard this story, and he was surprised by the whole thing and wanted to see the film, which I arranged the next day. Meanwhile, I met with Susan Milano and a Japanese director, Kumiko Igarashi, who were interested in doing a film about the underground and wanted Bernard involved. They wanted to film a sequence with Bernard back in the underground and coming out for the last time. This would also be the last time I would see Bernard alive.

Appendix A

INCOME AND HOUSING IN NEW YORK CITY, 2002–2014

Table A.1 indicates that while the median annual incomes for all households increased by 29 percent from 2002 to 2014, the median income for households paying for private nonregulated units increased by 47 percent during the same period. The median monthly gross rents increased from $788 in 2002 to $1,325 in 2014, constituting an increase of more than 68 percent. The median monthly rent for private nonregulated units rose by 59 percent, from $942 in 2002 to $1,500 in 2014. The median gross rent–income ratios rose from 28.80 percent to 33.80 percent, indicating that half of the households were paying over 33 percent of their income for rent and that every three in ten households were paying more than 50 percent of their income for rent. The last category of households increased from 25.50 percent in 2002 to 33.10 percent in 2014, showing a rising trend that half of all households are now paying a larger percentage of their income for rent in New York City.

TABLE A.1 INCOME AND HOUSING IN NEW YORK CITY FROM 2002 TO 2014

	2002	2005	2008	2011	2014
Median annual income for all households	$39,000	$40,000	$45,000	$48,040	$50,400
Median income for renter households	$31,000	$32,000	$36,000	$38,500	$41,500
Median income for private nonregulated units	$39,457	$46,000	$50,000	$52,260	$58,000
Median monthly gross rent (includes utilities)	$788	$920	$1,054	$1,204	$1,325
Median monthly contract rent for private nonregulated units	$942	$1,100	$1,200	$1,369	$1,500
Median gross rent–income ratio (%)	28.60	31.20	31.90	33.80	33.80
Percentage of households paying more than 50 percent of their income for rent (%)	25.50	28.80	29.40	33.10	33.10

Source: NYC Housing and Vacancy Survey (HVS)

Note: The survey is performed in New York City on a triennial basis by the U.S. Census Bureau.

Appendix B

BEHAVIOR MAPPING AND CARTOGRAPHY

Maps for the underground and aboveground areas are utilized in the text to supplement the ongoing research I conducted. These maps include Grand Central Terminal and Seventy-Second Street to 125th Street below Riverside Park. Also included are photographs and the tape recordings made by the homeless themselves. The maps display key features of the underground areas as well as important landmarks and streets above. The purpose is to create a visual representation of the areas in the form of maps and ancillary graphics (e.g., photographs, including aerial photography where possible). This method includes hand drawings and other hard-copy materials of the under- and aboveground regions, which are scanned digitally and geo-referenced to create base maps that are to scale. Recent aerial photography is used as backdrops to digitize aboveground features such as street centerlines and other key landmarks. Detailed maps (fifteen in total) of the study site provide a proper sense of locational reference.

The maps are an essential element in telling the underground story, and in essence, they comprise one of the characters in the narrative. How does mapping aid in the illumination of spatial concepts and methods for research in culturally unique, complex

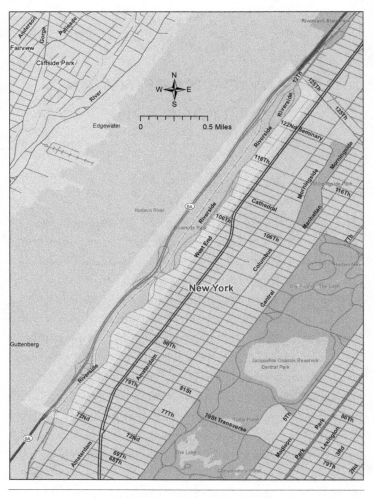

FIGURE A.1. Riverside Park.

Source: Maps by Rick Bunch.

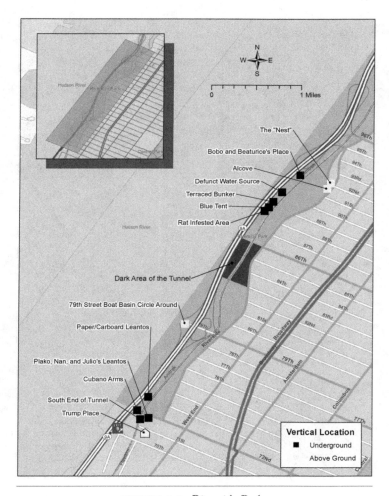

FIGURE A.2. Riverside Park.

Source: Maps by Rick Bunch.

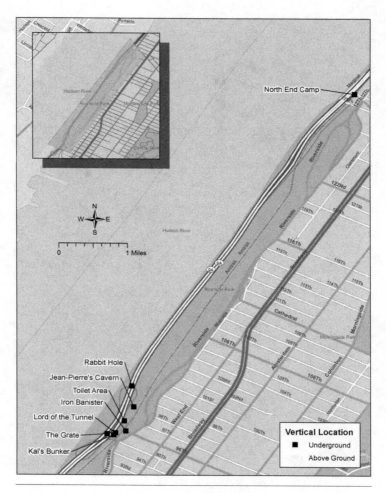

FIGURE A.2. (*continued*)

FIGURE A.3. The rabbit hole, Riverside Park.

FIGURE A.4. The grate, Riverside Park.

settings? I am in search of ways to understand the spatial dimensions of the human-environment relationship in a hidden community, in the spirit of helping enlighten the ethnographic enterprise; cartography is one of those ways.

Appendix C

INTERVIEW QUESTIONS FOR BERNARD, PRINCETON UNIVERSITY, 2012

BACKGROUND: LIFE STORY MATTERS

- How did you end up in the tunnel as a homeless person?
- How did you get the moniker "Lord of the Tunnel"?

DRUGS

- What role did illegal drugs play in your life?
- Is crack use the preferred drug because people need something to dull the experiences of homelessness and poverty?

PERSONAL RESPONSIBILITY ISSUES

- What would you say to people who would argue that you are totally responsible for your own situation and that it is not the fault of the "system," "capitalism," "democracy," or anything else? That people are homeless because they are lazy and don't want to work? Or that they are drug addicts who have chosen a lifestyle that brought them down?

INEQUALITY

- Does inequality make people sick?
- What do you make of the new dumpster-diving phenomenon by middle- and upper-class kids who find it fashionable to take food from the street as a form of rebellion or as a statement about consumption and wastefulness?
- The old days had hobos who moved from place to place. Today, people stay in the cities and don't go anywhere. Can you tell me why you decided to stay in the tunnel for so long rather than moving to a shelter?

ETHNOGRAPHY

- You have been the subject of several books now. Margret Morton's book, done by Yale University Press; Teun Voeten wrote about you, and you blurbed his book, *The Tunnel People*; I've written about you and visualized some of your story in the film *Harlem Diary*. You knew Jennifer Toth when she came to the tunnel to research her book on the underground. Do you see yourself representing a trend in ethnographic work where the "subject" is becoming more of the author of their own story? Take, for example, Hakim Hasan in Mitch Duneier's book *Sidewalk* or Lee Stringer in *Grand Central Winter*. You mentioned to me one time that you were thinking about writing your own book about life underground; how is your work coming along?
- When I first encountered you, I gave you the name Glaucon, after Plato's character in the Allegory of the Cave. But everywhere I turned, you were using your real name. We as

ethnographers are taught to protect the people we encounter by providing confidentiality. Is there a reason you wanted your real name out there, in spite of the conditions and situation you found yourself in?

Appendix D

BERNARD'S DREAM AND POSTCARD

I met people who offer a cross-section of life underground in terms of age, gender, and ethnicity, and their journals became useful as cultural artifacts. I became interested in the dream life these individuals said they had, especially as I'd heard people say they had "big dreams" while living underground. I received a few dream accounts, and they offered interesting reflections on the life of the unconscious mind in this setting. With some carefully applied guidance, I asked several underground residents to relate their dreams using tape recorders I provided and to write down their stories and dreams in journals.

Through writing in journals and recording their thoughts at night and other times, they became less inhibited and more reflective. During their first four months underground, Bernard and Bobo never slept without interruption for more than five hours. But of the twenty-four hours in the day, sixteen at least and sometimes more were spent in sleep, with three of those hours spent dreaming. In the last six months of being underground, they slept twelve hours on average, with three hours of day dreaming. Bernard recalls:

> Dream tonight was about a mushroom tea that a friend told
> me to take so I can be healthy. She said it would help my kidneys,

help my heart, help my liver and other parts of my body. The tea is called Kambocha. It tasted like vinegar, but I wanted to try it by myself, so I went home, and this is where the dream really starts crazy. When I came underground, the whole place was bright and full of light, not dark like I know it is. My place here was bigger, with rooms all over, and I tried to get some sleep, but I felt like the mushroom had gotten into my body because I touched it early that day.

I felt the tea pulling me out of bed, and it was a powerful force like I never felt before. When I got up in my dream and went to the kitchen, I could smell the tea all around, and I saw this bright light come in through the window that I don't have. The tea materialized into a woman with powerful hands and small feet. She walked up to me, kicked me, and patted my head. She said she was sorry and kissed me passionately. At that point two dogs arrived on a postcard with the inscription "tunnel dogs."

Appendix E

LEGACIES OF HARM: POLICY AND POLICING

There was time when the hobo and the bum were considered folk heroes. Such figures appear in the novels of Jack London and the songs of Woody Guthrie and Bob Dylan. The sociologist Nels Anderson's *Hobo* is classic in the literature. What happened to the glorified homeless person in America? What happened to the deserving poor?

Residents see the underground as having a "hierarchy of misery," or what the sociologist Loic Wacquant refers to in his 2009 book *Prisons of Poverty* as part of the spread of neoliberalism, which "aims to criminalize poverty—and thereby normalize insecure work at the bottom of the class structure." This "was incubated in the United States and is being internationalized, indeed globalized."[1]

"In New York we know who the enemy is," declared William Bratton, the city's chief of police, in a conference delivered in 1996 at the Heritage Foundation, one of the new right-wing think tanks closely allied to the Manhattan Institute and its campaign to dismantle the welfare state. Bratton is referring here to the "squeegee men," those destitute street entrepreneurs who accost drivers at traffic stoplights to offer to clean windshields for loose change, people not unlike Jason and Kal. Rudolph

Giuliani turned them into the reviled symbols of the social and moral decline of the metropolis during his victorious mayoral campaign in 1993, and the popular press openly likened them to social vermin or "squeegee pests," "petty drug retailers," "prostitutes," "beggars," "the homeless," "drifters," and "perpetrators of graffiti." "In short, the enemy is the sub proletariat that mars the scenery and menace or annoys the consumers of urban space."[2]

THE GIULIANI ADMINISTRATION

Thomas J. Main argues in his 2016 book *Homelessness in New York City* that the Giuliani administration began with the continued development of the paternalistic paradigm but ended by showing that paradigm's limitations and initiating the beginnings of the "housing first" approach, as developed by Sam Tsemberis.

Whereas David Dinkins, Giuliani's predecessor, hesitated to implement the Cuomo Commission's recommendations regarding housing policies, Rudy Giuliani, sworn in on January 1, 1994, enthusiastically embraced them. This meant trying to impose stricter eligibility requirements, while working within the legal framework of the "right to shelter." Giuliani initially proposed ending the right to shelter outright and limiting shelter stays to ninety days. His commissioner of the DHS, Joan Malin, advised against this, stating, "The public doesn't want us to walk away from the right to shelter. They just want us to do it better."[3]

The problem then became how to legally impose more limitations on shelter use. Adopting the ideas of the Cuomo Commission, this meant putting into practice the paternalistic ideas of "a mutuality of obligation" and a "balance of rights and responsibilities." Thomas Main, however, points out that in the "highly competitive political climate" of New York at the time, Giuliani was acting more as a "political entrepreneur" who used these ideas to shore up "electoral support."[4] In May 1994, his administration released a document entitled "Reforming New York City's System of Homeless Services," which articulates this exact political agenda:

> Eligibility rules ensure that those most in need of assistance and services have access to them. . . . Mutual responsibility will be established through an agreement known as an independent living plan, signed by both the provider and recipient, which indicates the homeless persons' acceptance of the responsibility to participate in programs provided to assist them in resolving their crisis and in moving toward independent living, mutual responsibility.[5]

The city first attempted to "enforce" these measures through legal means, rescinding state regulation 83 ADM-47, which stipulated that shelter be provided "immediately," and replacing it with a stipulation (94 ADM-20) that shelter be provided within forty-eight hours, giving the city time to determine eligibility. This new regulation would also stipulate that "clients" be required to sign an "independent living plan" as part of the "stronger eligibility process." The city was not initially successful in convincing the courts of the legality of this approach, because even though the "Callahan consent decree" established a legal right to shelter for homeless individuals in New York City, it also gave the state the right to "promulgate regulations for shelter." New York State Supreme Court Justice Helen E. Freedman temporarily blocked the measure, and the Coalition for the Homeless requested that the measure be declared "null and void," arguing that the restrictions would potentially disqualify from assistance needy individuals unable to guide themselves through the eligibility process. Such "eligibility requirements" were in 1997 ruled incompatible with the Callahan consent decree.

The Giuliani administration found an alternative way to pursue its agenda through privatizing the shelter system; that is, essentially, it contracted a city-operated system out to not-for-profit organizations. Once under way, privatization proceeded rapidly:

> In 1988, 73.1 percent of single men's shelters were operated by the city, and 26.8 percent were privately operated. By 1996, 45.7 percent were city run, and 54.3 were privately run. Family shelters were also privatized. By 1996, 72 percent of homeless families were sheltered in private, not-for-profit shelters. By the end of 1998, most of the eighty family shelters had been turned over to not-for-profit organizations.[6]

Overall, Main speaks of these developments approvingly, describing how both "quality of life" and "practices" improved dramatically. He uses the example of the Men's Shelter at East Third Street, noting how the "institution seemingly transformed as thoroughly as any pumpkin ever was by a fairy godmother." It was cleaner and smelled better, and the same could be said for the residents. In terms of practices, "The men were issued laminated ID cards, and everybody wore them, visible for all to see. There was no pointless waiting or wandering." Main describes how a "client" had even greeted him upon entering the building. "Incoming clients signed a contract specifying the cardinal rules they must obey, which included prohibitions on violence, substance abuse, and sexual activity. Clients also agreed to shower daily, keep a neat appearance, and provide urine for drug testing on staff request."[7] Compliance was continually monitored and ensured through punitive measures, such as dismissal from the shelter. Main does note that some clients viewed signing the contract as largely an involuntary and empty gesture.

The significance of the privatization of the shelter system for the Giuliani administration was that it "made possible the development of a more paternalistic system." While the city could not set any requirements for shelter, the nonprofit system could. With privatization, a "two-track system" also developed. "General" shelters run by the city served as intake points, where clients could not be denied entry, thus satisfying the city's legal requirement to provide shelter for all that asked. An interesting aspect of this system is the degree of choice it offered, while at the same time enabling an exercise of authority that "is less drastic, but perhaps more effective, than the impermissible denial of city shelters."[8]

For Main, choice and "a usable sanction" go hand in hand. Because entry into a "program shelter," the second track of the system, is voluntary, there can be a reasonable expectation of compliance. "However, admission to one of these shelters is predicated on the client's signing a contract calling for the client to 'establish and comply' with a service program tailored to his individual needs." What the contract also does is establish a tie between the client and the institution, a crucial aspect of the contract's enforceability. According to the anthropologist Janice M. Hirota, whom Main cites, "The contract system is emblematic of what is, from a social service point of view, the ideal relationship between worker and resident. Within such as system a client's problems are recognized and resolved by worker and resident working together in an individualized relationship of mutual respect and reciprocal accountability."[9] Thus, such a

contract reflects the "underlying problem" approach to homelessness and contains the assumption that some form of help is necessary if the client is going to "do the right thing," meaning a
structured rehabilitative program is necessary.

Yet according to policy analysts and housing scholars, with
the development of paternalism emerged its obvious limitations,
along with the limitations of enforcing compliance to the "right
to shelter" mandate through levying fines and contempt charges
by the court. During the Giuliani administration, "McCain
[which covered homeless families and set minimum standards
of decency for their shelter] continued to operate and act as a
driver of policy."[10] The continued practice of allowing homeless
families to stay overnight at Emergency Assistance Units (EAUs)
brought with it the threat of legal action.

The Giuliani administration sought to avoid this, and later
the city was fined for what was found to be deplorable conditions at its EAUs. However, two legal developments would alter
shelter provisions. On December 27, 1996, Governor Pataki
revised 94 ADM-20, which "removed the language that required
the city to comply with court decisions. So in fact that regulation's provision that the city had 48-hours to provide assistance
was good."[11] Another portion of the regulation, establishing
work-for-shelter requirements and stipulating that if the parents
of children became homeless because of noncompliance with this
regulation the children could be placed in foster care, was stalled
in court. However, on May 27, 1997, Justice Freedman, the same
judge that was instrumental in establishing the "right to shelter," upheld the legality of this provision, arguing that such measures were legal, if not rational, yet they could not be applied by
the city "arbitrarily or irrationally."

This allowed the city to develop "an effective eligibility-
determination process."[12] However, full implementation of this

policy would be delayed until after the winter of 1999–2000. This was a result of litigation and, possibly, negative press attention coming from the *New York Times*, which stated, "For the first time since the turn of the century, homeless people in New York City will be required to work as a condition of shelter, under a Giuliani administration policy to be put into effect before the end of the year. . . . The homeless who are able to work and who fail to comply with the rules will be refused shelter, and in the case of families, the children could be put into foster care."[13]

By the end of the Giuliani administration, the limitations of the eligibility process and the ideology of paternalism became apparent. Despite the implementation of the eligibility requirements, the shelter population continued to rise, reaching above "twenty-five thousand, higher than it had been since the late 1980s.

Although available shelters addressed a variety of needs for clients, from substance abuse to employment, thus increasing the number of options a client had, as Mark Hurwitz, then an assistant commissioner at the DHS put it,

> Program shelters, rather than being designed to serve anyone who had a mental illness or anyone who had an addiction problem, they were designed to serve those who were most, in the words of the providers, were most amenable to treatment or who were likely to respond well to treatment. That created this problem of the people with the worst problems got stuck in the general shelters and never left.[14]

Main speaks approvingly of Sam Tsemberis's "housing first" approach as a remedy to this problem, as it focused on providing housing regardless of any addiction or mental health problems a client may have and then later providing treatment, operating under the assumption that someone will be more likely to get treatment and respond better to treatment if they are first housed with no strings attached. There is evidence that this approach is effective. Conducted in 1997, the New York Housing Study found that "after five years, 88 percent of clients who participated in the Housing First model provided by Pathways remained housed, compared to only 47 percent of those who participated in the traditional treatment-first approach."[15]

We can see in the Giuliani administration the concretization of the policies and practices that have since shaped the treatment of the homeless population in New York City. As Main recognizes, many of these policies, perhaps more humane as they seemed following the 1996 welfare reform, would nevertheless be left to the subsequent administration—Bloomberg's—to rectify.

MATTERS OF APPROACH? FROM DINKINS TO GIULIANI

Dinkins's approach to homelessness, as seen, shows some surprising similarities to Giuliani's. Part of the perception that Dinkins was somehow sitting on his hands while New York became engulfed in crime and homeless shantytowns was a perception that Giuliani actively fed. During the mayoral campaign, Giuliani attacked Dinkins's inability to resolve the homeless problem, even as Dinkins's approach took a more conservative turn. On October 2, 1993, an article entitled "New York Rivals Differ Strikingly on Dealing with City's Poorest" appeared in the *New York Times*, highlighting Dinkins's struggles:

> The number of people on welfare has risen to almost 1.1 million, its highest level since the Depression. There are 273,000 more

New Yorkers on welfare than when Mr. Dinkins took office. . . .
The number of families in the city's shelter system has risen
54 percent, to 5,700, and dozens of families sleep each night on
floors, chairs and tables in city offices.[16]

At least part of this situation can be attributed the wider economic recession, which affected every American city, not just
New York. Nonetheless, the circumstances gave Giuliani plenty
of ammunition for his campaign. Perhaps the biggest difference
between the two candidates, as highlighted in the article, was
that Dinkins planned to rely on incentives to get more homeless off the streets and into shelter programs, such as subsidized
housing, education, training, drug treatment, and work placement. His opponent, on the other hand, argued that the homeless needed more a of "push," and he proposed to tighten requirements for shelter and require recipients of public benefits to
look for work immediately: "We need people to [do] for themselves, reform their own behavior,"[17] he's quoted as saying.

Also, while Dinkins appeared to be unsure of how to enforce
eligibility requirements, Giuliani would use the threat of removal
from shelter as a penalty for noncompliance. Giuliani also linked
the presence of the homeless to "quality of life" and promised to
get them off the streets, by force if necessary, responding in part
to growing public impatience with the intractability of the problem. An interesting point of convergence between the two is
that they both proposed to privatize the shelter system and were
influenced, Dinkins more reluctantly, by the Cuomo Commission's recommendations. Dinkins's reluctance provided Giuliani
an opportunity to claim the mayor was indecisive about the issue.

Indeed, after taking office, Giuliani wasted little time in
devising a plan to remove homeless from the streets. On
August 18, 1994, the *New York Times* printed an article entitled
"Police to Start New Program for Homeless," assigning a team

of police officers to "persuade the homeless to move to shelters." As mentioned before, Dinkins also implemented an outreach program, yet Giuliani's program appears to differ from Dinkins's in the sense that rather than simply offering an incentive, the threat of jail accompanied the efforts. Initially, though, the administration attempted to assure the public and homeless advocates of the "altruistic" nature of the program and kept the jailing of the homeless under the radar. The deputy mayor is quoted as saying, "The prime motivation is to get the homeless into shelters because it's not safe on the streets," adding that the priority was to get the homeless in programs so that they could receive help. But Police Captain Jay Kopstein made Giuliani's conviction clear: the homeless do not have a right to the streets. "The sidewalk is not a mattress," he's quoted as saying. A different police captain, William Bayer, was quoted as saying, speaking of homeless people living in Central Park, "The answer is, we have to cut off the head of the enemy and the enemy is the homeless. . . . They are predators."[18]

Within a month, on September 4, 1994, the *New York Times* ran another article, "Special Unit Ushers Homeless from Subways," documenting the city's efforts to date. Again, "persuasion" is mentioned as the primary tool, and concerns for public safety and getting the homeless help are invoked. Yet the article highlights a difficulty repeated in many different articles: given concerns for the safety and loss of autonomy, many of the homeless seek to avoid shelters. The reporter, who followed police during one night's efforts, writes: "Only one of the seven accepted a van ride to a shelter, where social workers tried to coax them into treatment. The six others, including one who voluntarily dropped his pants to show them a hernia the size of a golf ball, were gently hustled out of the tunnels to find their way through the wet streets and parks." The article also makes clear that this program was used and even was escalated during the Dinkins years, although the special unit itself was founded in 1982. "The number of homeless people transported by the police rose to a high of 5,100 last winter from 1,400 in the winter of 1990–1991."[19]

On November 12, 1995, the *New York Times* article "The Homeless Huddle at City's Margins" made it evident that Giuliani's program was not moving the homeless into shelters but simply moving them into the city's "margins," that is, less visible locations, which indeed was part of the intent. The psychological toll on the homeless was made evident: One homeless woman is quoted as saying, "You get worn down. . . . It's a message sent to you: you're no good, you're not acceptable, you're perverted, you're disgusting. So you go with your tail between your legs, and want to give up." Being repeatedly chased from place to place was also making the homeless less trusting and more difficult to "reach." There is no mention of arrests occurring, although the police did make the threat of arrest if any homeless returned to the place they had been evicted from. This aspect of the outreach effort would not be brought to public awareness until the end of the Giuliani administration.[20]

Down underground, the "tunnel people" would also be evicted, as documented in the April 15, 1996, *New York Times* article "Forced from Tunnel Shanties, Dwellers Are Trying Out Life Above," although it is made clear that Amtrak and not the city was the main force behind their removal. In this instance, the Coalition for the Homeless would intervene, buying time so that living arrangements could be made. The organization managed to revive an underutilized $9 million federal voucher program set aside for homeless living underground, including subway systems.[21] In a different article, "Homes for the Invisible," published on October 7, 1995, the photographer Margaret Morton celebrated the fact that several of the tunnels' then population of fifty would be placed into housing, not shelters: "There are solutions to homelessness. The people leaving the tunnel are proof," she emphatically states.[22] Interestingly, a reply by Kim Hopper, directed at Morton, would be written to the editor, entitled "Tunnel Dwellers Give Us No Easy Answers on Homelessness," in which he would criticize Morton's stance. Stated as it is in opaque academic language, it is difficult to discern exactly what he is arguing, yet his main point seems to be a concern that this development gives a different kind of perverse incentive to the homeless:

> Nor is the successful relocation she documented a demonstration of the economies of housing over shelter: the tunnel dwellers avoided the public shelters, after all. What we have is an object lesson in the futility of making policy through gestures. . . . For city officials, the tunnel dwellers are a standing reproach to the public shelter system. This comes as the terms and conditions of access to the shelters are being tightened, the better to force those who have recourse elsewhere to make use of it. . . . The message to the street-dwelling homeless? Hide better.[23]

In November 1999, a twenty-seven-year-old office worker, Nicole Barrett, was hit in the back of the head with a brick, in Midtown, and sustained serious injuries.[24] Giuliani responded with an even more aggressive sweep of New York City's streets.[25] "Mayor Rudolph W. Giuliani declared yesterday that the homeless had no right to sleep on the streets and his police commissioner added that they could be arrested if they refused shelter. Their remarks came three days after an office worker in Midtown Manhattan was critically injured in a random attack by a man the police say may have been homeless." The mayor is quoted as saying: "Streets do not exist in civilized societies for the purpose of people sleeping there," adding that the right to sleep on the streets "doesn't exist anywhere. The founding fathers never put that in the Constitution."[26]

This appears to be the point where something that had been going on throughout Giuliani's tenure was brought decisively to public attention. On November 22, 1999, the *New York Times* ran an article entitled "A Homeless Man Challenges New York City Crackdowns," which stated:

> Almost three years ago, on the cold night of Feb. 27, 1997, Mr. Betancourt tucked himself into cardboard and fell asleep on a bench in a small park across the street from the Criminal Courts building in Lower Manhattan. About 1:30 a.m., he was awakened by two police officers. And for the first time in his life, he was arrested. "Direct order from Giuliani," an officer told Mr. Betancourt before taking him to jail, according to court affidavits. "You're not supposed to be sleeping here."[27]

This homeless man sued the city in court, yet when faced with the legality of this now authoritarian approach to removal of the homeless from the streets, a judge ruled in the city's favor. A regulation that barred people from leaving "any box, barrel, bale of merchandise or other movable property" on city streets or erecting a "shed, building or other obstruction" was found to legally apply to homeless individuals as well. It also blocked people from abandoning "any motor vehicle, not otherwise lawfully parked," on city streets.[28]

CONTEXT: WELFARE CUTS

Whereas Dinkins had to contend with an economic recession, Giuliani presided over the dotcom boom, and even as his policies toward the homeless were unpopular among New Yorkers,[29] a January 14, 1999, *New York Times* article entitled "In a Year of Acrimony, Giuliani Is Defined by the Economy" summarized the mayor's popularity by saying: "Crime is down. Jobs are up. Little else matters, experts say."[30]

Yet the poorest did not share in this economic boom. An important piece of the context, beginning at the national level, is that on August 23, 1996, Bill Clinton signed welfare reform into law.[31] The law eliminated the "Aid to Families with Dependent Children" program and placed more of the burden of the expense for poverty alleviation on the states. The bill also put into place work requirements for receiving welfare. It was not long before the effects were felt in New York City. The journalist Rachel Swarns wrote, "Four years later [after Giuliani promised to 'put the jobless back to work'], there are 320,000 fewer people on the welfare rolls. Nearly 200,000 welfare recipients have swept streets and cleaned parks in what has become the nation's largest workfare program. The homeless men and women who begged for pennies have greatly decreased, at least in the busy center of town, and some shelters now require work in exchange for beds." On the other hand, "Homeless adults have been swept from Manhattan's busy streets, but their numbers in city shelters have surged by 15 percent over the last two years, to 7,119 on an average night. It is the first increase since 1990 and it results, in part, from the city's failure to develop enough affordable, permanent housing."[32]

In August 1999, the Coalition for the Homeless provided an answer to the question of where those kicked off of welfare had gone. In a report entitled "Legacy of Neglect: The Impact of Welfare Reform on New York's Homeless," the organization outline the devastating impact Bill Clinton's measure had on the homeless. Increasingly cut off from benefits, they turned to overwhelmed service providers. They cite a claim often made to cite

welfare reform's success: "The number of people receiving welfare in New York State fell by 41 percent between January 1995
and April 1999, from a reported 1,643,832 recipients to 972,292"
(4). Yet rather than returning to work, more had been turning
to service providers and staying longer at shelters, and more were
being turned away because of "insufficient capacity." The top
reason for loss of benefits reported was "difficulty complying
with work requirements" (5), an ironic fact given that welfare
cuts were to supposedly lead to an increased incentive to work.[33]

Not surprisingly, toward the end of Giuliani's term, New York
City's shelter population stood at 25,693, its highest level since
the mid-1980s. According to an article published on February 8,
2000, "Officials say no single factor explains the increase in families seeking shelter. Likely explanations include sharply rising
housing costs in an economic boom, a subway advertisement
campaign that encourages victims of domestic violence to seek
help, more court orders for eviction, and declines in subsidized
housing." Martin Oesterreich, the city's commissioner of homeless services, said, "Whereas the debate for the last few years
has been about work programs, what we're seeing now is that
work isn't enough to keep people out of the shelter system."[34]
That is, the minimum wage of $5.15 per hour was insufficient to
pay New York City's exorbitant rents.

Appendix F

WHERE ARE THEY NOW?

Bernard	After leaving the underground, Bernard lived first in Dunbar Housing and later in the Carver public housing project. Although he was not working full-time at the time of his untimely death in 2017, his interest was in the human services area, and he was seeking a full-time job in the helping profession.
Kal	Resides at a halfway house in Times Square.
Beatrice	Lives in a New York City welfare hotel.
Bobo	Lives in the same New York City welfare hotel.
Jason	Moved to North Carolina.
Jean-Pierre	Last seen leaving the underground.
Tin Can Tina, aka MM	Unknown.
Kovacs	Left the underground; whereabouts unknown.

NOTES

PROLOGUE

1. "The Canal du Midi today is a modest but pretty tree-lined waterway that threads through Languedoc in southwestern France. Most people who glimpse it from the nearby highway have little idea what was entailed to build it. Many assume that British canals predated it, or that it was contemporary to the Eric Canal. But it preceded them by nearly two centuries and was hailed at its opening in the 1680s as a wonder of the world. The world harbored a mystery. It was not technically possible according to the formal engineering knowledge of the period. Some called it a work of the Devil; the entrepreneur who built it, Pierre-Paul Riquet, attributed its success to God; and propagandists touted it as measure of glory of Louis the XIV. It was otherworldly in its modernism, and huge by period standards. It did not just dominate the landscape but also haunted it with the foreignness of its powers." Chandra Mukerji, *Impossible Engineering: Technology and Territoriality on the Canal du Midi* (Princeton, NJ: Princeton University Press, 2021), xix.

2. Harry Stack Sullivan, *Clinical Studies in Psychiatry*, ed. Helen Perry et al. (New York: Norton , 1956), 3–190.

3. Allen R. Pred, *Place, Practice and Structure: Social and Spatial Transformation in Southern Sweden* (London: Polity, 1986). See too Michel Foucault, "Questions on Geography," in *Power/Knowledge: Selected Interviews and Other Writings, 1972–1977* (New York: Pantheon, 1980);

and Doreen Massey, ed., *Geography Matters* (New York: Cambridge University Press, 1984).

4. *Ethnography* (from the Greek *ethnos*, nation, people, folk + *graphei*, to write) is a method. The term *ethnology* (*ethnos* + *logos*, speech, the study of a subject), first used in the late eighteenth century, refers to the study of people or groups, and *anthropology* (*anthropos*, man + *logos*) refers to the study of man. Malinowski distinguished between ethnography, "the empirical and descriptive results of the science of Man," and ethnology, "speculative and comparative theories," but for Lévi-Strauss ethnography was a data collection tool, ethnology the analysis of ethnographic data, and anthropology the comparative analysis of societies. The term *ethnology* is rarely used today, as the real distinction made presently is between cultural and social anthropology, connected to national traditions: the former with American scholarship (Boas, Morgan, Mead), the latter with British (i.e., Malinowski, Evans-Pritchard, Radcliffe-Brown). Finally, the distinction between sociology and social anthropology can be read as one between industrial versus so-called primitive societies rather than between differences in method. Scholars like Radcliffe-Brown and Emile Durkheim argued that maintaining such boundaries between sociology and social anthropology was useless.

INTRODUCTION

1. The original reference to the "mole people" derived from a 1964 comic book, *The Mole People*, illustrated by Marvel Comics artists, drawn from a 1956 sci-fi B-movie of the same name. The Marvel Comics character Mole Man is the ruler of a race of "moloids," who live in Subterranea, an underground location. Mole Man appeared in an earlier comic book series, The Fantastic Four, in 1962. The comic book cover reads, "The Mole People Meet Superman; Wonder Woman Battles the Mole People."

2. Maxim Gorky, *The Lower Depths and Other Plays*, trans. Alexander Bakshy (New Haven, CT: Yale University Press, 1945).

3. John Dos Passos, *Midcentury: A Contemporary Chronicle* (Cambridge, MA: Riverside, 1960), 5.

4. William Kornblum, "Discovering Ink: A Mentor for a Historical Ethnography," *Annals of the American Academy of Political and Social Science* 595, no. 1 (2004).

5. Anne Sutherland, *Gypsies: The Hidden Americans* (Prospect Heights, IL: Waveland, 1975); Michael Burawoy, *Ethnography Unbound: Power and Resistance in the Modern Metropolis* (Berkeley: University of California Press, 1991); Ruth Behar and Deborah A. Gordon, *Women Writing Culture* (Berkeley: University of California Press, 1995).

6. Carol Ellis and Arthur Bochner, *Composing Ethnography: Alternative Forms of Qualitative Writing* (Walnut Creek, CA: Altamira, 1996).

7. Norman K. Denzin, *Interpretive Autoethnography* (Thousand Oaks, CA: Sage, 2014).

8. Personal conversations with Charles Tilly.

9. James Duncan, "Men Without Property: The Tramp's Classification and Use of Urban Space," in *Readings in Urban Analysis* (New York: Routledge, 1983), 166.

10. Jean Schensul, Merrill Singer, et al., *Mapping Social Networks, Spatial Data, and Hidden Populations* (Walnut Creek, CA: Altamira, 1999), 125.

11. James Clifford, *On the Edges of Anthropology: Interviews* (Chicago: Prickly Paradigm, 2003).

1. DESCENT

1. Located underground are 7,000 miles of gas mains; 7,400 miles of sewer pipes; 2,000 miles of television cables; and 19,000 miles of electrical cables. Pamela Jones, *Under the City Streets: A History of Subterranean New York* (New York: Holt, Rinehart and Winston, 1978).

2. Thomas J. Main, *Homelessness in New York City: Policy Making from Koch to de Blasio* (New York: New York University Press, 2016), 9.

3. From Teun Voeten, *Tunnel People* (Oakland, CA: PM, 1996), 13.

4. Jack London, "To Build a Fire, first published in *The Youth's Companion*, May 29, 1902; see Earle Labor and King Hendricks, "Jack London's Twice-Told Tale," *Studies in Short Fiction* 4 (Summer 1967).

2. GENESIS

1. Robert Fitch, *The Assassination of New York* (New York: Open Road Media, 2014).
2. Thomas J. Main, *Homelessness in New York City: Policy Making from Koch to de Blasio* (New York: New York University Press, 2016), 69.
3. Main, *Homelessness in New York City*, 79.
4. Overall, however, Main is cautious about deploying what A. O. Hirschman referred to as the "perversity thesis," or the idea, often endorsed by conservatives, that "the attempt to push society in a certain direction will result in its moving . . . in the opposite direction." He nonetheless finds it a potentially useful tool in assessing the "total set of incentives" that a policy initiative may create.
5. Main, *Homelessness in New York City*, 81.
6. Main, *Homelessness in New York City*, 87.
7. Main, *Homelessness in New York City*, 87.
8. Main, *Homelessness in New York City*, 92.
9. Main, *Homelessness in New York City*, 87.
10. Dennis P. Culhane, "The Quandaries of Shelter Reform: An Appraisal of Efforts to 'Manage' Homelessness," *Social Service Review*, September 1992, 428–40.
11. Main, *Homelessness in New York City*, 8.
12. Peter Steinfels, "Apathy Is Seen Greeting Agony of the Homeless," *New York Times*, January 20, 1992, http://www.nytimes.com/1992/01/20/us/apathy-is-seen-greeting-agony-of-the-homeless.html.
13. Steinfels, "Apathy Is Seen Greeting Agony of the Homeless."
14. David M. Herszenhorn, "Charities Fear Climate of Cynicism Around Poor," *New York Times*, January 27, 1997, http://www.nytimes.com/1997/01/27/nyregion/charities-fear-climate-of-cynicism-around-poor.html.
15. Celia W. Dugger, "A Roof for All, Made of Rulings and Red Tape," *New York Times*, July 4, 1993, http://www.nytimes.com/1993/07/04/nyregion/a-roof-for-all-made-of-rulings-and-red-tape.html.

3. UNDERGROUND ECOLOGY

1. Human ecology studies how social relationships are affected by their environment. For a good review and historical look at this perspective, see Michael P. Smith, *The City and Social Theory* (New York: St. Martin's, 1979), chap. 2.

2. Louis Wirth's 1938 essay "Urbanism as a Way of Life," in *On Cities and Social Life*, ed. Albert J. Reiss Jr. (Chicago: University of Chicago Press, 1938).

3. See, for example, William F. Whyte, *The Street Corner Society* (Chicago: University of Chicago Press, 1962); and Oscar Lewis, *La Vida: A Puerto Rican Family in the Culture of Poverty* (New York: Random House, 1966).

4. Murray Melbin, *Night as Frontier: Colonizing the World After Dark* (New York: Free Press, 1987).

5. Robert and Helen Lynds, *Middletown* (New York: Harcourt, Brace, Jovanovich, 1929); Amos Hawley, *Human Ecology: A Theory of Community Structure* (New York: Ronald, 1950).

6. George Theodorson, *Urban Patterns: Studies in Human Ecology* (State College, PA: Penn State University Press, 1982), 5.

7. J. G. Millais, "The True Position of *Mus Rattus* and Its Allies," *Zoologist* (1905).

8. See Eugene V. Walter, *Placeways: A Theory of the Human Environment* (Chapel Hill: University of North Carolina Press, 1988), 48: "While the neolithic pioneers of agricultural life gathered the livestock they wanted to bind to their houses, uninvited beasts such as rats and mice followed the grain and domesticated themselves. They occupied the places constructed by humans in order to enjoy a regular food supply, and in those places they also found shelter from natural predators. Nature rewarded the drive that linked rodent fortunes with human destiny by giving rodents a security unknown in the wilderness."

9. Joseph Mitchell, *Up in the Old Hotel* (New York: Random House, 1993).

10. Pierre Huber, *Recherches sur le moeurs des fourmis indigènes* (Geneva, 1810); Sir J. Lubbock, *Ants, Bees, and Wasps* (London, 1882).

11. *Encyclopedia Britannica*.

12. David Levinson, ed., *Encyclopedia of Homelessness* (Berkshire Publishing Group, 2004).

13. R. Lindner, *The Reportage of Urban Culture* (New York: Cambridge University Press, 1996).

14. James Duncan, "Men Without Property: The Tramp's Classification and Use of Urban Space," in *Readings in Urban Analysis: Perspectives on Urban Form and Structure*, ed. Robert W. Lake (New York: Routledge, 1983).

4. MEN UNDERGROUND:
BERNARD, KAL, AND JASON

1. Yuval Harari, *Sapiens: A Brief History of Human Kind* (Toronto: McClelland and Stewart, 2014), 12: "Foods that humans cannot digest in their natural forms—such as wheat, rice and potatoes—became staples of our diet thanks to cooking. Fire not only changed food's chemistry, it changed its biology as well. Cooking kills germs and parasites that infested food. Humans also had a far easier time chewing and digesting old favorites such as fruits, nuts, insects and carrion if they were cooked."

2. In 1989–1990, I was a visiting scholar at the Russell Sage Foundation, and Robert Merton was resident scholar emeritus.

3. See figure A.1 in appendix A.

4. Paul Radin, *The Trickster: A Study in American Indian Mythology* (New York: Schocken, 1988); Lewis Hyde, *Trickster Makes This World: Mischief, Myth, and Art* (New York: North Point, 1999), 10.

5. WORKING LIFE

1. Bob Herbert, "In America: Bullying the Homeless," *New York Times*, November 29, 1999, http://www.nytimes.com/1999/11/29/opinion/in-america-bullying-the-homeless.html.

2. Jonathan P. Hicks, "Hillary Clinton Attacks Arrests of the Homeless," *New York Times*, December 1, 1999, http://www.nytimes.com/1999/12/01/nyregion/hillary-clinton-attacks-arrests-of-the-homeless.html.

3. Elisabeth Bumiller, "Mayor Defends Homeless Efforts as a Carefully Coordinated Plan," *New York Times*, December 9, 1999, http://www.nytimes.com/1999/12/09/nyregion/mayor-defends-homeless-efforts-as-a-carefully-coordinated-plan.html.

4. Eric Lipton, "Computers to Track 'Quality of Life' Crime, Giuliani Says," *New York Times*, November 15, 2000, http://www.nytimes.com /2000/11/15/nyregion/computers-to-track-quality-of-life-crime-giuliani -says.html.

5. James Duncan, "Men Without Property: The Tramp's Classification and Use of Urban Space," in *Readings in Urban Analysis* (New York: Routledge, 1983).

6. Personal communication with Brian Bartholomew, January 2021.

7. George James, "Beggar Hit by Cab, Giving Up Streets," *New York Times*, April 22, 1992.

8. In Milan, Italy, and Budapest, Hungary, children beg on buses and finer restaurants but are quickly ushered out. On buses, women grab their purses as soon as Roma children show up. The Roma are usually recognizable by their appearance: dark hair, women with long colorful dresses, and the men poorly dressed, with a head scarf.

9. Fernand Braudel, *The Structures of Everyday* (New York: Harper and Row, 1979), 75.

10. Terry Williams, *Harlem Supers: The Social Life of a Community in Transition* (New York: Palgrave-Macmillan, 2016).

6. FOOD: RESTAURANTS AND SOUP KITCHENS

1. See Coalition for the Homeless, https://www.coalitionforthehomeless .org/get-help/i-need-food-old/soup-kitchen-and-food-pantry-listings/, for a listing of soup kitchens in the city. Also see Food Bank NYC, https://www.foodbanknyc.org/get-help/.

2. William Difazio, *Ordinary Poverty: A Little Food and Cold Storage* (Philadelphia: Temple University Press, 2006), 84.

3. The Food Bank for New York City–Community Kitchens.

4. Terry Williams, *Harlem Supers: The Social Life of a Community in Transition* (New York: Palgrave-Macmillan, 2016).

7. WOMEN UNDERGROUND:
BEATRICE AND TIN CAN TINA

1. Elliot Liebow, *Tell Them Who I Am: The Lives of Homeless Women* (New York: Penguin, 1995).
2. Kai T. Erikson, *Everything in Its Path: Destruction of Community in the Buffalo Creek Flood* (New York: Simon and Schuster, 1976), 177.
3. Larry Hogue, "The Wild Man of 96th Street," *Daily News*, May 1993.

8. BEATRICE AND BOBO

1. Elliot Liebow, *Tell Them Who I Am: The Lives of Homeless Women* (New York: Penguin, 1995), 34, 35.
2. Peter Schrag, "The Forgotten American," *Harpers*, August 1969, 27–34.

11. REFLECTIONS ON LIFE UNDER
THE STREET

1. Joseph Campbell, *The Power of Myth* (New York: Doubleday, 1988).
2. Personal communication.

ENDNOTE

1. Terry Williams and William Kornblum, *The Uptown Kids: Struggle and Hope in the Projects* (New York: G. P. Putnam's Sons, 1994).
2. Michael B. Katz, *The Undeserving Poor* (New York: Pantheon, 1986).
3. Katz, *The Undeserving Poor*, 185–86, 139, 143, 172–73.
4. Kimberly A. Tyler, Barrett A. Lee, and James D. Wright, "The New Homelessness Revisited," *Annual Review of Sociology* 36 (2010): 501–21.
5. Mitchell Duneier, *Sidewalk* (New York: Farrar, Straus and Giroux, 1999), 115.
6. Coalition for the Homeless, *Undercounting the Homeless*, briefing paper, 2004.
7. Kim Hopper, "Counting the Homeless: S-Night in New York," *Evaluation Review* 16, no. 4 (1992): 367–77.
8. Coalition for the Homeless, *Undercounting the Homeless*, 15.

9. Tyler, Lee, and Wright, "The New Homelessness Revisited," 507.

10. Tyler, Lee, and Wright, "The New Homelessness Revisited," 507.

11. Tyler, Lee, and Wright, "The New Homelessness Revisited," 509.

12. Tyler, Lee, and Wright, "The New Homelessness Revisited," 507, 511.

13. Tyler, Lee, and Wright, "The New Homelessness Revisited," 514.

14. Peter Rossi, *Down and Out in America: The Origins of Homelessness* (Chicago: University of Chicago Press, 1989).

15. Peter Rossi, *Down and Out in America: The Origins of Homelessness* (Chicago: University of Chicago Press, 1989); Richard H. Ropers, *The Invisible Homeless: A New Urban Ecology,* (Edmonton, OK: InSight, 1988); G. Barak, *Gimme Shelter* (New York: Praeger, 1991); Crystal Nix, "Taking Account of the Hidden Homeless," *New York Times,* June 22, 1986, https://www.nytimes.com/1986/06/22/weekinreview/taking-ac count-of-the-hidden-homeless.html.

16. Rossi, *Down and Out in America,* 197; Sam Roberts, "What Led to Crackdown on Homeless," *New York Times,* November 28, 1991; M. Rosenbaum, *Women on Heroin* (New Brunswick, NJ: Rutgers University Press, 1981); L. Maher, "Punishment and Welfare: Crack Cocaine and the Regulation of Mothering," *Women and Criminal Justice* 3, no. 2 (1991): 35–70.

17. Ropers, *The Invisible Homeless;* Eloise Dunlap, "Impact of Drugs on Family Life and Kin Networks in the Inner-City African-American Single-Parent Household," in *Drugs, Crime, and Social Isolation: Barriers to Urban Opportunity,* ed. A. Harrell and G. Peterson (Washington, DC: Urban Institute Press, 1992), 181–207; Kim Hopper and Jill Hamberg, "The Making of America's Homeless: From Skid Row to New Poor, 1945–1984," in *Critical Perspective on Housing,* ed. R. Bratt, C. Hartman, and A. Meyerson (Philadelphia: Temple University Press, 1986).

18. Ropers, *The Invisible Homeless;* Nix, "Taking Account of the Hidden Homeless."

19. Rossi, *Down and Out in America;* Steven Vanderstaay, *Street Lives: An Oral History of Homeless Americans* (Gabriola Island, BC: New Society Publishing, 1992). Data for homeless families came from Coalition for the Homeless, https://www.coalitionforthehomeless.org/facts-about -homelessness/.

20. Vanderstaay, *Street Lives*, 59–60.

21. For example, during the Giuliani administration, in compliance with a law prohibiting "the use of hotels with more than one hundred units and without kitchens in each unit," the residents of a "non-compliant" facility, the Kennedy Inn in Jamaica, were moved to compliant hotels or shelters, yet not without protests. Some residents blocked traffic and even refused to move. The hotel was later transformed into a luxury hotel. Thomas J. Main, *Homelessness in New York City: Policy Making from Koch to de Blasio* (New York: New York University Press, 2016), 132.

22. Suzanne Keller, *Community* (Princeton, NJ: Princeton University Press, 2003); Roy F. Baumeister and Mark R. Leary, "The Need to Belong: Desire for Interpersonal Attachments as a Fundamental Human Motivation," *Psychological Bulletin* 117, no. 3 (1995): 497–529.

23. In the documentary *Dark Days*, one former underground dweller is quoted as saying, "That was the saddest part of my journey through life. You know what I'm saying? Those were dark days, real dark. But during the time, it didn't bother me at all. But once I sit down and think about it, I let myself down. How could I have done that? Let myself go like that? . . . You don't realize until you get out of it, and then, you know, you look back on it every now and then. I used to do that? That used to be me? No way." This can be contrasted with another man who, when it became clear that they were no longer welcome in the underground, defiantly declared, "Leave us alone!" Of course, it shouldn't be assumed that all unhoused people would see things this way.

24. Rick Bragg, "Fleeing the World Underneath," *New York Times*, March 28, 1994, http://www.nytimes.com/1994/03/28/nyregion/fleeing -the-world-underneath.html; John Tierney, "A Thanksgiving Feast, Under the Highway," *New York Times*, November 23, 1990, http://www .nytimes.com/1990/11/23/nyregion/a-thanksgiving-feast-under-the -highway.html.

25. John Tierney, "In Tunnel, 'Mole People' Fight to Save Home," *New York Times*, June 13, 1990, https://www.nytimes.com/1990/06/13 /nyregion/in-tunnel-mole-people-fight-to-save-home.html.

26. Gary Hustwit, dir., *Urbanized*, documentary, 2011.

APPENDIX E: LEGACIES OF HARM: POLICY AND POLICING

1. Loic Wacquant, *Prisons of Poverty* (Minneapolis: University of Minnesota Press, 2009), 2.
2. Wacquant, *Prisons of Poverty*, 15–16.
3. Thomas J. Main, *Homelessness in New York City: Policy Making from Koch to de Blasio* (New York: New York University Press, 2016), 106.
4. Main, *Homelessness in New York City*, 107.
5. Main, *Homelessness in New York City*, 107.
6. Main, *Homelessness in New York City*, 110.
7. Main, *Homelessness in New York City*, 110–11.
8. Main, *Homelessness in New York City*, 112.
9. Main, *Homelessness in New York City*, 113–15.
10. Main, *Homelessness in New York City*, 118.
11. Main, *Homelessness in New York City*, 127.
12. Main, *Homelessness in New York City*, 128.
13. Main, *Homelessness in New York City*, 136.
14. Main, *Homelessness in New York City*, 137.
15. Main, *Homelessness in New York City*, 138.
16. Celia W. Dugger, "New York Rivals Differ Strikingly on Dealing with City's Poorest," *New York Times*, October 2, 1993, http://www.nytimes.com/1993/10/02/nyregion/new-york-rivals-differ-strikingly-on-dealing-with-city-s-poorest.html.
17. Dugger, "New York Rivals Differ Strikingly on Dealing with City's Poorest."
18. Celia W. Dugger, "Police to Start New Program for Homeless," *New York Times*, August 18, 1994, http://www.nytimes.com/1994/08/18/nyregion/police-to-start-new-program-for-homeless.html.
19. Clifford Krauss, "Special Unit Ushers Homeless from Subways," *New York Times*, September 4, 1994, http://www.nytimes.com/1994/09/04/nyregion/special-unit-ushers-homeless-from-subways.html.
20. Carey Goldberg, "The Homeless Huddle at City's Margins," *New York Times*, November 12, 1995, http://www.nytimes.com/1995/11/12/us/the-homeless-huddle-at-city-s-margins.html.
21. Robin Pogrebin, "At the End of the Tunnel, a Home; Forced to Leave Shanties, Dwellers Try Out Life Above Ground," *New York Times*,

April 15, 1996, http://www.nytimes.com/1996/04/15/nyregion/end
-tunnel-home-forced-leave-shanties-dwellers-try-life-above-ground
.html.

22. Margaret Morton, "Homes for the Invisible," *New York Times*, October 7, 1995, http://www.nytimes.com/1995/10/07/opinion/homes-for
-the-invisible.html.

23. "Tunnel Dwellers Give Us No Easy Answers on Homelessness," *New
York Times*, October 13, 1995, http://www.nytimes.com/1995/10/13/opi
nion/l-tunnel-dwellers-give-us-no-easy-answers-on-homelessness
-421995.html.

24. Andy Newman, "Woman on Midtown Street Is Hit by Man with a
Brick: Critically Injured in an Afternoon Attack," *New York Times*,
November 17, 1999, http://www.nytimes.com/1999/11/17/nyregion
/woman-on-midtown-street-is-hit-by-man-with-a-brick.html.

25. Deborah Feyerick, "New York Mayor Reacts to Attack with Crackdown on Homeless," CNN, November 22, 1999, http://www.cnn.com
/US/9911/22/ny.homeless/.

26. Elizabeth Bumiller, "In Wake of Attack, Giuliani Cracks Down on
Homeless," *New York Times*, November 20, 1999, http://www.nytimes
.com/1999/11/20/nyregion/in-wake-of-attack-giuliani-cracks-down
-on-homeless.html.

27. Nina Bernstein, "A Homeless Man Challenges New York City Crackdowns," *New York Times*, November 22, 1999, http://www.nytimes.com
/1999/11/22/nyregion/a-homeless-man-challenges-new-york-city-crack
downs.html.

28. David Rhode, "Judge Upholds Policy on Arresting the Homeless Who
Sleep in Boxes," *New York Times*, December 29, 2000, http://www
.nytimes.com/2000/12/29/nyregion/judge-upholds-policy-on-arrest
ing-the-homeless-who-sleep-in-boxes.html.

29. Coalition for the Homeless, "New Yorkers Critical of Giuliani Homeless Policy," 1999, https://shnny.org/uploads/New_Yorkers_Critical
_of_Giuliani_Homeless_Policy.pdf.

30. Dan Barry, "Political Memo; In a Year of Acrimony, Giuliani Is
Defined by the Economy," *New York Times*, January 14, 1999, https://
www.nytimes.com/1999/01/14/nyregion/political-memo-in-a-year-of
-acrimony-giuliani-is-defined-by-the-economy.html.

31. Francis X. Clines, "Clinton Signs Bill Cutting Welfare; States in New Role," *New York Times*, August 23, 1996, http://www.nytimes.com/1996 /08/23/us/clinton-signs-bill-cutting-welfare-states-in-new-role.html.

32. Rachel L. Swarns, "The 1997 Elections: The Issues; 320000 Have Left Welfare, but Where Do They Go from Here?," *New York Times*, October 29, 1997, http://www.nytimes.com/1997/10/29/nyregion/1997-elec tions-issues-320000-have-left-welfare-but-where-they-go-here.html.

33. Coalitions for the Homeless, *Legacy of Neglect: The Impact of Welfare Reform on New York's Homeless*, August 1999, https://www.coalition forthehomeless.org/wp-content/uploads/2014/06/LegacyofNeglect -finalreport1999.pdf.

34. Nina Bernstein, "Homeless Shelters in New York Fill to Highest Level Since 80's," *New York Times*, February 8, 2001, http://www.nytimes .com/2001/02/08/nyregion/homeless-shelters-in-new-york-fill-to -highest-level-since-80-s.html.

INDEX

TreeNotes

TreeNotes
A YEAR IN THE
COMPANY OF TREES

Nalini Nadkarni

NATIONAL
GEOGRAPHIC

WASHINGTON, D.C.

Published by National Geographic Partners, LLC
1145 17th Street NW Washington, DC 20036

Text Copyright © 2025 University of Utah. Compilation Copyright © 2025 National Geographic Partners, LLC. All rights reserved. Reproduction of the whole or any part of the contents without written permission from the publisher is prohibited.

NATIONAL GEOGRAPHIC and Yellow Border Design are trademarks of the National Geographic Society, used under license.

Financially supported by the National Geographic Society.

"Bäume," from: Hermann Hesse, *Sämtliche Werke in 20 Bänden*. Edited by Volker Michels, Band 11: *Autobiographische Schriften 1.* © Suhrkamp Verlag Frankfurt am Main 2003. All rights reserved by and controlled through Suhrkamp Verlag AG, Berlin. Reprinted with kind permission of Suhrkamp Verlag Berlin.

Illustrations: Cover: (leaf border), devilkiddy/Adobe Stock; (tree), Ghen/Adobe Stock. 3, Ghen/Adobe Stock; 13 (Winter), Elena Medvedeva/Adobe Stock; 35 (Spring), nurofina/Adobe Stock; 57 (Summer), Salnikova Watercolor; 83 (Fall), Anna Nekotangerine/Adobe Stock; 107 (Winter), NightCreativity/Adobe Stock.

Since 1888, the National Geographic Society has funded more than 14,000 research, conservation, education, and storytelling projects around the world. National Geographic Partners distributes a portion of the funds it receives from your purchase to National Geographic Society to support programs including the conservation of animals and their habitats.

Get closer to National Geographic Explorers and photographers, and connect with our global community. Join us today at nationalgeographic.org/joinus

For rights or permissions inquiries, please contact National Geographic Books Subsidiary Rights: bookrights@natgeo.com

Interior design: Elisa Gibson

ISBN: 978-1-4262-2441-6

Printed in the United States of America
24/WOR/1

*To the eight wonderful maple trees
that grew in my front yard and
on which I climbed as a child,
and to the 3.1 trillion other remarkable trees
that now grow on our planet*

CONTENTS

introduction

On a brisk autumn day when I was nine years old, I saw that trees could dance. I had spent hours that afternoon in the crown of one of the eight maples that lined our driveway, watching leaves descend to the ground, each one free and suspended for a time, before arching to rest with its sisters.

After most of the leaves had fallen, the golds and reds made a long quilt of the driveway. Aloft, I watched squirrels jump from branch to branch and was envious of how easily they moved through the treetops. Where did they go when I couldn't see them? I dreamed up ways to attach a spool of red thread to their backs to track their movements—the world's first ever squirrel tracker. It was the earliest of the many questions that arose every time I climbed into a tree.

I wrote my first book in those branches: *Be Among the Birds: A Child's Guide to Tree Climbing,* 12 pages of stapled-together notebook paper. In my most careful penmanship accompanied by smudged pencil illustrations, I gave advice to other tree climbers in chapters titled "How to Cross Over Trunks on a Double-Trunked Tree" and "What to Wear to Avoid Skin-scrapes." I lost the single copy long ago.

From that treetop refuge, I took a solemn oath that when I was a grown-up, I would do something to cherish and protect trees, in thanks for the beauty and delight they gave me.

I suppose that those events are the roots of this book, *TreeNotes.* I've turned into a grown-up who has spent 40 years using science to understand and protect trees. Climbing trees on four continents to study canopy-dwelling plants and animals, I have documented the complex interactions of trees with birds, animals, microbes, the atmosphere, *and* people.

I've become increasingly aware of the challenges that trees now face as the planet warms and humans relentlessly reduce the size of primary forests along with the integrity of what remains of them. Over the arc of my scientific career, I have felt compelled to engage people of all kinds to instill the sense of forest protection that I developed among the limbs of my front yard maples.

One effort was to create a radio program that would remind people of the many ways tree lives touch human lives. I modeled it on the structure and tone of *BirdNote,* the radio program about birds created by the Seattle chapter of the National Audubon Society in partnership with the Tacoma public radio station. I approached my local public radio station, KUER, and happily, they agreed to produce and broadcast it. National Geographic has now turned two years of these broadcasts into the book you are reading.

The title, *TreeNotes,* signifies that this is not an exhaustive anthology of the ways people interact with trees. Just as the single note of a flute in an orchestra is a tiny part of the whole symphony, so each episode in this book is a modest indicator of the larger arena in which people and trees interact. Each episode could expand to a chapter, a volume, a compendium about its subject.

Many tree books describe arboreal extremes: the tree with the greatest height, girth, or volume; or the tree that grows at the southernmost or northernmost reaches of our planet; or the remote forests studied by intrepid explorers. In contrast, this book celebrates everyday trees and their relationships with everyday people who encounter them. It focuses on the often overlooked functions those trees provide: telephone poles, railroad track ties, orchestra conductors' batons, disposable chopsticks.

Writing this book has revealed to me not only the interconnectedness of trees and their associates but also the dendritic structure of our knowledge about trees. Each episode begins with the topic as a trunk and then branches into other arenas of arboreal and human life. For example, when I began writing about cinnamon, I became immersed in the limbs of other topics: the Silk Road and the spice trade in China, the biochemistry of bark, the evolutionary history of the avocado family of plants, recipes for gingersnaps.

My hope is that these *TreeNotes* will awaken in each reader a sense of appreciation for the multiple values that trees embody and the diverse ways that trees touch our lives. When you hear the sound of a cello, or encounter the fuzz on a peach, or open a bottle of wine with a stopper from a cork oak in Spain, or sit in the solacing shade of a cemetery tree, you'll think, "Ahhh! Trees!" And I imagine you'll be inspired to come up with *TreeNotes* of your own.

WINTER

JANUARY–MARCH

the body
language of trees

Cedar of Lebanon *(Cedrus libani)*; spruce *(Picea)*

I have a small white scar on my elbow. It's from a dog bite I
got on my newspaper route in seventh grade. I've long imagined throwing a "scar party," in which my guests take turns
describing the marks left on their bodies by events that might have
been otherwise forgotten.

So, what about trees—what of their history can we read from
their bodies?

On a recent walk through my local city park, I noticed an odd
branch on a small maple tree. It had started growing horizontally
but then took a sharp vertical turn. A raised circular collar of
scar tissue revealed that the branch above it had broken off. In
response, the lower branch grew upward instead of outward, a
record of an earlier injury.

Mountain trees strategically grow different types of wood that
resolve the stresses imposed by wind and heavy snow loads. A
spruce *(Picea)* tree grows "tension wood" on its trunk's uphill
side and wider-ringed "compression wood" on its lower side,

which creates a big-bellied trunk to let the tree straighten up and stand tall.

One tree that silently conveys its history is the 70-year-old cedar of Lebanon that stands at the east entrance to Temple Square in Salt Lake City, Utah. Years ago, the tree survived a potentially fatal blow when a chunk of ice fell from the temple's roof, completely shearing off the tree's top. Gardeners guided a lateral branch to grow vertically, leaving a distinct wiggle in its trunk.

Anytime you walk in your own city or forests, take a moment to appreciate the body language of trees. Without words, the arc of a branch or the slant of a trunk reveals that trees can survive damage and carry on living—their scars giving voice to their stories.

a birthday for trees

Almond *(Prunus dulcis)*; carob *(Ceratonia siliqua)*; date palm
(Phoenix dactylifera); olive *(Olea europaea)*; pomegranate *(Punica granatum)*

One of my favorite ways to honor trees is celebrating Tu BiShvat, the Jewish holiday that commemorates the "New Year for the Trees." In 2024, it began at sunset on January 24, the 15th day of the Hebrew month of Shevat.

The origins of Tu BiShvat lie with the people who were guided by the tenets decreed in the Torah, their holy book. The Book of Leviticus forbids Jews from eating fruit produced by trees during the first three years after the trees are planted. Fruit produced in the fourth year goes to the temple and the poor. After five years, tree owners can take the fruit for themselves. To get the accounting right, followers needed a date to mark time, like the beginning of a fiscal year, a sort of birthday for all trees.

In the 16th century, members of the mystical Jewish sect the Kabbalah instituted a feast of fruits as a ceremonial meal, or seder. Participants ate fruits associated with the land of Israel, which were described in the Book of Deuteronomy: figs, dates, raisins, pomegranates, olives, carob, and almonds.

Celebrants also drank four cups of wine, ranging from white to red, each color a symbol of a different season. They recited particular blessings, which they believed would bring human beings and the world closer to spiritual perfection.

In the 1970s, Tu BiShvat took on an ecological flavor and became the "Jewish Earth Day," with communities implementing actions related to environmental care. In many Jewish congregations today, Tu BiShvat is celebrated as a time to plant trees—in Israel and elsewhere. Many contribute money to the Jewish National Fund, an organization devoted to reforesting Israel.

For me, this holiday reveals the many different values and ways of understanding trees. It started as a way to account for the economic value of trees. Then it manifested symbolic links to Jewish spirituality. And now it's both an opportunity to celebrate the many benefits that we receive from trees and an inspiration to return those gifts.

petrified wood

Ginkgo *(Ginkgo biloba)*; Norfolk pine *(Araucaria heterophylla)*

O n a recent camping trip in Nevada, I visited a display of petrified wood. A tall chain-link fence surrounded the logs—as if they were in prison—to protect them from people who might grab pieces as souvenirs.

What makes these logs so special? Petrified wood is a very particular type of fossilized wood. Those logs are more than 200 million years old but, amazingly, still retain the same shape and structure as when they were alive. Biologically, the original trees are related to our current-day ginkgoes and Norfolk pine trees.

The process of trees turning to stone started pretty simply: Water washed logs into ancient river systems, burying them so deeply that oxygen was cut off. Then, bacteria and fungi—which need oxygen—couldn't decompose them. Instead, water, containing all kinds of dissolved minerals, flowed through the porous wood, replacing every single cell of organic material with crystals.

Petrified forests can be found all around the world, including in

Petrified Forest National Park in Arizona, Curio Bay in southern New Zealand, and Xinjiang Province in China.

One reason petrified wood must be protected is because of its beauty. Each piece is a giant sparkly quartz crystal, with a rainbow of colors produced by embedded minerals: Cobalt creates greens, iron oxides create reds, and manganese makes pinks and oranges.

So, trees can turn into rocks. Can rocks turn into trees? Yes! Trees get their nutrients, water, and support from soil, which is originally derived from rock.

The dynamic process of soil formation happens through the slow but unstoppable forces of physical, chemical, and biotic weathering. When moisture seeps into cracks and then freezes and expands, it literally busts the rocks apart. And when water combines with carbon dioxide, either from the air or in the soil, that reaction creates carbonic acid, which can chemically dissolve rocks.

So, trees can turn into rocks, and rocks can turn into trees, if we give them enough time.

But rock time and tree time pass in different scales. As poet Bill Yake once said to me, rocks see trees as "just passing through."

drumsticks

Birch *(Betula)*; hickory *(Carya)*; maple *(Acer)*;
oak *(Quercus)*; rosewood *(Dalbergia)*

My favorite Beatle is Ringo. As a tree lover, I've long wondered which wood this famous drummer chose for his drumsticks, and what other trees percussionists use.

Although some drumsticks are made of metal or resin, the majority of them are turned from a single piece of wood. Most come from three tree species: maple, hickory, and oak. Some specialized sticks are made of birch or rosewood.

Maple is 10 percent lighter than hickory, so the drummer can play a bit faster, but the sticks wear out more quickly. Hickory is a harder, more durable wood and, since it is more resilient, hickory drumsticks can absorb the shock of a hard-hitting drummer. Oak is the heaviest wood option and can withstand more intense playing styles.

Aluminum and polyurethane sticks are extremely durable, but wood absorbs vibrations and is more flexible, so most drummers—including Ringo—prefer the "feel" of wood.

Drumsticks are lacquered to seal the wood, stabilize the moisture content, and give the sticks a grabby feel. And that's another tie-in to trees, because one of the ingredients for lacquer, nitrocellulose, is a by-product of manufacturing paper from wood pulp.

But back to Ringo. The musical instrument manufacturer Avedis Zildjian Company has collaborated with Ringo Starr to create a drumstick made of hickory wood lacquered with a vibrant purple color. It's imprinted with Ringo's signature and his trademark star.

brazil: the tree that named a nation

Brazilwood *(Paubrasilia echinata)*

When Portuguese explorers landed in South America in the early 1500s, they encountered a tree with red-colored sap. It was similar to a tree native to Asia whose sap was used to dye luxury garments in Europe. Because the cost of importing the sap from India was much higher, the South American source quickly became a valuable trading commodity.

The value of its deep red wood was already known to the people native to those forests. The colonizing merchants named the tree *pau brasil—pau* means "wood" and *brasil,* "a glowing red charcoal ember." It inspired the name Land of Brazil.

Pernambuco is the common name for this orange-red wood. Its interlocked grain gives it fine texture, remarkable elasticity, and a lovely natural luster. For centuries, those properties made it the top choice for making violin and cello bows. But global demand for the tree—first for dye and then for making music—has pushed the species to near extinction.

However, demand from musicians is only a tiny part of the problem. The real issue is the rampant conversion of its habitat for farming and human development. The tree can thrive only in Brazil's Atlantic Forest, which has shrunk to just 5 percent of its original area. In 2007, the International Union for Conservation of Nature (IUCN) listed brazilwood as an endangered species.

Still, hope remains. Music lovers and conservationists have collaborated to create a group called Trees of Music that empowers farmers to regenerate these trees and their ecosystem and advocates using alternative woods and carbon fiber for musicmaking.

Today, Brazil is well known for its vast rainforests and the music-loving people who live there. Little did those Portuguese colonizers know when they named this nation how appropriate that name would be.

the mysteries
of pykrete

I think of sawdust as a by-product of woodworking, kind of a
nuisance that I have to sweep up and dispose of after a session in the woodshop.

There's lots of it! At the industrial level, about 10 percent of the
logs processed in U.S. lumber mills end up as sawdust—three million tons (2.7 million metric tons) every year. We use this sawdust
to make particleboard, to generate warmth as woodstove pellets,
and even as an ingredient in cat litter.

But to me, the most intriguing use of sawdust is pykrete. This
concrete-like material is made of 15 percent sawdust and 85 percent water and frozen into sheets. It is much stronger, is less brittle, and has a slower melting rate than real ice. It also floats on
water and can be molded into any shape.

Pykrete was developed during World War II, when steel for war-
ships was in short supply. Geoffrey Pyke, an engineer who advised
the Royal Navy of the United Kingdom, proposed it to make huge,
unsinkable aircraft carriers.

He argued that if the military could make a pykrete hull thick enough, torpedo damage would have no effect. They could build mile-long floating islands, adding refrigeration coils to keep them from melting. And they could repair any damage with water. Well, this didn't happen, but they did build one small test ship before the war ended.

Pykrete remains an unexploited curiosity. Occasionally, architects submit pykrete designs for gigantic offshore construction projects. But the material has proved unreliable, as it tends to sag under its own weight at temperatures above 40°F (4.4°C).

So, although the world has plenty of sawdust, finding novel ways to use it continues to elude us.

arborsculpture

American sycamore *(Platanus americanus)*; poplar *(Populus)*; willow *(Salix)*

We've all seen beautiful pieces of wood crafted by sculptors into artistic shapes. But have you ever heard of arborsculpture?

Artists of this remarkable practice shape living trees into intricate forms by grafting different parts of trees together. The subset of trees that self-graft—what botanists call "inosculate" trees—includes fruit trees, sycamores, poplars, and willows. They don't need much human help to create dramatic loops, ladders, diamonds, and knots.

You've observed inosculate species when you've seen a tree with two separate branches fused together. How does self-grafting work? When branches of a single tree or neighboring inosculate trees are placed together, their rubbing wears off the outer bark, which allows the inner layer of their trunks, called the cambium, to join. Over time, these trees' vascular systems intermingle and get covered in new bark, thus creating a living connection.

The grand master of arborsculpture was Axel Erlandson. Born

in 1884, he observed a natural graft between two sycamore trees in a city park, inspiring him to shape trees—first as a hobby and then as a passion and livelihood. He sculpted 70 trees in his own backyard in Santa Clara, California, which became known as the Tree Circus. It opened for paying visitors in 1947 and went on intriguing guests for more than 40 years. After Erlandson's death, the trees were replanted into the Gilroy Gardens Family Theme Park in Central California, marketed as the place "Where Fun Grows on Trees."

But anyone with time, patience, and a few saplings of inosculate trees can create arborsculpture. A how-to book called *How to Grow a Chair* by Richard Reames and Barbara Delbol teaches the fundamentals of this art form. It will take you a few years, but just imagine sitting on your arborsculpture chair of an afternoon, watching the clouds, as your own living tree sculpture grows around you.

termites

I recently visited some friends who built a lovely wooden home at the edge of a forest glade. But instead of inviting me in for a cup of tea, they enlisted me to help move every stick of furniture to the shed outside their house.

The reason for this strange request was the discovery of piles of wood shavings at the base of each wooden beam of their house. Termites. They had to fumigate without delay. A colony of termite workers can consume more than 11 pounds (5 kg) of wood a month.

A termite colony starts with a pair of winged termites, a male and a queen, known as alates, who set off on their nuptial flight. When they find a good nesting spot, they shed their wings. The queen lays eggs, which hatch into nymphs, who then divide into workers, soldiers, or reproductive termites.

The growing colony needs wood to eat—and lots of it. But how do termites, or any insects, manage to consume wood? Cellulose, which gives wood its durable structure, is extremely difficult to break down, and termites themselves don't have the capacity to do so.

They can live off cellulose only because they harbor protozoa in their stomachs. Those microorganisms produce an enzyme that breaks down cellulose into sugars that the termites can digest. And the termite gut provides the microbes with a stable environment.

But termites aren't all bad for forests. Termites prefer wood that is already starting to decay, so their actions enhance the cycling of nutrients, helping to keep forests productive and healthy.

Thankfully, my friends were able to save their house before the termites consumed it. And that interaction reminded us that trees—living in the forest or serving as our shelter—foster complex interactions at multiple levels, whether they be human, termite, or microscopic.

trees and trains

Douglas fir *(Pseudotsuga menziesii)*; hemlock *(Tsuga heterophylla)*;
hickory *(Carya)*; maple *(Acer)*; oak *(Quercus)*

I recently took the train from Salt Lake City, Utah, to Sacramento, California, my first such experience in decades. Each mile, my train passed more than 3,000 railroad ties, nearly all of them made from trees.

Railroad ties, or crossties, are a critical component of railway tracks. They transfer the tremendous weight of cars and cargo to the crushed-gravel bed (known as a track ballast) that underlies the rails and helps maintain the correct distance between the tracks (called the gauge).

In the 1830s, the first railroads were secured onto stone blocks. But as locomotives became heavier, wooden railroad ties were introduced. Workers hand-cut rough ties from trees with cross saws and broadaxes, jobs that were replaced by sawmills in the 1940s. Today, crossties have a uniform size and thickness: 10 inches (25 cm) thick and 10 feet (3 m) long.

Nationwide, freight trains now move nearly two billion tons (1.8 billion metric tons) of goods across an astounding 450 million railroad ties. Nearly all of them are made from wood—less than 2 percent are made of steel or concrete.

Ties from trees persist because wood is strong, flexible, and renewable, and it doesn't conduct electricity or interfere with electronic rail monitoring. But because wood is subject to decay, crossties must be treated with liquid wood preservatives, like creosote, a type of coal tar. Treated crossties can last for more than 30 years.

If a rail company chooses ties made from deciduous trees—such as oak, maple, or hickory—the liquid preservative can easily permeate throughout the wood because of the open-ended cells that transport water within deciduous trees.

If the company goes for ties made from conifer trees—such as Douglas fir or hemlock—they'll be less expensive and lighter weight but less absorptive of the preservative, since their transport cells have closed ends that allow for one-way transfer of liquids.

On my recent railroad voyage, I encountered members of the Railroad Tie Association, who are as enthusiastic about railroad ties as I am about trees. That organization was founded in 1919 to promote the sound use of wood crossties. Their annual meeting takes place each October. I think I might attend. And I'll take the train there, counting those wooden ties as I go.

SPRING

APRIL–MAY

to every tree
a purpose

Chestnut *(Castanea);* cocobolo *(Dalbergia retusa);*
ebony *(Diospyros);* hickory *(Carya);* lignum vitae *(Guaiacum officinale);*
trembling aspen *(Populus tremuloides)*

When you're contemplating a remodel of your house, or trying to decide which cutting board to buy, how do you know which wood is best?

I suggest turning to the wood hardness scale. Created in 1906 by Austrian scientist Gabriel Janka, this rating indicates hardness by measuring how much force is needed to push a small steel ball exactly halfway into a piece of wood.

The more force required, the higher the number, and the more resistant the wood is to denting and wear. For example, hickory has a Janka rating of 1,820, while chestnut has a rating of only 540. So, hickory is the more resistant wood and is a better flooring choice for, say, your kitchen, which gets heavy foot use.

But if you want to add warmth and style to your bedroom, where the issue of wear is not as important, then chestnut is a good option.

Among the hardest woods in the world are lignum vitae, ebony, and cocobolo, with Janka scores of more than 3,000. The trembling aspen, one of the most common trees in the western United

States, has a hardness of only 380, so it's not much used for construction. But it is useful for traditional medicines, animal bedding, snow fences, and matches.

But remember: The Janka score is simply another way to evaluate wood, so don't think that just because a wood has a higher score that it's superior to those with lower numbers. It all comes down to what you are using the wood for. Hard or soft, every tree has a different role—not unlike the rest of us.

trees and towers

Strangler fig (*Ficus tuerckheimii*)

I just returned from a field trip in Costa Rica. For decades, I've oriented myself in my study plots there by sighting on a group of emergent strangler fig trees that I call the "Four Sisters," so named because they seem to lean toward one another, just as my sisters and I do.

But last year, that family of four was reduced to just three. Construction of a hotel killed one of them, and in its place, a cell phone tower now stands. I still take my spatial bearings by it, but I miss the beauty of that magnificent tree crown.

Our brave new world of internet communication has created a sort of counterpart to this story. On a trek to Big Mountain, a popular hiking spot in Utah's Wasatch Mountains, I spied what seemed to be an odd-looking tree, one that stretched far higher than the surrounding forest. Perfectly straight, stubby branches with spiky foliage poked out at precise horizontal angles from its trunk.

It was actually a cell phone tower that had been disguised as a conifer tree to blend in with the habitat. If you were driving by, you might be fooled, but anyone walking by would instantly spot it as a fake.

Cell towers disguised as trees are increasingly common, especially in cities and suburbs, where residents demand fast cell service but don't want unsightly cell towers in the places they live and work.

Camouflaged cell towers originated with companies that built artificial landscapes for theme parks. Since the 1990s, tens of thousands of disguised cellular transmission sites have sprouted up around the country.

Many people prefer these fake trees over those metal monopoles topped with tangles of cables. In fact, city officials are willing to spend twice as much money to camouflage the regular cell towers in our landscapes.

The spread of these stealth towers presents philosophical questions about the use—or exploitation—of nature in our lives. I'm not sure how I'd feel if that tower in Costa Rica had been disguised as the beloved "fourth sister" fig tree it replaced.

It's these conundrums that make us think deeply about the complex relationships that continue to shift between people and trees.

tree pollen:
the perfect clue

Y ou've heard of counting tree rings: one ring for every year of the tree's life. Count up the rings and you know how old the tree is.

But if you want to understand the long-term history of a whole forest, you'll need the help of a palynologist, a scientific detective who uses tiny pollen grains as clues to help reconstruct a forest's history over thousands or even millions of years.

Pollen is the perfect clue for two reasons. First, it's basically the fingerprint of a species. At the microscopic level, every grain of pollen has a unique and identifiable structure.

Second, pollen stays true to its original shape over millennia because its shell is made of a highly resistant compound called exine. When trees release their pollen, the grains drift through the air, settle on the surfaces of nearby lakes, and sink to the bottom. Over centuries, those grains of pollen become covered with sediments.

To get samples of this ancient pollen, palynologists plunge metal augers into lake bottoms and extract the sediment containing the preserved grains. Then, they freeze and slice these sediment cores into very thin sections, counting up each species' individual pollen grains under a microscope.

That creates a picture—called a pollen diagram—of the communities of plants that once grew in the vicinity of that lake. And by knowing the environments of where those plants grow now, these pollen detectives can infer what the climate conditions were in that place long ago.

What can pollen records tell us about our own environments? For my state, Utah, we consider the Great Salt Lake as one huge body of intermixed water and minerals. But pollen diagrams suggest that starting one million years ago, the North Basin and South Basin differed substantially in their water cycles, their chemical properties, and the crustacean communities they supported. In the Pacific Northwest, pollen diagrams have revealed striking changes in vegetation since the retreat of continental glaciers, shifting from tundra parklands to the current mix of tall conifers, hardwoods, and herbs, all happening over the course of just 15 generations of trees.

So, the next time you sweep pollen off your car or deck, consider that it's actually a tiny package that can hold big answers.

how trees
breathe

Birch *(Betula)*; cherry *(Prunus avium)*

W hat's the first thing you do when you get into your car after it's been sitting in the hot sun all day? Open the windows! Well, trees also need windows in their trunks and branches to let air circulate.

If you're thinking "Wait! I learned in botany class that the exchange of gases occurs in the leaves of trees, not the bark," you are correct. Leaves have tiny holes in their surfaces—called stomata, or "little mouths"—that open and close to let tree leaves draw in carbon dioxide and release oxygen for photosynthesis.

But trees also respire, just as we do, pulling in oxygen and releasing carbon dioxide. And respiration occurs in the cells of all living tree tissues, not just the leaves.

So how can this exchange take place in the parts of trees that aren't leaves, like trunks and branches, tissues that don't have stomata? It's a puzzle, because tree bark is the first line of protection for a tree. It acts as an impermeable layer that prevents insects and diseases from getting to a tree's interior structures.

Think of the trunk of a cherry tree, with its narrow lines etched into the bark. Those lines—called lenticels, or "little windows"—are actually portals in the bark that let the tree breathe. These lens-shaped slits in the bark allow gases to pass between living cells on the inside and the air outside.

Botanists also use the shape of lenticels to identify trees. Some trees, like cherry and birch, have prominent lenticels, but most are invisible to the human eye. Even if you can't see them, they're there, helping trees survive through even the hottest days they encounter.

tree
architecture

The diversity of tree species in tropical forests is mind-boggling. Costa Rica alone hosts nearly 2,000 types of trees! A perennial challenge for tropical biologists like me is learning how to identify the tree species we study.

Traditional plant taxonomy—the science of categorizing and naming living botanical things—is based on a classification system that uses the shape and color of trees' flowers, fruits, and leaves to give each species a unique two-word Latin name.

But often, trees don't have accessible flowers, fruits, or leaves. One classification alternative is the approach of tree architecture.

This concept was developed in the 1970s by a trio of botanists who recognized that tropical trees, like buildings, have distinctive forms.

These botanists grew a variety of trees from seeds and then categorized the trees from aspects of growth. Do limbs grow from the base or throughout the trunk? Is growth continuous or seasonal? And so on. Then they narrowed these tree forms to just

23 "architectural models" and labeled each one after a famous botanist—naming the first three models after themselves.

The system was wildly attractive because it simplified the huge diversity of tropical forests. But its application is limited, since trees conform to this model for only a short time. As trees grow, their shapes change because of external factors like shade and wind. So today, botanists don't rely on tree architecture as a way to classify trees. But it has advanced our theoretical understanding of trees, especially how trees repair themselves after damage.

On your next walk, look at the structures of the trees you pass. You probably won't classify them by their form, but it's another way to see and appreciate trees.

what about telephone poles?

Douglas fir *(Pseudotsuga menziesii)*; loblolly pine *(Pinus taeda)*

O ur country has more than 150 million telephone poles—
that's almost half a pole for every person!

Although we don't much notice them under normal
conditions, windstorms wake us up to the importance of the poles
that support telephone and power lines. After Hurricane Katrina,
New Orleans needed 72,000 pole replacements from around the
country.

That kind of spike in demand makes pole growing a complex
business. Pole tree plantations, which grow loblolly pines and
Douglas firs, must be thinned and pruned to create trees that are
at least 60 feet (18 m) tall and free of knots.

As smart grids and underground power lines become more prev-
alent, I wonder: How much longer will we be using traditional
wooden poles? Well, don't expect to see them disappear anytime
soon. Wooden poles are more affordable, are easier to transport,
and need less energy to manufacture than steel or concrete poles.
They're also nonconductive, which makes them safer for utility

workers. Plus wooden poles store carbon, a small but real contribution to mitigate climate change.

And many birds use these structures! Swallows, crows, ospreys, and mourning doves all roost on poles. In the wide-open spaces of the West, many raptors hang out on the wires for an uninterrupted view of the prey that scuttles below.

But perching on these wires does carry risks. Power lines electrocute tens to hundreds of thousands of birds annually. Many power companies have taken measures to mitigate these dangers, such as insulating existing wires and adding fiberglass perch guards on transformer poles.

Electrical and telephone poles are so ubiquitous in our landscape that we hardly even see them. But each one started its life as a seedling and ended up providing us with a more connected world.

the tree of life

Baobab *(Adansonia digitata)*

The baobab tree has many intriguing nicknames: the camel tree, the bottle tree, the upside-down tree, and the Tree of Life.

These trees grow in dry areas of mainland Africa, Madagascar, and Australia. Their branches are skinny and few, and their trunks are disproportionately wide for their height. The record circumference of a baobab is 150 feet (45.7 m)—almost the width of a football field!

Although these trees produce only faint growth rings, we know that baobabs live amazingly long lives. Carbon dating has determined that the oldest baobab is more than 2,500 years old.

Local people call the baobab the Tree of Life because they have so many uses for it: eating its iron-rich leaves, drinking a coffee substitute produced from its seeds, and making beer and juice from the pulp of its large fruits, which have six times more vitamin C than oranges. And the ideal spot for markets in many rural villages? The shade of the baobab's crown.

A single baobab can store more than 1,000 gallons (3,785 L) of water, which helps keep soil humid and stable. During droughts, elephants consume the juicy wood beneath the bark of the baobab.

I first read about baobabs as a child, in Antoine de Saint-Exupéry's classic book *The Little Prince*. The young prince roots out baobabs as seedlings to prevent them from taking over his tiny planet, a metaphor that instructs us to take action against destructive forces as early as possible to avoid terrible consequences.

It's appropriate advice for us today, considering that we've lost nine of Africa's 13 oldest baobab trees to increasing drought brought on by climate change.

The baobab tree has earned each of its nicknames, but the one I love the most is the Tree of Life. My hope is that we heed the Little Prince's advice and act now to allow the skinny limbs of the amazing Tree of Life to continue reaching upward.

little apples
of death

Black walnut *(Juglans nigra)*; manchineel *(Hippomane mancinella)*

I 've often been called a tree hugger. But I know that getting anywhere near (let alone hugging) the poisonous manchineel tree is a very bad idea.

This tall, handsome tree grows in sandy soils along the coastlines of the Caribbean and South America, but it literally oozes toxic chemicals from all of its parts.

And I do mean all: Its fruit, *manzanillas de la muerte,* or "little apples of death," has a deceptively sweet flavor. But after one bite, you'll notice a weird peppery taste, which then turns into a burning, painful tightness in your throat. Contact with the sap can cause your skin to blister. And smoke from burning manchineel wood can cause temporary blindness.

The poisonous nature of this tree seems counter to the principles of evolution. Most trees have evolved fruits to attract animals to spread their seeds to places that are safe for germination. But this tree's toxicity means that typical dispersers—birds and mammals—completely avoid it. Instead, these seashore-dwelling trees drop their fruit into the water, and the tides and currents of the ocean disperse the seeds to successfully colonize new places.

What about trees that are toxic to other plants? Some trees, like black walnuts, exhibit allelopathy, a sort of chemical warfare among plants in which one plant releases chemicals that suppress the germination or growth of other plants. These compounds move into the soil from decomposing leaves or roots, which stunts or kills the neighboring plants, leaving more nutrients, water, and sunlight available for the plant aggressor.

But some poisonous trees have positive properties. People use the wood of the manchineel tree to make furniture, felling the trees while wearing gloves and long sleeves to avoid skin blisters. And these trees act as natural windbreaks, countering the forces of beach erosion, which is critical in the face of rising sea levels. Indigenous groups have also used manchineel fruits as a diuretic.

So, although there are a few trees that cause harm, even the most toxic of them have redeeming uses.

how many kinds of trees are there?

O nce, on a road trip, I counted the number of different types of cars that whizzed by, responding to that human urge to tally the diversity around us.

I came up with 42 models, a tiny fraction of the many cars manufactured over the years.

As a tree lover, of course I wondered: How many different types of trees are there? A recent scientific paper—co-authored by 143 scientists from 62 countries—gave me the answer.

Based on an exhaustive inventory of five million trees in 100,000 forest plots, their estimate was more than 73,000 tree species. And that's just the number of species living today. It doesn't include those that have gone extinct since trees evolved 380 million years ago.

Not surprisingly, tree diversity is highest in the tropics, where life has evolved without the glacial interruptions that polar and temperate regions have experienced over geologic time. And South America is the champion continent for tree diversity, hosting a whopping 43 percent of the world's estimated tree species.

Based on their statistical analyses, the authors also suggested that there are another 9,000 species yet to be discovered, many of which they predict will be extremely rare, and thus vulnerable to human changes in land use and climate.

Why did these 143 scientists invest years in tallying tree species? From the standpoint of conservation, we need to know what currently exists before we can figure out how to protect species that might have value for us in the future. Think about automobile dealers. They need accurate inventories of their cars to avoid running out of the models their customers want. In the same way, this tree species inventory serves as a critical step to guide the protection of trees and the resources they provide for animals, plants, water, air, soil—and people.

SUMMER

JUNE–AUGUST

the old old oak

White oak *(Quercus alba)*

I n the summer of 2023, I was saddened to receive a newspaper clipping from my younger brother.

The brief report announced the removal of the Linden Oak that lived in the neighborhood where I grew up, just outside Washington, D.C. The 300-year-old white oak tree had been in declining health for several years, forcing Montgomery County, Maryland, arborists to schedule its removal.

It was a special tree for me. Every Saturday morning during my middle school summers, my two older sisters and I would walk down Grosvenor Lane to catch the T6 bus to our weekly piano lessons. We would wait at the bus stop beneath the tree. I was grateful for the shade it cast during those hot, muggy afternoons. Even more, I treasured the sense of peace and stillness I felt beneath it.

At the time, I never even imagined that one day, it would die. But there it was in the newspaper, the soon-to-be demise of that giant, silent friend of mine. The article noted that the oak's trunk would be left in place as a memorial, with a plaque that commemorated its status as a 1976 Bicentennial Tree.

Do you have a tree that holds a sense of history and of place for you? If you do, you'll understand that stumps and plaques can't replace the meaning and presence of a special living tree.

What does comfort me, though, is the knowledge that an individual oak tree can produce about 10,000 acorns every year. So, over its long lifetime, that big Linden Oak produced about three million acorns. My hope is that at least one of those seeds will germinate, sprout, and flourish, to provide shade—and a sense of stillness—for my great-great-grandchildren, just as it did for me.

tiny utensil, big impact

Birch *(Betula)*; poplar *(Populus)*; spruce *(Picea)*

Take a look at the packet of disposable chopsticks you get with your next order of sushi—you know, the snap-apart kind, tucked in a paper sleeve. These throwaway chopsticks are clean and convenient, but they contribute to a bento box of environmental problems.

Chopsticks originated in China nearly 5,000 years ago. In Japan, jade and ivory chopsticks were originally used only for religious ceremonies. Chopsticks made of chestnut wood and persimmon wood were said to bring wealth and long life.

But in the late 1800s, as chopsticks became more common, the Japanese started using disposable utensils made of bamboo and wood, called *wari-bashi*. Today, nearly 80 billion pairs of disposable chopsticks are produced each year (about 10 pairs for every person in the world), costing the planet an estimated 10 to 20 million trees a year.

Some disposable chopsticks are made from quick-growing bamboo, but nearly half come from the wood of birch, poplar, and spruce trees. Because domestic wood in Japan is protected by financial incentives, 90 percent of the wood for the country's chopsticks comes from Southeast Asia, Canada, and the United States.

The wood used for disposable chopsticks is bleached and treated with chemicals like hydrogen peroxide and sulfur, making the chopsticks nonbiodegradable, so that millions of them end up in landfills when they're discarded.

I'm happy that we're now exploring innovative alternatives to this throwaway situation. Wood fibers from chopsticks are being added to biodegradable plastics and used to produce sustainable battery electrodes. And the Chinese government has imposed new taxes on disposable chopsticks to protect the environment. But we're still a long way from sustainably dealing with both the production and waste from these single-use utensils.

So, next time you go out for sushi, think about embracing the idea of BYOC—bring your own chopsticks—allowing more trees to live longer.

the space
between trees

When we describe trees, we generally focus on their solid place within a landscape. For an exact description, we measure the size and shapes of their trunks, their foliage, and their flowers.

But one forest researcher, Roman Dial, studies the negative space of the forest by literally measuring the forest parts that are not occupied.

Dial first shoots a horizontal line over two tree canopies with a crossbow and ties vertical ropes at intervals along that line. Then, hanging from a harness on each of those ropes, he uses a laser range finder to measure the distance between his eye and the nearest solid object, like a branch, a leaf, or a trunk, at eight compass directions around him.

He calculates the volume and shape of the air space around him and then creates images that look like giant asymmetrical vases placed among the solid trees. Those images help us understand how a bird or grain of pollen or even a molecule of air would "see" and navigate its way through the forest interstices.

His work has also shed light on the evolution of forest-dwelling animals. Scientists have wondered why rainforests in South America support many species of canopy-dwelling mammals, like opossums and sloths, which can hang from branches with prehensile tails or claws. But very few mammals in those forests have evolved to glide from tree to tree.

In contrast, rainforests in Asia have almost no hanging animals. But those habitats support many species of gliding mammals, along with snakes, lizards, and frogs. Being able to glide from one treetop to another lets an animal move more quickly in search of food or in flight. Dial's images document that there are far larger volumes of air space between trees in Asian forests than in South American forests.

Measuring the air space between trees provides insights about many subtle aspects of forests, helping us think about how pollen grains, birds, and gliding lizards navigate the complex three-dimensional spaces of forests.

tree houses

Elm *(Ulmus)*

When I was a kid, my father built a magnificent tree house, 60 feet (18 m) high, in the air space between two elm trees in our backyard.

Its platform was only half the size of our one-car garage—but it seemed not a cubit smaller than Noah's ark. We installed a pulley system to haul up snacks and flashlights for our treetop sleepovers. Up there, the world was ours. It was our ark.

Today, tree houses are no longer just for kids—they've popped up all over the world, as romantic getaways for adventurous couples and as "rooms with a view" for those seeking seclusion and reflection.

They're far more sophisticated than my dad's tree fort. Some come with king-size beds, air conditioners, refrigerators, and ironing boards—sometimes even a hot tub to unwind under the stars.

Bookstores and websites offer manuals on how to build tree houses. Each structure must be tailored to the unique architecture of its supporting tree, with knowledge and respect for the biology of the tree. Placing bolts into the tree's cambium can introduce disease, and constrictions around a trunk must allow for movement and growth.

If you don't want to build one, you can make reservations at tree house hotels around the world and cozy up in these arboreal resorts for a night of good dreams in the treetops.

My own childhood memories and the rising popularity of tree houses tell me that they fulfill our dual desires for shelter and adventure. As Peter Nelson, a master tree house builder and author of *Treehouses: The Art and Craft of Living Out on a Limb,* once said, "If we can't fly with the birds, at least we can nest with them."

trees and
lightning

E nvision a bolt from the sky striking a single tall tree in an open field.

That electric charge travels through the layer of moist sap just beneath the bark, heating and expanding as it goes and then blasting off the bark and killing the tree.

That's what lightning can do to just one tree. But what about a whole forest?

Over the past two decades, a team of researchers in Panama monitored the number of lightning strikes at their research site. They then estimated that tropical forests around the globe experience more than 60 million strikes each year, which can kill up to 40 percent of the largest trees in those forests.

Obviously, the tallest trees are the most directly vulnerable. But these researchers discovered another mortality factor—the presence of woody vines, or lianas. These plants germinate in the forest floor soil and then grow into the tree canopy, using understory stems for support. Researchers found that the greater the density of lianas, the larger the number of small trees that lightning damaged or killed.

With their long stems filled with water, lianas act as superconductors for electricity. They physically connect canopy trees to the forest understory, like jumper cables between cars, delivering deadly electrical currents from tall trees to the small trees that would otherwise be unaffected by a lightning strike. The death of those smaller trees and saplings can ultimately change the future composition of the whole forest.

As their research deepens, these scientists better understand the complex interconnections among trees, knowledge that comes not as a bolt of lightning but through careful observations over time.

peach fuzz

Peach tree *(Prunus persica)*

Peach season is here! A first bite into one of those luscious orange globes is a high point of our tree harvests.

But there can be one small problem when eating a peach: The fine hair on peach skin can be irritating to some of us. Actually, that might be exactly the point of it.

Biologists have speculated that peaches have evolved those fuzzy hairs—called indumenta—to create a physical barrier that prevents flies and other pests from laying eggs in their flesh.

Is this true? In 2014, four researchers at the University of California, Berkeley, carried out a lab experiment to test that idea. They presented populations of the spotted wing fly, an economic pest of fruit crops, with peaches that had three different fruit surfaces: peaches with natural fuzz, peaches from which the fuzz had been shaved off with a wet tissue and a razor, and peaches that had already been damaged by other insects.

Then they counted the number of eggs laid on each substrate. They found that flies did not lay eggs in the fuzzy fruits. But they readily laid eggs in the peaches without fuzz and the peaches with insect damage. This suggests that peach fuzz puts up a real barrier to the damage that could be imposed by flies.

However, many commercial fruit producers understand that their customers prefer their peaches with less fuzz, and so they remove it during processing with high-pressure streams of water.

But don't worry! The presence or absence of fuzz after a peach is picked doesn't affect its lifespan, because the hair is there to help the fruit while it's growing, not when it's safely mature.

So, let's enjoy our splendid peaches this season, with or without the fuzz.

may the best tree win

I once worked as a surveyor for the U.S. Forest Service in Southeast Alaska.

My co-workers were snuff-chewing, big-bearded men who felled huge spruce and hemlock trees. The highlight of the summer was the Fourth of July logger sports competition. There were competitions for axe throwing, choker setting, and "topping the spar," a timed event that measured who could zip up a tree the fastest with pole spikes and then slice off the top with a chain saw.

These contests started more than a century ago, when lumber-jacks did the dangerous work of cutting and hauling timber. In their isolated camps, they competed to see who could throw a double-bit axe the most accurately, chop through a piece of wood the fastest, and stay on top of a rolling log the longest.

Those matches evolved to formal competitions at county fairs and festivals and, later, were televised on ESPN. New events arose, like the springboard chop, in which contestants literally hack their way to the top of a pole with only a plank and an axe.

And then there's the "hot saw," where competitors see how fast they can cut logs using chain saws powered by motorcycle engines that run on jet fuel.

The Lumberjack World Championships is held annually in Wisconsin, with 21 events for men, women, and teams. Lumberjack pros usually come from a long line of loggers, with teams often made up of siblings or parents, sons, and daughters.

And there's real money at stake! The best lumberjacks and lumberjills can win as much as $50,000.

But logger sports enthusiasts will tell you the competition is not about the money; it's about pride in the work—and the chance to work with trees in any way. I can certainly understand that.

are trees good
for business?

W ould you rather shop in a business district set on tree-
lined streets or in an area without trees? A recent
study shows that consumers respond in remarkably
positive ways to shopping environments that are nestled within a
healthy urban forest. Social scientists at the University of Washington studied how the presence of trees influences the ways that
we perceive and behave when we're out shopping.

Customers shopping in business districts that had tree-lined
sidewalks reported that they had an 80 percent higher comfort
level compared to how they felt when shopping on treeless streets.
Consumers also perceived that retailers who incorporated trees
into their property contribute to the well-being of the community,
and rated interactions with those merchants more positively than
with other merchants.

Consumers also stated that they were willing to pay more for
parking and even more for goods in a shopping area that had
trees than one without trees—both for low-priced goods like

a tuna sandwich and for bigger-ticket items like sports shoes or eyeglasses.

None of this really surprises me. Our physical surroundings, both outdoor and indoor, affect many of the decisions we make. This study—and other research on the economic values of trees—suggests that people carry their favorable perceptions of trees with them when they decide where they shop, where they recreate, where they work, and where they live.

So the value of trees isn't only about their many ecological contributions, their beauty in urban and wildland settings, and their practical uses in lumber for our houses and furniture. They provide real economic value because of the many direct and indirect contributions they make in the lives of people around the world. Caring for trees makes dollars and sense.

crown shyness

I magine that you're in a forest on a windless day. You lie on your back and look up at the treetops high above you. Notice that none of the individual tree crowns touch each other, so tracks of blue sky show in between them.

That phenomenon is what botanists call crown shyness. It occurs in forests around the world where trees are all the same age. But the type of tree doesn't seem to make a difference; those open tracks can appear between different species, between the same species, and even within the same tree.

But why?

For more than a century, scientists have posed different theories.

Some suggest that competition for light is the key. Tree leaves contain photoreceptors, proteins that can detect and interpret the quality of light that arrives on leaf surfaces. When receptors detect an increase in the far-red light that bounces off the leaves of their neighbors rather than direct light that originates from the sun, a tree can shift its growth away from its neighbors' light. The resulting gaps minimize direct competition for light capture. So, crown shyness might be all about plant physiology.

But there's another hypothesis that makes sense if you returned to that same forest on a windy day. You'd see that the air movement in the canopy makes one tree's crown hit up against its neighbor's, scraping against its buds and twigs—creating wind-driven pruning.

In 2008, researchers photographed the crown-shy canopy of a Canadian pine forest and then roped individual trees to prevent their crowns from colliding in the wind. Six years later, the crowns had grown toward each other, filling in the empty spaces between them, evidence that crown shyness might instead be about the physical effects of those crown collisions.

So, is it physiology? Bud-bumping? Or both?

That's part of the fun of learning about trees: Scientists see patterns in nature and arrive at different conclusions. It's the search for answers that makes it interesting.

reading the
tree rings

he messiest laboratory I have ever seen is the prep room of the Center for Tree-Ring Science at the University of Missouri. Shaggy-barked cross sections of trees are stacked from floor to ceiling, each giant tree "cookie" labeled and wrapped in raggedy gray duct tape.

But this messy room holds important work. Here, scientists work to both quantify the ages of trees and chart their disturbances, a field of study called dendrochronology. They do this by extracting cores from live trees or residual stumps, or timber from human structures. Fire scars provide cross-checks with data banks from other trees in other forests, providing a timeline that can extend back for centuries.

On a recent visit, Mike Stambaugh, the director of the Center for Tree-Ring Science, told me about a project he's working on—this one to determine when a local Missouri farmhouse and grist mill were built by European settlers. By coring wood samples cut from the ends of the timbers, his team learned that the logs for the mill were cut in 1847. Scars in that wood also presented a rare opportunity to date the frequency of fires before European settlement.

Stambaugh's research also helps future trees. By working with wood chemistry experts, he's able to explore the potential for new kinds of forest products generated after fires move through the forests in the Southeast and the West. His team is identifying novel compounds that arise from the resin that pine trees create in response to wildfire exposure.

So counting tree rings is not just about knowing how old a single tree is—it's a way to understand trees that provides insights to our past and to our future.

wonderful
willows

Euphrates poplar *(Populus euphratica)*; willow *(Salix)*

W illow trees are wonderful. They take root easily and grow remarkably quickly. But their lifespans are short, evoking the motto that James Dean made famous: "Live fast, die young."

With more than 300 species worldwide, willows show huge variation in their size. In the high Arctic, you'll find willows that are just a few inches tall at full maturity. In the United States' eastern forests, the largest species, the black willow, can grow up to 60 feet (18 m) high. Their scientific name, *Salix,* comes from the Celtic word meaning "near water," which is apt, since we find them near streams and riversides.

Probably the most famous of the group is the weeping willow, whose branches and foliage suggest the falling of tears from crown to ground. The Swedish botanist Carl Linnaeus gave them the scientific name of *Salix babylonica.*

Why Babylon? Well, due to a mistranslation, Linnaeus mistakenly believed that weeping willows were the willows of Babylon described in Psalm 137 of the Bible—the trees where enslaved Hebrews wept for Zion. Instead, the true weeping willow originated in China. The biblical willow was actually the Euphrates poplar, a relative of our cottonwood tree.

And willows have medicinal uses: For thousands of years, Egyptians, Greeks, and Native Americans used the extracts of willow bark to soothe aches and pains. The active ingredient in the bark? Salicin, the chemical that was developed into aspirin in 1899 and is now the most commonly used drug in the world.

But even without its history and the healing properties of its chemicals, just sitting under a willow tree soothes and calms us when we need it most.

FALL

SEPTEMBER–NOVEMBER

bark cloth:
the fashion of trees

Mutuba tree *(Ficus natalensis)*

It's hard to know exactly when humans started using bark cloth, but it's likely that it predates weaving. Historians have found examples of bark cloth from across the Pacific, Indonesia, Africa, and Asia.

Some of the earliest evidence of bark cloth comes from Uganda, where skilled workers still create the textile through processes they developed centuries ago. First making a slit at the base of the mutuba tree, workers cut through the top layer of bark. From there, they separate the inner bark from the tree in one large piece and wrap the tree trunk in mutuba leaves to protect it as it heals.

Then, they scrape and boil the inner bark to make it flexible. After beating it down to a single layer, they wring it out and stretch it taut. After several days of drying in the sun, the fabric—now strong and soft—is ready.

Although most tree species would die from this process, mutuba trees can live through annual harvests for 40 years, with a single tree producing 8,000 square yards (6,690 sq m) of cloth in its lifetime—enough to cover more than a New York City block.

Historians have found evidence of bark cloth dating back 700 years, when only royalty were allowed to wear it. But its uses have diversified—it's been used as currency, in religious ceremonies, and as a symbol of protest against colonialism.

In 2005, UNESCO named Ugandan bark cloth a "masterpiece of intangible cultural heritage." And today, you can find bark cloth on the fashion runway! Uganda-born designer José Hendo creates bark cloth for her London-based collections, fostering a culture of environmentally friendly and sustainable fashion.

The clothing we wear is a necessity, a fashion statement, and sometimes a symbol about what we value. I can't imagine wearing anything better than an elegant garment made entirely of trees.

the survivor tree

Callery pear *(Pyrus calleryana)*

O n September 11, we remember the terrorist attacks at the World Trade Center. One way to commemorate that event is through the messages that trees can communicate to those who survived.

In the aftermath of the attack, a tree that had been growing at Ground Zero was discovered alive but severely damaged. Its roots had snapped, and its branches were burned and broken. The New York City Department of Parks and Recreation took over its care, excavating and removing the tree, a Callery pear, for rehabilitation.

In time, new limbs sprouted from its stump, and in 2010, it was replanted at the site of the 9/11 Memorial and Museum. Now called the Survivor Tree, it stands as a living example of resilience of life in the face of death.

But its message goes beyond that tree. From that Callery pear came the Survivor Tree seedling program, which is coordinated by an arborist firm and a high school in Queens. Each year, they provide seedlings from this tree to three communities that have endured tragedy. The young saplings are planted and nurtured as an inspiration for hope and regrowth.

In 2022, Ukraine was one recipient, to help commemorate the casualties and refugees that have stemmed from the war with Russia. In 2021, the World Health Organization received seedlings for its response to the COVID-19 pandemic. Other groups in many countries have derived inspiration from the seeds to recover from hurricanes, shootings, and wildfires.

Of course, the presence of a single tree can neither prevent nor make up for the great losses that emerge from such tragedies. But this Survivor Tree program—and similar efforts that harness the quiet power of trees—inspires a sense of hope, solace, and promise in people and places around the world.

vote for cork!

Cork oak *(Quercus suber)*

People have used cork for millennia. It's light, buoyant, and elastic, thanks to the 40 million air cells that occupy each cubic inch. Today, we use cork for fishing floats, floor tiles, and, of course, bottle stoppers.

The tree that produces it is called cork oak, which has evolved a spongy bark to protect against fire and disease. Unlike other trees, the cork oak has bark that separates along the dead cambium, so the inner bark can regrow for many harvests.

Most of the 13 billion corks produced each year come from Spain and Portugal. Each cork oak lives for 250 years and makes enough cork for 60,000 bottles of wine.

Skilled workers harvest the bark, slicing and peeling it into sheets the size of a yoga mat. The bark weathers for a year and is then soaked, flattened, and sorted. Wine corks are punched by hand, printed with logos, and then sent off to candlelit dinners in our homes and restaurants. The process provides jobs for some 30,000 people.

Cork forests also offer critical habitat for two endangered animals: the Iberian lynx and the Iberian eagle.

But recently, the wine industry has started using synthetic corks made from petroleum to reduce costs and the risk of contaminants. Cork oak forests are being replaced by pine plantations to make wood pulp, with negative impacts on centuries-old human and animal communities.

So the next time you order a bottle of wine, let your server know you'd like a bottle with a real cork, from a real tree. As with so many of our actions, this seemingly simple decision can affect people and trees half a world away.

why leaves change colors

W hy *does* a tree drop its leaves?

During the long days of spring and summer, leaves convert all of that sunlight into energy, a process that requires a lot of water. Short winter days mean there isn't enough sunlight to make it worth using the extra water the tree would need for the conversion process.

But instead of just tossing those leaves away like old candy wrappers, trees prepare for the cold weather by breaking down the leaves' chlorophyll and transporting the nutrients to their roots for recycling in the spring.

The process of moving out the chlorophyll reveals the yellow and orange of other leaf pigments. They were there all along, just masked by the chlorophyll. Timing is critical. Trees must maximize leaf-time to capture energy but avoid the risk of freezing before completing that nutrient recycling process.

So how do trees tell seasonal time without a calendar? You might think that the air temperature is the trigger. But the answer is photoperiod: the balance of daytime and nighttime, a far more reliable indicator of seasonal change.

What's cool is that trees don't assess the length of the day—rather, they measure the duration of the night!

A pigment called phytochrome is the key. It has two interconvertible forms. One is activated by red light, which leaves get during the day. The other is activated by far-red light, which dominates at night. A change in the proportion of these two is the trigger that signals it's time for the leaves to fall.

So, when you check out the brilliant autumn colors, remember that it's not the temperature that triggers the show—it's the length of the night.

the puzzle of
acorn masting

Oak *(Quercus)*

Ask any squirrel: Acorns are delicious! Over our long, cold winters, these portable packets of oak fruit provide nourishment for mammals and birds. On average, a single oak tree can produce more than 10,000 of these nuggets each year.

But that's an average. Oaks bear superabundant fruit crops only every three to five years, what botanists call mast years. These masting events are preceded and followed by years of very small crops—sometimes by complete crop failure. What's the reason for this irregular seed production?

One theory is predator satiation, an idea grounded in the fact that making acorns is a huge energy investment. The tree's payoff comes when animals transport their offspring to places far from their own crowns, where the acorns will have a better chance of thriving, free from competition with their parents. And the animals get a food source that is rich in carbohydrates and nutrients and that can be stored for months at a time.

When oak trees produce lots of fruits during a mast year, they make more food than acorn-consuming animals can possibly eat, so there are plenty of acorn leftovers that can germinate and grow into the next generation. And during low-crop years, some animals will starve, which effectively keeps those populations in check. This pattern ensures that, in the long term, some acorns make it into the next generation.

But still, oak masting puzzles remain: How do oak trees across populations coordinate the timing of their masting events? How do local weather patterns affect acorn variability? And how is climate change affecting these patterns? Happily, long-term studies are now probing these questions to better understand the complex dance between trees and their associates.

a home for ants

Gambel oak *(Quercus gambelii)*

My husband, Jack, studies ants, and he often charms me with his inexhaustible supply of insect stories. On a recent stroll, we found a scattering of Gambel oak acorns littering the trail. Stooping down to pick one up, Jack told me the story of the acorn ants.

These well-named *Temnothorax* ants—*temno* meaning "slight"—are so tiny that a colony of 200 of them can make their home in a single acorn! They are perhaps the cutest species of ant I've ever seen.

Acorn ants are described as being extremely peaceful. They gather sugar that comes from the bodies of plant-sucking aphids and collect small protein sources like springtails and flies.

But Jack described a more complex picture. These little ants are too weak to be able to bust through the hard outer core of the acorn shell, so they have to rely on the acorn weevil to provide a home for them.

These half-inch-long (1.27 cm) brown weevils have long, slender snouts called rostrums. The females bore holes into young summer acorns with the chewing mouthparts at the end of their rostrums. Then, the weevil does an about-face and deposits her eggs right into the kernel of the acorn. The eggs hatch into pale, legless, stubby grubs.

The larvae live there until fall, when the acorns drop to the ground. Then it's go-time for the grubs! These little creatures bore through the acorn shell and out into the wide world of the forest floor, where they live for a year before emerging as new adult weevils to repeat their own small circle of life.

And that leftover hollow in the acorn shell? Perfect for the next tenants: an active colony of *Temnothorax* ants.

This is what I love about trees. Whether you are observing them from the huge landscapes of our mountain forests or in the miniature arena of a single acorn, you'll always find something to amaze you.

departed:
on trees and death

Black walnut *(Juglans nigra)*; cherry *(Prunus avium)*;
mahogany *(Swietenia macrophylla)*; pine *(Pinus)*; poplar *(Populus)*; willow *(Salix)*

M any cultures and religions celebrate the Tree of Life (page 49), but trees also have deep associations with death. People all over the world have laid their dead to rest inside caskets and coffins made of wood, a tradition that traces back to the burial boxes created in ancient China and Egypt.

In the mid-1800s in the United States, local furniture makers moonlighted as undertakers, making each coffin individually. During the Civil War, thousands of coffins were needed to transport the thousands of dead soldiers, which opened the era of mass-produced caskets in the United States. Since then, their manufacture has evolved into a $660 million industry.

Caskets and coffins are made from of a variety of tree species, each type reflecting the resources of the departed. On the high-cost end, black walnut, cherry, and mahogany are used. Less expensive are those of poplar and pine, symbols of frugality and simplicity.

In the last two decades—partly due to rising funeral costs—people have increasingly sought funeral arrangements that don't include caskets, such as cremation.

Since conventional burials involve toxic embalming fluids, the option of a green burial is increasingly appealing to those who want to reduce their impact on the Earth, even after they die. Those burial containers are made of quickly decomposing bamboo and willow, and a tree is often planted in a hand-dug burial space, a symbol that life can spring from death. More than 200 green burial cemeteries exist in the United States.

Trees participate in the natural cycles of life and death, in the past and present, and in real and symbolic ways.

guns
and gunstocks

Beech *(Fagus)*; maple *(Acer)*; myrtle *(Myrtus)*;
thin-shelled walnut *(Juglans regia)*

F all is here! And for deer hunters like me, that means it's time for our annual trip to hunt for wild game in our bountiful wildlands.

The connection between trees and hunting isn't obvious, but don't forget: Deer and elk depend on forests for their food and habitat.

Also, certain tree species provide wood for the gunstock, the part of the gun that gives it structural support. The best wooden gunstocks are made from thin-shelled walnut, thanks to the species' exceptional strength and dense grain, and the fact that it can absorb the force of a rifle's recoil.

Cheaper wood stocks are made of beech, maple, and myrtle wood, but gunmakers often stain these to resemble walnut.

And just as with any crafted object, looks matter! Hunters keep an eye out for what they call figure: gunstocks that have curly, ropy, or swirly designs in the wood. One of the most sought-after designs is the fiddleback, in which closely grown layers of curly wood grain reflect the light in waves.

These wooden gunstocks also take time to age before they are shaped—up to three years minimum, although there are some gunstock aficionados who won't use wood that's aged any less than six.

And, as is true for so many objects, I'm sorry to say that synthetic stocks are now replacing wood. These molded fiberglass shells are filled with plastic foam, and while manufacturers still dress them up with elaborate, colorful patterns at little expense, these synthetic stocks can warp in hot weather and freeze in cold, becoming so brittle that they shatter.

So, despite the higher cost, many hunters stick to wood, because, as we say, "It just feels right in the arms."

out of many, one: our national tree

Oak *(Quercus)*

Nearly 250 years ago, our country adopted the American bald eagle as the national bird, giving it a place on the Great Seal of the United States. In the early 1900s, the buffalo nickel featured the American bison, which later became our official national mammal. But it was only 20 years ago that the Arbor Day Foundation invited everyone in the country to vote for our national tree. The winner? The mighty oak, which received more than 101,000 votes.

According to then senator Ben Nelson of Nebraska, the oak represents "our nation's strength, as it grows from just an acorn into a powerful entity whose many branches continue to strengthen and reach skyward with every passing year."

I like to think that Americans chose the oak tree because, like our own population, it's incredibly diverse, with more than 90 species native to our country. You can find oaks in all shapes and sizes, from New England's stately red oaks to the scrub oaks of California.

Oak trees can also adapt to their environment: California's blue oaks are deciduous, while Arizona's silverleaf oaks are evergreen. The willow oak thrives in our southern states' wet climate, whereas Utah's gambel oaks do well in the arid Mountain West.

And don't forget that oaks played a role in American history. The USS *Constitution* battleship got the nickname "Old Ironsides" not because its sides were made of iron but for its resistance to British cannonballs, thanks to its hull's solid oak timbers.

Given that a mature oak tree can create more than two million acorns during its lifetime (only one of which needs to survive for the tree's reproductive success), I can't help thinking of our country's motto, *E pluribus unum*—Out of many, one. It's a reminder that despite our great diversity, we are stronger when we come together—a message that our mighty oaks help us remember.

the great ginkgo leaf dump

Ginkgo *(Ginkgo biloba)*

lthough most trees lose their leaves just a few at a time, the leaves of ginkgo trees drop in synchrony over the span of a day or two. Ginkgoes develop a leaf-shedding layer, or abscission zone, all at once, so at the first hard frost, they rain to the ground in a saffron shower.

My husband, Jack, and I have a running bet—of a dollar—on the timing of "the Great Ginkgo Leaf Dump," checking the ginkgo tree we encounter on our walk to work to see who will win.

Ginkgoes are also known as maidenhair trees because their leaf veins radiate out in long, parallel strands. Their separated leaf tips create the form of twin Japanese fans—hence the scientific name *Ginkgo biloba*, or "two lobes."

Their ancestors existed during the Jurassic period, coexisting with dinosaurs more than 170 million years ago. People have cultivated ginkgoes for more than 3,000 years, and because they are resistant to disease and drought, they grow well in urban settings like Salt Lake City, Nashville, and New York City.

They have separate male and female trees. Because the pulp that covers the seeds of female trees smells putrid—not something you want to encounter on a stroll—city planners have to be careful about which individuals they plant.

And yet, more than 800 mature female trees line the streets of our nation's capital. So, how do they deal with the stinky fruits? Washington, D.C., has a special license from the Environmental Protection Agency to spray those female ginkgoes with a chemical that prevents their fruits from maturing. Happily, it's harmless to humans.

As the days grow colder, Jack and I will be watching our ginkgo every day. Whoever wins that dollar, we'll both enjoy witnessing those leaves shedding in a symphony of gold.

WINTER

DECEMBER

scent of the season

Cinnamon *(Cinnamomum verum)*; clove *(Syzygium aromaticum)*;
ponderosa pine *(Pinus ponderosa)*; vanilla *(Vanilla planifolia)*

With the winter holidays approaching, I'm baking festive goodies, a joyful counterpoint to our shortening days.

As you might expect of an ecologist, many of my recipes involve trees. But I'm not alone! After all, the bark of the cinnamon tree flavors pumpkin pies, and the sharp aroma of hot mulled cider comes from cloves, the flower buds of a tree in the myrtle family.

And there's vanilla. Natural vanilla comes from a vinelike orchid, which gets its support by hanging from tree branches and trunks.

Native to Mexico, vanilla is now cultivated in tropical areas worldwide with labor-intensive practices. Trained workers must transfer pollen from male flowers to female flowers by hand. The seed pods are then fermented, causing them to release vanillin, the active ingredient.

Because the fragrance and pharmaceutical industries also use vanillin, the annual demand of more than 20,000 tons (18,145 metric tons) has long exceeded the supply of vanilla beans.

So, chemists synthesized vanillin, using coal and oil as sources early on. But these compounds were carcinogenic, and producers needed healthier, sustainable sources.

Chemists later discovered that vanillin could be made from coniferin, found in the bark of pine trees. So now, 15 percent of vanillin comes from by-products of the paper pulp manufacturing process.

In a way, this isn't a surprise. Walk up to a ponderosa pine tree and take a deep breath. You'll get a strong whiff of vanilla!

As you consider all the things you're thankful for this holiday, add trees to your list—especially when you take a bite of your favorite dessert.

deck the halls

Cedar *(Thuja)*; fir *(Abies)*; holly *(Ilex)*

M ost of our wreath greens in the United States are harvested from Pacific Northwest forests, where the climate is ideal for growing fir, cedar, and holly.

Wreath materials are a non-timber forest product, meaning that they are harvested without cutting down trees—similar to nuts, berries, mushrooms, and medicinal plants. Nationwide, these products generate about $5 billion a year, with roughly half coming from the evergreen boughs and pine cones collected for the winter holidays.

Although wreaths are small in size, the business of harvesting, shaping, and shipping them is huge. Each year, harvesters gather more than 10,000 tons (9,070 metric tons)—that's 20 million pounds (90 million kg)!—of evergreen boughs and nearly 14,000 bushels of pine cones to create the five million wreaths and garlands that are sent around the world.

Most harvesters obtain state or federal permits to gather greens from public land or from land owned by private timber companies.

And many greenery companies proudly emphasize their sustainable practices of trimming boughs, not cutting whole trees or using old-growth forests.

As with agricultural crops, wild greenery is subject to the weather. Evergreen trees require cold temperatures to trigger dormancy, as harvesting limbs while trees are still actively growing can stress the parent tree, causing them to shed their foliage more quickly. In 2015, trees in the Pacific Northwest experienced a "Godzilla El Niño" year, with record-high winter temperatures. That delayed the harvest and created large economic losses for the whole industry.

Some companies are now experimenting with bough orchards. In Denmark, for example, trees are managed for greenery production by leaving a skirt of branches on the lower part. As the tree grows taller, limbs are harvested from the skirt, a practice that can be repeated for 30 years.

So, when you deck your halls with boughs of holly—or another tree species—give a holiday cheer to the forests of the Pacific Northwest for the beauty they provide.

the silent instrument

Birch *(Betula)*; Brazilian rosewood *(Dalbergia)*; ebony *(Diospyros)*; maple *(Acer)*; oak *(Quercus)*; walnut *(Juglans)*

Even though it's the smallest—and most silent—instrument in the orchestra pit, the conductor's baton is what unifies and shapes the composer's score for listeners.

Batons are almost always made from trees. These lightweight wooden shafts taper down to a teardrop grip called a bulb that gives the conductor something substantial to hold on to.

Early on, batons were made from exotic hardwoods, like ebony and Brazilian rosewood, trees that grow in the forests of South America and Africa. But these species are now threatened or endangered, so conductors use other woods, like oak and walnut, because of ethical concerns about forest destruction and the rights of the Indigenous people who live in rainforests.

Leonard Bernstein, the legendary conductor of the New York Philharmonic, began his career with batons made of maple. But they tended toward brittleness, so he switched to birch. It's reported that Bernstein was buried along with the score of Mahler's Fifth Symphony and his beloved birch baton.

Jared Oaks, the music director and conductor of Utah's Ballet West Orchestra, said that for him, the baton is not just about keeping the beat—it's also about expression. When he gestures with his baton, he thinks of it as an invitation to the musicians, guiding them to join him in creating music.

Oaks uses a baton with a shaft of fiberglass, but the bulb he cradles in his palm is made of compressed wood of different species. He plans to make his own baton out of driftwood that he collected years ago.

Every orchestra is full of instruments made of wood, but the piece most of us overlook is that slim little shaft made of a tree that brings all the instruments together to make the sound of music.

an afterlife for urban trees

Shamel ash *(Fraxinus uhdei)*

We think of trees as belonging in the wildlands of our country. But more than five billion trees live in the urban forests of our cities.

The trees that occupy our neighborhood streets, schoolyards, and parks supply us with many health and aesthetic benefits when they stand alive and healthy.

But those trees are subject to damage and death from weather, insects, and plain-old old age. What happens to trees when they threaten public safety and need to be removed?

Traditionally, they've just been cut down and disposed of in landfills, at taxpayers' expense. But some city planners now realize that trees are unrecognized city treasures. A lot of valuable timber can also be salvaged from the beams and joists of old, abandoned homes—wood from old-growth forests that no longer exist. Deconstructing homes creates six times more jobs than just demolishing them.

And dead urban trees can create live music! An enterprising

guitar-making company, Taylor Guitars, partnered with West Coast arborists to create the Street Tree Revival Project.

After exploring which tree species would create acceptable tone woods, the guitar makers created a dedicated model in their guitar line that's crafted from the wood of a common urban tree called shamel ash, in the olive family. The wood is a terrific mix of the right density and drying attributes and responds well to sanding and finishing.

These initiatives showcase that even when city lumber and trees reach the end of their long lives, we can still gain valuable resources—and sweet harmonies—from our urban forests.

the meaning of
mistletoe

Douglas fir *(Pseudotsuga menziesii)*;
lodgepole pine *(Pinus contorta)*; oak *(Quercus)*

The Celtic Druids observed that mistletoe could flourish in sacred oak trees during the harsh winters of the British Isles. It became their symbol of vitality and fertility. The custom of kissing under mistletoe arose in England in the mid-1800s. And today, we chime in on popular songs about mistletoe like the tune "I Saw Mommy Kissing Santa Claus."

Knowing the biology of mistletoe reveals some contradictions about it as a symbol for love. After all, mistletoes are parasites. They infect trees to get resources from their hosts by penetrating the bark with a rootlike tissue called a haustorium, which connects the mistletoe to the tree's transport systems, diverting water, nutrients, and sugars to itself.

Mistletoe can reduce the growth of some economically important trees, like lodgepole pine and Douglas fir. But from an evolutionary standpoint, all parasites—from tapeworms to malarial vectors—are moderate in their takings, since diverting too much from the host would mean literally eating themselves out of house and home.

Nearly 250 species of birds disperse mistletoe. The seeds are surrounded by a sticky goo called viscin, which cements the seeds where they fall. Some birds wipe their bills onto branches. Other birds excrete seeds in their droppings, manifesting the Old English origin of the word "mistletoe": *mistel* meaning "dung" and *tan* meaning "twig." Hence: dung-on-a-stick.

Many other animals, including porcupines and lizards, eat mistletoe berries and leaves as a critical part of their diet. In one experiment in Australia, mistletoe was removed entirely from study sites. Those areas ended up with 25 percent fewer bird species than neighboring sites where mistletoe was left intact.

So, as with many interactions with trees, the meaning of mistletoe is wonderfully complex. Mistletoes can reduce growth of their hosts, but they also provide a bounty of resources for the organisms surrounding them.

That's something to reflect on when you're invited beneath that dung-on-a-stick for a holiday kiss.

our nation's christmas tree

Juniper *(Juniperus)*; Norway spruce *(Picea abies)*

Every year, my family takes an afternoon to drive out to Utah's East Tintic Mountains to choose our holiday tree. After a few hours of fierce debate, we end up with a native juniper tree that graces our living room for the holidays.

But selecting the national Christmas tree for the U.S. Capitol is a *year*-long process. It is sourced from one of 154 U.S. national forests, which make up nearly 200 million acres (80 million ha) throughout the country.

Like the tree we choose for our home, the winner is based on height, shape, and fullness. Officials ensure that the tree isn't critical for endangered species or water sources.

And the tree must be accessible to the 100-foot-long (30 m) flatbed truck that moves it across the country, escorted by law enforcement.

In 2023, this arboreal honor went to a 63-foot-tall (19 m) Norway spruce tree from Monongahela National Forest in West Virginia. Locals gathered to watch two sawyers cut the trunk with a vintage Forest Service crosscut saw—in homage to the historic timber industry there.

When it arrived, crews hoisted it vertically, decorated it with splendor, and prepared it for the lighting ceremony ... just as we do with our living room juniper.

the most
exemplary
of things

As an ecologist, I have shelves full of scientific and literary books on trees.

One of my favorite books has an essay by the German writer Hermann Hesse, who received the Nobel Prize in Literature in 1946. As we head into the New Year, I share with you this selection from Hesse's piece titled "On Trees." I hope you find it as powerful as I do.

For me, trees have always been the most penetrating preachers. I revere them when they live in tribes and families, in forests and groves. And even more I revere them when they stand alone. They are like lonely persons. Not like hermits who have stolen away out of some weakness, but like great, solitary men, like Beethoven and Nietzsche. In their highest boughs the world rustles, their roots rest in infinity ... Nothing is holier, nothing is more exemplary than a beautiful, strong tree. When a tree is cut down and reveals its naked death-wound to the sun, one can read its whole history in the luminous, inscribed disk of its trunk: in the rings of its years, its scars, all the struggle, all the suffering, all the sickness, all the happiness and prosperity stand truly written, the narrow years and the luxurious years, the attacks withstood, the storms endured. And every young farm boy knows that the hardest and noblest wood has the narrowest rings, that high on the mountains and in continuing danger the most indestructible, the strongest, the ideal trees grow.

Trees are sanctuaries. Whoever knows how to speak to them, whoever knows how to listen to them, can learn the truth ...

So the tree rustles in the evening, when we stand uneasy before our own childish thoughts: Trees have longer thoughts, long-breathing and restful, just as they have longer lives than ours ... But when we have learned how to listen to trees, then the brevity and the quickness and the childlike hastiness of our thoughts achieve an incomparable joy. Whoever has learned how to listen to trees no longer wants to be a tree. He wants to be nothing except what he is. That is home. That is happiness.

acknowledgments

Like a tree that flourishes by drawing on its surrounding elements of water and soil and sun, this book grew from the contributions of many.

Cristy Meiners, the station manager at KUER, contributed intellectually and logistically, skillfully editing each piece and mentoring me to better engage with a broad audience. David Childs was the production coordinator who recorded the radio episodes. The KUER team, with Maria O'Mara as executive director, supported and promoted the program.

The National Geographic Society (NGS) supported the creation of this book through my role as an NGS Explorer at Large. At National Geographic Books, editorial director Lisa Thomas and senior editor Susan Tyler Hitchcock offered guidance. Editorial project manager Ashley Leath provided amazing editorial help. The book design is by creative director Elisa Gibson, and we had further editorial help from senior production editor Michael O'Connor and copy editor Maureen Klier.

Finally, I am grateful for the trees that I have encountered in the past and those I have yet to meet in the future.

about the author

University of Utah

Nalini Nadkarni is an ecologist, an avid science communicator, and, as a National Geographic Explorer at Large, an ambassador who represents science and nature awareness throughout the world. She has pioneered novel access techniques to study the plants, animals, and microbes that live in the tropical and temperate rainforest treetops in Costa Rica and Washington State, galvanizing biologists to study what has been called the "last biotic frontier." A professor at the University of Utah, she has published more than 150 journal articles and three books. She has appeared on public media such as *Science Friday, Wait Wait ... Don't Tell Me!,* and *Radiolab,* and she is the subject of the PBS documentary *Between Earth and Sky.* Her awards include a Guggenheim Fellowship, the American Association for the Advancement of Science Award for Public Engagement, the National Science Board Public Service Award, the William Julius Wilson Award for the Advancement of Social Justice, the Archie F. Carr Medal for Conservation, and the Rachel Carson Award for Conservation. She divides her time between Salt Lake City, Utah, and Monteverde, Costa Rica.

tree index

National Geographic Society

The National Geographic Society is a global nonprofit organization that uses the power of science, exploration, education, and storytelling to illuminate and protect the wonder of our world.

Since 1888, the Society has pushed the boundaries of exploration to better understand our world. We have awarded more than 15,000 grants to National Geographic Explorers—scientists, conservationists, innovators, educators, and storytellers—for work across all seven continents. Today, Explorers are advancing new knowledge and leading conservation programs with outsize impact to protect nature, wildlife, historical places, and communities. They're documenting the wonder of our world—including its beauty, its mystery, and the threats it faces—and inspiring people to care and act on behalf of our planet and its people.

Known as the "Queen of the Forest Canopy," Explorer at Large and forest ecologist Nalini Nadkarni has created novel canopy access techniques to study the plants, animals, and microbes that live in the tropical and temperate rainforest treetops across the Americas. Nadkarni discovered that while the forest canopy—the "last biotic frontier"—is a deeply interrelated part of forest ecosystems, it is also a separate world to be studied. An avid communicator and advocate of making nature and science accessible to people from all backgrounds, she has collaborated with preachers, policymakers, artists, and individuals who are incarcerated, enhancing their awareness of trees and forests and sharing her inspiring message more broadly.

To learn more about our Explorers and how you can join us, visit *natgeo.com/impact*.